Mountain Bike ™
AMERICA

NEW HAMPSHIRE
MAINE

Contact

Dear Readers:

Every effort was made to make this the most accurate, informative, and easy-to-use guide-book on the planet. Any comments, suggestions, and/or corrections regarding this guide are welcome and should be sent to:

Outside America™
c/o Editorial Dept.
300 West Main St., Ste. A
Charlottesville, VA 22903
editorial@outside-america.com
www.outside-america.com

We'd love to hear from you so we can make future editions and future guides even better.

Thanks and happy trails!

Mountain Bike
AMERICA™

NEW HAMPSHIRE
MAINE

An Atlas of New Hampshire & Maine's Greatest
Off-Road Bicycle Rides
by Bob Fitzhenry

The
Globe
Pequot
Press

Guilford, Connecticut

Published by
The Globe Pequot Press
P.O. Box 480
Guilford, CT 06437
www.globe-pequot.com

Mountain Bike America is a trademark of Beachway Press Publishing, Inc.

Produced by
Beachway Press Publishing, Inc.
300 West Main St., Ste A
Charlottesville, VA 22903
www.beachway.com

Cover Design   Beachway Press

Photographs throughout the book provided by the author

Maps designed and produced by Beachway Press

Find Outside America™ at **www.outside-america.com**

Cover Photo: The author riding the trails of Mount Agamenticus

Library of Congress Cataloging-in-Publication Data
is available

ISBN 0-7627-0700-3

Manufactured in the United States of America
First Edition/First Printing

Acknowledgments

I owe thanks to Schwinn Cycling for providing me with clothing and a discounted Schwinn Homegrown for racing and book research. Thanks also to Norm at Portsmouth, New Hampshire's Breakout Attitude, Inc. for spreading the BOA philosophy that achievement comes from the workings of the body, the mind, and the soul.

Thanks to the bike shop employees and owners, cycling clubs, the Wojciks, Bill Altenburg, and every other cyclist with whom I spoke to gather information for this book. Without exception, these people were courteous and helpful. I'm sorry I couldn't answer yes to all your invitations to join you on the trails of New Hampshire and Maine.

Bill Nichols deserves special thanks for advice he's given me over our years of friendship and through the thousands of trail and road miles.

Another debt of gratitude goes to Scott Bailey for showing me the way to the Job, and for meeting me at the Four Corners for rides on the coldest and most memorable winter mornings either of us will ever know.

Deep thanks goes to my parents for nurturing within me the talent and character to be a mountain biker, a writer, and an arguably decent human being. What they instilled lets me enjoy the world and gave me the wisdom and patience to develop the love I share with my wife Michelle. She rode many trails with me and read chapter drafts, both of which are small things compared to the difficult ones we have gone at together.

I'd like to thank my son, who was a toddler through much of the writing of this book, for the many times he helped maintain the family bikes, and for becoming such a pro at dumping my toolbox over so I could reorganize it more efficiently.

And I thank God for allowing me all that I am thankful for.

Table Of

Contents

Preface

Scratches cover their forearms. Chainring gouges scar their calves. Tattoos, nose-rings, goatees on the men. It's the way real mountain bikers look. Or is it? It could be that you or the rider in your life flows with the mainstream. You eat mud like the others, but brush, floss, and even shower before returning to the regular world.

Perhaps all you want to do is ride your bicycle off-road, without devouring a loamy entree, but no one will answer your question: "Are there trails someplace I can enjoy?" Of course there are. They're described in these pages, mixed in with the rides for the mud-eaters and for everyone in between.

The hardened treadheads out there are saying: "Dude, I don't need a book to find an epic ride."

Is that ride the abandoned cart path that looks awesome every time you drive by, but cuts through the Civic Garden Club's flower patch after the first corner and ends at a swamp a half-mile in?

Don't be drained by disappointment when you've set aside a chunk of time for riding, only to find the new loop you're exploring is much shorter than your best friend described it. It might make you stop having best friends. Equally bad emotions can come from taking your boyfriend, girlfriend, father, family, or family dog out for a ride that's beyond their ability or fitness level. For this book, I've researched New Hampshire and Maine for enough trails to make any mountain biker on the planet happy. Are you feeling happy yet?

On many of these routes, my wife rode point while I pulled my son in the bike trailer (where he usually falls asleep). Other loops I went at alone, up to eight hours at a time. I repaired flats and broken-off derailleurs, portaged a river by way of the rusted I-beams of a washed out bridge, climbed mountains that still haven't ended, and I spent more money on snacks than I'll ever make back. I did all of these things because I love to cycle. I love those endless, middle-ring ascents and steep, singletrack downhills. I love spring rides that start at 5 A.M. and last long after the sun rises. I love for other people to cycle. I love for them to ride to work or to the store on errands. I smile when I see them pedal past cars on the gridlocked boulevard through Conway, and through the center of Freeport, Maine, when L.L. Bean is having a sale. It's just cool to me.

Writing is cool to me too. It's the part of my living which I work at so that someday I'll make my 9 to 5 job go away. Regardless, my great fortune is that doing this book let me combine my intended vocation with my avocation, mountain biking. It took me from the mountains to the rivers to the sea. It brought my family together for shared times on the trails, picnics in the most beautiful places of New England, and kept us happy just sitting around home with the good feelings which come from being healthy.

I wrote this book so that I could ride, and so that you would. But I can only describe the trails to you and wait until the day when we meet on one of them. The chances of that are pretty good, because cycling is a life-long sport. Read, ride, and care deeply about whatever you do.

Bob Fitzhenry

Introduc

A note from the folks behind this endeavor...

We at Outside America look at guidebook publishing a little differently. There's just no reason that a guidebook has to look like it was published out of your Uncle Ernie's woodshed. We feel that guidebooks need to be both easy to use and nice to look at, and that takes an innovative approach to design. You see, we want you to spend less time fumbling through your guidebook and more time enjoying the adventure at hand. At any rate, we hope you like what you see and enjoy the places we lead you. And most of all, we'd like to thank you for taking an adventure with us.

Happy Trails!

Welcome to the new generation of bicycling! Indeed, the sport has evolved dramatically from the thin-tired, featherweight-frame days of old. The sleek geometry and lightweight frames of racing bicycles, still the heart and soul of bicycling worldwide, have lost much ground in recent years, unpaving the way for the mountain bike, which now accounts for the majority of all bicycle sales in the U.S. And with this change comes a new breed of cyclist, less concerned with smooth roads and long rides, who thrives in places once inaccessible to the mortal road bike.

The mountain bike, with its knobby tread and reinforced frame, takes cyclists to places once unheard of—down rugged mountain trails, through streams of rushing water, across the frozen Alaskan tundra, and even to work in the city. There seem to be few limits on what this fat-tired beast can do and where it can take us. Few obstacles stand in its way, few boundaries slow its progress. Except for one—its own success. If trail closure means little to you now, read on and discover how a trail can be here today and gone tomorrow. With so many new off-road cyclists taking to the trails each year, it's no wonder trail access hinges precariously between universal acceptance and complete termination. But a little work on your part can go a long way to preserving trail access for future use. Nothing is more crucial to the survival of mountain biking itself than to read the examples set forth in the following pages and practice their message. Then turn to the maps, pick out your favorite ride, and hit the dirt!

WHAT THIS BOOK IS ABOUT

Within these pages you will find everything you need to know about off-road bicycling in New Hampshire and Southern Maine. This guidebook begins by exploring the fascinating history of the mountain bike itself, then goes on to discuss everything from the health benefits of off-road cycling to tips and techniques for bicycling over logs and up hills. Also included are the types of clothing to keep you comfortable and in style, essential equipment ideas to keep your rides smooth and trouble-free, and descriptions of off-road terrain to prepare you for the kinds of bumps and bounces you can expect to encounter. The major provisions of this book, though, are its unique perspectives on each ride, it detailed maps, and its relentless dedication to trail preservation.

Without open trails, the maps in this book are virtually useless. Cyclists must learn to be responsible for the trails they use and to share these trails with others. This guidebook addresses such issues as why trail use has become so controversial, what can be done to improve the image of mountain biking, how to have fun and ride responsibly, on-the-spot trail repair techniques, trail maintenance hotlines for each trail, and the worldwide-standard Rules of the Trail.

Each of the 40 rides is complete with maps, photos, trail descriptions and directions, local history, and a quick-reference ride information guide including such items as trail contact information, park schedules, fees/permits, local bike stores, dining, lodging, entertainment, alternative map resources and more. Also included at the end of each regional section is an "Honorable Mentions" list of alternative off-road rides (61 rides total).

1

It's important to note that mountain bike rides tend to take longer than road rides because the average speed is often much slower. Average speeds can vary from a climbing pace of three to four miles per hour to 12 to 13 miles per hour on flatter roads and trails. Keep this in mind when planning your trip.

MOUNTAIN BIKE BEGINNINGS

It seems the mountain bike, originally designed for lunatic adventurists bored with straight lines, clean clothes, and smooth tires, has become globally popular in as short a time as it would take to race down a mountain trail.

Like many things of a revolutionary nature, the mountain bike was born on the west coast. But unlike Rollerblades, purple hair, and the peace sign, the concept of the off-road bike cannot be credited solely to the imaginative Californians—they were just the first to make waves.

The design of the first off-road specific bike was based on the geometry of the old Schwinn Excelsior, a one-speed, camel-back cruiser with balloon tires. Joe Breeze was the creator behind it, and in 1977 he built 10 of these "Breezers" for himself and his Marin County, California, friends at $750 apiece—a bargain.

Breeze was a serious competitor in bicycle racing, placing 13th in the 1977 U.S. Road Racing National Championships. After races, he and friends would scour local bike shops hoping to find old bikes they could then restore.

It was the 1941 Schwinn Excelsior, for which Breeze paid just five dollars, that began to shape and change bicycling history forever. After taking the bike home, removing the fenders, oiling the chain, and pumping up the tires, Breeze hit the dirt. He loved it.

His inspiration, while forerunning, was not altogether unique. On the opposite end of the country, nearly 2,500 miles from Marin County, east coast bike bums were also growing restless. More and more old, beat-up clunkers were being restored and modified. These behemoths often weighed as much as 80 pounds and were so reinforced they seemed virtually indestructible. But rides that take just 40 minutes on today's 25-pound featherweights took the steel-toed-boot- and-blue-jean-clad bikers of the late 1970s and early 1980s nearly four hours to complete.

Not until 1981 was it possible to purchase a production mountain bike, but local retailers found these ungainly bicycles difficult to sell and rarely kept them in stock. By 1983, however, mountain bikes were no longer such a fringe item, and large bike manufacturers quickly jumped into the action, producing their own versions of the off-road bike. By the 1990s, the mountain bike had firmly established its place with bicyclists of nearly all ages and abilities, and now command nearly 90 percent of the U.S. bike market.

There are many reasons for the mountain bike's success in becoming the hottest two-wheeled vehicle in the nation. They are much friendlier to the cyclist than traditional road bikes because of their comfortable upright position and shock-absorbing fat tires. And because of the health-conscious, environmentalist movement of the late 1980s and 1990s, people are more activity minded and seek nature on a closer front than paved roads can allow. The mountain bike gives you these things and takes you far away from the daily grind—even if you're only minutes from the city.

MOUNTAIN BIKING INTO SHAPE

If your objective is to get in shape and lose weight, then you're on the right track, because mountain biking is one of the best ways to get started.

One way many of us have lost weight in this sport is the crash-and-burn-it-off method. Picture this: you're speeding uncontrollably down a vertical drop that you realize you shouldn't be on—only after it is too late. Your front wheel lodges into a rut and launches you through endless weeds, trees, and pointy rocks before coming to an abrupt halt in a puddle of thick mud. Surveying the damage, you discover, with the layers of skin, body parts, and lost confidence littering the trail above, that those unwanted pounds have been shed—*permanently*. Instant weight loss.

There is, of course, a more conventional (and quite a bit less painful) approach to losing weight and gaining fitness on a mountain bike. It's called the workout, and bicycles provide an ideal way to get physical. Take a look at some of the benefits associated with cycling.

Cycling helps you shed pounds without gimmicky diet fads or weight-loss programs. You can explore the countryside and burn nearly 10 to 16 calories per minute or close to 600 to 1,000 calories per hour. Moreover, it's a great way to spend an afternoon.

No less significant than the external and cosmetic changes of your body from riding are the internal changes taking place. Over time, cycling regularly will strengthen your heart as your body grows vast networks of new capillaries to carry blood to all those working muscles. This will, in turn, give your skin a healthier glow. The capacity of your lungs may increase up to 20 percent, and your resting heart rate will drop significantly. The Stanford University School of Medicine reports to the American Heart Association that people can reduce their risk of heart attack by nearly 64 percent if they can burn up to 2,000 calories per week. This is only two to three hours of bike riding!

Recommended for insomnia, hypertension, indigestion, anxiety, and even for recuperation from major heart attacks, bicycling can be an excellent cure-all as well as a great preventive. Cycling just a few hours per week can improve your figure and sleeping habits, give you greater resistance to illness, increase your energy levels, and provide feelings of accomplishment and heightened self-esteem.

BE SAFE—KNOW THE LAW

Occasionally, even the hard-core off-road cyclists will find they have no choice but to ride the pavement. When you are forced to hit the road, it's important for you to know and understand the rules.

Outlined below are a few of the common laws found in New Hampshire and Maine's Vehicle Code books.

- *Bicycles are legally classified as vehicles in New Hampshire and Maine.* This means that as a bicyclist, you are responsible for obeying the same rules of the road as a driver of a motor vehicle.
- *Bicyclists must ride with the traffic—NOT AGAINST IT!* Because bicycles are considered vehicles, you must ride your bicycle just as you would drive a car—with traffic. Only pedestrians should travel against the flow of traffic.
- *You must obey all traffic signs.* This includes stop signs and stoplights.

- *Always signal your turns.* Most drivers aren't expecting bicyclists to be on the roads, and many drivers would prefer that cyclists stay off the roads altogether. It's important, therefore, to clearly signal your intentions to motorists both in front and behind you.
- *Bicyclists are entitled to the same roads as cars (except controlled-access highways).* Unfortunately, cyclists are rarely given this consideration.
- *Be a responsible cyclist.* Do not abuse your rights to ride on open roads. Follow the rules and set a good example for all of us as you roll along.

THE MOUNTAIN BIKE CONTROVERSY

Are Off-Road Bicyclists Environmental Outlaws? Do We have the Right to Use Public Trails?
Mountain bikers have long endured the animosity of folks in the backcountry who complain about the consequences of off-road bicycling. Many people believe that the fat tires and knobby tread do unacceptable environmental damage and that our uncontrollable riding habits are a danger to animals and to other trail users. To the contrary, mountain bikes have no more environmental impact than hiking boots or horseshoes. This does not mean, however, that mountain bikes leave no imprint at all. Wherever man treads, there is an impact. By riding responsibly, though, it is possible to leave only a minimum impact—something we all must take care to achieve.

Unfortunately, it is often people of great influence who view the mountain bike as the environment's worst enemy. Consequently, we as mountain bike riders and environmentally concerned citizens must be educators, impressing upon others that we also deserve the right to use these trails. Our responsibilities as bicyclists are no more and no less than any other trail user. We must all take the soft-cycling approach and show that mountain bicyclists are not environmental outlaws.

ETIQUETTE OF MOUNTAIN BIKING

When discussing mountain biking etiquette, we are in essence discussing the soft-cycling approach. This term, as mentioned previously, describes the art of minimum-impact bicycling and should apply to both the physical and social dimensions of the sport. But make no mistake—it is possible to ride fast and furiously while maintaining the balance of soft-cycling. Here first are a few ways to minimize the physical impact of mountain bike riding.

- *Stay on the trail.* Don't ride around fallen trees or mud holes that block your path. Stop and cross over them. When you come to a vista overlooking a deep valley, don't ride off the trail for a better vantage point. Instead, leave the bike and walk to see the view. Riding off the trail may seem inconsequential when done only once, but soon someone else will follow, then others, and the cumulative results can be catastrophic. Each time you wander from the trail you begin creating a new path, adding one more scar to the earth's surface.
- *Do not disturb the soil.* Follow a line within the trail that will not disturb or damage the soil.
- *Do not ride over soft or wet trails.* After a rain shower or during the thawing sea-

son, trails will often resemble muddy, oozing swampland. The best thing to do is stay off the trails altogether. Realistically, however, we're all going to come across some muddy trails we cannot anticipate. Instead of blasting through each section of mud, which may seem both easier and more fun, lift the bike and walk past. Each time a cyclist rides through a soft or muddy section of trail, that part of the trail is permanently damaged. Regardless of the trail's conditions, though, remember always to go over the obstacles across the path, not around them. Stay on the trail.

- *Avoid trails that, for all but God, are considered impassable and impossible.* Don't take a leap of faith down a kamikaze descent on which you will be forced to lock your brakes and skid to the bottom, ripping the ground apart as you go.

Soft-cycling should apply to the social dimensions of the sport as well, since mountain bikers are not the only folks who use the trails. Hikers, equestrians, cross-country skiers, and other outdoors people use many of the same trails and can be easily spooked by a marauding mountain biker tearing through the trees. Be friendly in the forest and give ample warning of your approach.

- *Take out what you bring in.* Don't leave broken bike pieces and banana peels scattered along the trail.
- *Be aware of your surroundings.* Don't use popular hiking trails for race training.
- *Slow down!* Rocketing around blind corners is a sure way to ruin an unsuspecting hiker's day. Consider this—If you fly down a quick singletrack descent at 20 mph, then hit the brakes and slow down to only six mph to pass someone, you're still moving twice as fast as they are!

Like the trails we ride on, the social dimension of mountain biking is very fragile and must be cared for responsibly. We should not want to destroy another person's enjoyment of the outdoors. By riding in the backcountry with caution, control, and responsibility, our presence should be felt positively by other trail users. By adhering to these rules, trail riding—a privilege that can quickly be taken away—will continue to be ours to share.

TRAIL MAINTENANCE

Unfortunately, despite all of the preventive measures taken to avoid trail damage, we're still going to run into many trails requiring attention. Simply put, a lot of hikers, equestrians, and cyclists alike use the same trails—some wear and tear is unavoidable. But like your bike, if you want to use these trails for a long time to come, you must also maintain them.

Trail maintenance and restoration can be accomplished in a variety of ways. One way is for mountain bike clubs to combine efforts with other trail users (i.e. hikers and equestrians) and work closely with land managers to cut new trails or repair existing ones. This not only reinforces to others the commitment cyclists have in caring for and maintaining the land, but also breaks the ice that often separates cyclists from their fellow trailmates. Another good way to help out is to show up on a Saturday morning with a few riding buddies at your favorite off-road domain ready to work. With a good attitude, thick gloves, and the local land manager's supervision, trail repair is fun and very rewarding. It's important, of course, that you arrange a trail-repair outing with the local land manager before you start pounding shovels into the dirt. They can lead you to the most needy sections of trail and instruct you on what repairs should be done and how best to accomplish the task. Perhaps the most effective means of trail maintenance, though, can be done by yourself and while you're riding. Read on.

ON–THE–SPOT QUICK FIX

Most of us, when we're riding, have at one time or another come upon muddy trails or fallen trees blocking our path. We notice that over time the mud gets deeper and the trail gets wider as people go through or around the obstacles. We worry that the problem will become so severe and repairs too difficult that the trail's access may be threatened. We also know that our ambition to do anything about it is greatest at that moment, not after a hot shower and a plate of spaghetti. Here are a few on-the-spot quick fixes you can do that will hopefully correct a problem before it gets out of hand and get you back on your bike within minutes.

Muddy Trails. What do you do when trails develop huge mud holes destined for the EPA's Superfund status? The technique is called corduroying, and it works much like building a pontoon over the mud to support bikes, horses, or hikers as they cross. Corduroy (not the pants) is the term for roads made of logs laid down crosswise. Use small-and medium-sized sticks and lay them side by side across the trail until they cover the length of the muddy section (break the sticks to fit the width of the trail). Press them into the mud with your feet, then lay more on top if needed. Keep adding sticks until the trail is firm. Not only will you stay clean as you cross, but the sticks may soak up some of the water and help the puddle dry. This quick fix may last as long as one month before needing to be redone. And as time goes on, with new layers added to the trail, the soil will grow stronger, thicker, and more resistant to erosion. This whole process may take fewer than five minutes, and you can be on your way, knowing the trail behind you is in good repair.

Leaving the Trail. What do you do to keep cyclists from cutting corners and leaving the designated trail? The solution is much simpler than you may think. (No, don't hire an off-road police force.) Notice where people are leaving the trail and throw a pile of thick branches or brush along the path, or place logs across the opening to block the way through. There are probably dozens of subtle tricks like these that will manipulate people into staying on the designated trail. If executed well, no one will even notice that the thick branches scattered along the ground in the woods weren't always there. And most folks would probably rather take a moment to hop a log in the trail than get tangled in a web of branches.

Obstacle in the Way. If there are large obstacles blocking the trail, try and remove them or push them aside. If you cannot do this by yourself, call the trail maintenance hotline to speak with the land manager of that particular trail and see what can be done.

We must be willing to sweat for our trails in order to sweat on them. Police yourself and point out to others the significance of trail maintenance. "Sweat Equity," the rewards of continued land use won with a fair share of sweat, pays off when the trail is "up for review" by the land manager and he or she remembers the efforts made by trail-conscious mountain bikers.

RULES OF THE TRAIL

The International Mountain Bicycling Association (IMBA) has developed these guidelines to trail riding. These "Rules of the Trail" are accepted worldwide and will go a long way in keeping trails open. Please respect and follow these rules for everyone's sake.

1. **Ride only on open trails.** Respect trail and road closures (if you're not sure, ask a park or state official first), do not trespass on private property, and obtain permits or authorization if required. Federal and state wilderness areas are off-limits to cycling. Parks and state forests may also have certain trails closed to cycling.

2. **Leave no trace.** Be sensitive to the dirt beneath you. Even on open trails, you should not ride under conditions by which you will leave evidence of your passing, such as on certain soils or shortly after a rainfall. Be sure to observe the different types of soils and trails you're riding on, practicing minimum-impact cycling. Never ride off the trail, don't skid your tires, and be sure to bring out at least as much as you bring in.

3. **Control your bicycle!** Inattention for even one second can cause disaster for yourself or for others. Excessive speed frightens and can injure people, gives mountain biking a bad name, and can result in trail closures.

4. **Always yield.** Let others know you're coming well in advance (a friendly greeting is always good and often appreciated). Show your respect when passing others by slowing to walking speed or stopping altogether, especially in the presence of horses. Horses can be unpredictable, so be very careful. Anticipate that other trail users may be around corners or in blind spots.

5. **Never spook animals.** All animals are spooked by sudden movements, unannounced approaches, or loud noises. Give the animals extra room and time so they can adjust to you. Move slowly or dismount around animals. Running cattle and disturbing wild animals are serious offenses. Leave gates as you find them, or as marked.

6. **Plan ahead.** Know your equipment, your ability, and the area in which you are riding, and plan your trip accordingly. Be self-sufficient at all times, keep your bike in good repair, and carry necessary supplies for changes in weather or other conditions. You can help keep trails open by setting an example of responsible, courteous, and controlled mountain bike riding.

7. **Always wear a helmet when you ride.** For your own safety and protection, a helmet should be worn whenever you are riding your bike. You never know when a tree root or small rock will throw you the wrong way and send you tumbling.

Thousands of miles of dirt trails have been closed to mountain bicycling because of the irresponsible riding habits of just a few riders. Don't follow the example of these offending riders. Don't take away trail privileges from thousands of others who work hard each year to keep the backcountry avenues open to us all.

THE NECESSITIES OF CYCLING

When discussing the most important items to have on a bike ride, cyclists generally agree on the following four items.

Helmet. The reasons to wear a helmet should be obvious. Helmets are discussed in more detail in the *Be Safe—Wear Your Armor* section.

Water. Without it, cyclists may face dehydration, which may result in dizziness and fatigue. On a warm day, cyclists should drink at least one full bottle during every hour of riding. Remember, it's always good to drink before you feel thirsty—otherwise, it may be too late.

Cycling Shorts. These are necessary if you plan to ride your bike more than 20 to 30 minutes. Padded cycling shorts may be the only thing preventing your derriere from serious saddle soreness by ride's end. There are two types of cycling shorts you can buy. Touring shorts are good for people who don't want to look like they're wearing anatomically correct cellophane. These look like regular athletic shorts with pockets, but have built-in padding in the crotch area for protection from chafing and saddle sores. The more popular, traditional cycling shorts are made of skin-tight material, also with a padded crotch. Whichever style you find most comfortable, cycling shorts are a necessity for long rides.

Food. This essential item will keep you rolling. Cycling burns up a lot of calories and is among the few sports in which no one is safe from the "Bonk." Bonking feels like it sounds. Without food in your system, your blood sugar level collapses, and there is no longer any energy in your body. This instantly results in total fatigue and light-headedness. So when you're filling your water bottle, remember to bring along some food. Fruit, energy bars, or some other forms of high-energy food are highly recommended. Candy bars are not, however, because they will deliver a sudden burst of high energy, then let you down soon after, causing you to feel worse than before. Energy bars are available at most bike stores and are similar to candy bars, but provide complex carbohydrate energy and high nutrition rather than fast-burning simple sugars.

BE PREPARED OR DIE

Essential equipment that will keep you from dying alone in the woods:

- **Spare Tube**
- **Tire Irons**—See the Appendix for instructions on fixing flat tires.
- **Patch Kit**
- **Pump**
- **Money**—Spare change for emergency calls.

- **Spoke Wrench**
- **Spare Spokes**—To fit your wheel. Tape these to the chain stay.
- **Chain Tool**
- **Allen Keys**—Bring appropriate sizes to fit your bike.
- **Compass**
- **First-Aid Kit**
- **Rain Gear**—For quick changes in weather.
- **Matches**
- **Guidebook**—In case all else fails and you must start a fire to survive, this guidebook will serve as excellent fire starter!

To carry these items, you may need a bike bag. A bag mounted in front of the handlebars provides quick access to your belongings, whereas a saddle bag fitted underneath the saddle keeps things out of your way. If you're carrying lots of equipment, you may want to consider a set of panniers. These are much larger and mount on either side of each wheel on a rack. Many cyclists, though, prefer not to use a bag at all. They just slip all they need into their jersey pockets, and off they go.

BE SAFE—WEAR YOUR ARMOR

While on the subject of jerseys, it's crucial to discuss the clothing you must wear to be safe, practical, and—if you prefer—stylish. The following is a list of items that will save you from disaster, outfit you comfortably, and most important, keep you looking cool.

Helmet. A helmet is an absolute necessity because it protects your head from complete annihilation. It is the only thing that will not disintegrate into a million pieces after a wicked crash on a descent you shouldn't have been on in the first place. A helmet with a solid exterior shell will also protect your head from sharp or protruding objects. Of course, with a hard-shelled helmet, you can paste several stickers of your favorite bicycle manufacturers all over the outer shell, giving companies even more free advertising for your dollar.

Shorts. Let's just say Lycra™ cycling shorts are considered a major safety item if you plan to ride for more than 20 or 30 minutes at a time. As mentioned in *The Necessities of Cycling* section, cycling shorts are well regarded as the leading cure-all for chafing and saddle sores. The most preventive cycling shorts have padded "chamois" (most chamois is synthetic nowadays) in the crotch area. Of course, if you choose to wear these traditional cycling shorts, it's imperative that they look as if someone spray painted them onto your body.

Gloves. You may find well-padded cycling gloves invaluable when traveling over rocky trails and gravelly roads for hours on end. Long-fingered gloves may also be useful, as branches, trees, assorted hard objects, and, occasionally, small animals will reach out and whack your knuckles.

Glasses. Not only do sunglasses give you an imposing presence and make you look cool (both are extremely important), they also protect your eyes from harmful ultraviolet rays, invisible branches, creepy bugs, dirt, and may prevent you from being caught sneaking glances at riders of the opposite sex also wearing skintight, revealing Lycra™.

Shoes. Mountain bike shoes should have stiff soles to help make pedaling easier and provide better traction when walking your bike up a trail becomes necessary. Virtually any kind of good outdoor hiking footwear will work, but specific mountain bike shoes (especially those with inset cleats) are best. It is vital that these shoes look as ugly as humanly possible. Those closest in style to bowling shoes are, of course, the most popular.

Jersey or Shirt. Bicycling jerseys are popular because of their snug fit and back pockets. When purchasing a jersey, look for ones that are loaded with bright, blinding, neon logos and manufacturers' names. These loudly decorated billboards are also good for drawing unnecessary attention to yourself just before taking a mean spill while trying to hop a curb. A cotton T-shirt is a good alternative in warm weather, but when the weather turns cold, cotton becomes a chilling substitute for the jersey. Cotton retains moisture and sweat against your body, which may cause you to get the chills and ills on those cold-weather rides.

OH, THOSE COLD NEW HAMPSHIRE AND MAINE DAYS

If the weather chooses not to cooperate on the day you've set aside for a bike ride, it's helpful to be prepared.

Tights or leg warmers. These are best in temperatures below 55 degrees. Knees are sensitive and can develop all kinds of problems if they get cold. Common problems include tendinitis, bursitis, and arthritis.

Plenty of layers on your upper body. When the air has a nip in it, layers of clothing will keep the chill away from your chest and help prevent the development of bronchitis. If the air is cool, a Polypropylene™ or Capilene™ long-sleeved shirt is best to wear against the skin beneath other layers of clothing. Polypropylene or Capilene, like wool, wicks away moisture from your skin to keep your body dry. Try to avoid wearing cotton or baggy clothing when the temperature falls. Cotton, as mentioned before, holds moisture like a sponge, and baggy clothing catches cold air and swirls it around your body. Good cold-weather clothing should fit snugly against your body, but not be restrictive.

Wool socks. Don't pack too many layers under those shoes, though. You may stand the chance of restricting circulation, and your feet will get real cold, real fast.

Thinsulate or Gortex™ gloves. We may all agree that there is nothing worse than frozen feet—unless your hands are frozen. A good pair of Thinsulate™ or Gortex™ gloves should keep your hands toasty and warm.

Hat or helmet on cold days? Sometimes, when the weather gets really cold and you still want to hit the trails, it's tough to stay warm. We all know that 130 percent of the body's heat escapes through the head (overactive brains, I imagine), so it's important to keep the cranium warm. Ventilated helmets are designed to keep heads cool in the summer heat, but they do little to help keep heads warm during rides in sub-zero temperatures. Cyclists should consider wearing a hat on extremely cold days.

Capilene skullcaps are great head and ear warmers that snugly fit over your head beneath the helmet. Head protection is not lost. Another option is a helmet cover that covers those ventilating gaps and helps keep the body heat in. These do not, however, keep your ears warm. Some cyclists will opt for a simple knit cycling cap sans the helmet, but these have never been shown to be very good cranium protectors.

All of this clothing can be found at your local bike store, where the staff should be happy to help fit you into the seasons of the year.

TO HAVE OR NOT TO HAVE... *(Other Very Useful Items)*

Though mountain biking is relatively new to the cycling scene, there is no shortage of items for you and your bike to make riding better, safer, and easier. We have rummaged through the unending lists and separated the gadgets from the good stuff, coming up with what we believe are items certain to make mountain bike riding easier and more enjoyable.

Tires. Buying yourself a good pair of knobby tires is the quickest way to enhance the off-road handling capabilities of your bike. There are many types of mountain bike tires on the market. Some are made exclusively for very rugged off-road terrain. These big-knobbed, soft rubber tires virtually stick to the ground with unforgiving traction, but tend to deteriorate quickly on pavement. There are other tires made exclusively for the road. These are called "slicks" and have no tread at all. For the average cyclist, though, a good tire somewhere in the middle of these two extremes should do the trick.

Toe Clips or Clipless Pedals. With these, you will ride with more power. Toe clips attach to your pedals and strap your feet firmly in place, allowing you to exert pressure on the pedals on both the downstroke and the upstroke. They will increase your pedaling efficiency by 30 percent to 50 percent. Clipless pedals, which liberate your feet from the traditional straps and clips, have made toe clips virtually obsolete. Like ski bindings, they attach your shoe directly to the pedal. They are, however, much more expensive than toe clips.

Bar Ends. These great clamp-on additions to your original straight bar will provide more leverage, an excellent grip for climbing, and a more natural position for your hands. Be aware, however, of the bar end's propensity for hooking trees on fast descents, sending you, the cyclist, airborne.

Fanny Pack. These bags are ideal for carrying keys, extra food, guidebooks, tools, spare tubes, and a cellular phone, in case you need to call for help.

Suspension Forks. For the more serious off-roaders who want nothing to impede their speed on the trails, investing in a pair of suspension forks is a good idea. Like tires, there are plenty of brands to choose from, and they all do the same thing—absorb the brutal beatings of a rough trail. The cost of these forks, however, is sometimes more brutal than the trail itself.

Bike Computers. These are fun gadgets to own and are much less expensive than in years past. They have such features as trip distance, speedometer, odometer, time of day, altitude, alarm, average speed, maximum speed, heart rate, global satellite positioning, etc. Bike computers will come in handy when following these maps or to know just how far you've ridden in the wrong direction.

Water Pack. This is quickly becoming an essential item for cyclists pedaling for more than a few hours, especially in hot, dry conditions. The most popular brand is, of course, the Camelback™, and these water packs can carry in their bladder bags as much as 100 ounces of water. These packs strap onto your back with a handy hose running over your shoulder so you can be drinking water while still holding onto the bars on a rocky descent with both hands. These packs are a great way to carry a lot of extra liquid on hot rides in the middle of nowhere.

TYPES OF OFF-ROAD TERRAIN

Before roughing it off road, we may first have to ride the pavement to get to our destination. Please, don't be dismayed. Some of the country's best rides are on the road. Once we get past these smooth-surfaced pathways, though, adventures in dirt await us.

Rails-to-Trails. Abandoned rail lines are converted into usable public resources for exercising, commuting, or just enjoying nature. Old rails and ties are torn up and a trail, paved or unpaved, is laid along the existing corridor. This completes the cycle from ancient Indian trading routes to railroad corridors and back again to hiking and cycling trails.

Unpaved Roads are typically found in rural areas and are most often public roads. Be careful when exploring, though, not to ride on someone's unpaved private drive.

Forest Roads. These dirt and gravel roads are used primarily as access to forest land and are generally kept in good condition. They are almost always open to public use.

Singletrack can be the most fun on a mountain bike. These trails, with only one track to follow, are often narrow, challenging pathways through the woods. Remember to make sure these trails are open before zipping into the woods. (At the time of this printing, all trails and roads in this guidebook were open to mountain bikes.)

Open Land. Unless there is a marked trail through a field or open space, you should not plan to ride here. Once one person cuts his or her wheels through a field or meadow, many more are sure to follow, causing irreparable damage to the landscape.

TECHNIQUES TO SHARPEN YOUR SKILLS

Many of us see ourselves as pure athletes—blessed with power, strength, and endless endurance. However, it may be those with finesse, balance, agility, and grace that get around most quickly on a mountain bike. Although power, strength, and endurance do have their places in mountain biking, these elements don't necessarily form the framework for a champion mountain biker.

The bike should become an extension of your body. Slight shifts in your hips or knees can have remarkable results. Experienced bike handlers seem to flash down technical descents, dashing over obstacles in a smooth and graceful effort as if pirouetting in Swan

Lake. Here are some tips and techniques to help you connect with your bike and float gracefully over the dirt.

Braking

Using your brakes requires using your head, especially when descending. This doesn't mean using your head as a stopping block, but rather to think intelligently. Use your best judgment in terms of how much or how little to squeeze those brake levers.

The more weight a tire is carrying, the more braking power it has. When you're going downhill, your front wheel carries more weight than the rear. Braking with the front brake will help keep you in control without going into a skid. Be careful, though, not to overdo it with the front brakes and accidentally toss yourself over the handlebars. And don't neglect your rear brake! When descending, shift your weight back over the rear wheel, thus increasing your rear braking power as well. This will balance the power of both brakes and give you maximum control.

Good riders learn just how much of their weight to shift over each wheel and how to apply just enough braking power to each brake, so not to "endo" over the handlebars or skid down a trail.

GOING UPHILL—*Climbing Those Treacherous Hills*

Shift into a low gear (push the shifter away from you). Before shifting, be sure to ease up on your pedaling so there is not too much pressure on the chain. Find the gear best for you that matches the terrain and steepness of each climb.

Stay seated. Standing out of the saddle is often helpful when climbing steep hills with a road bike, but you may find that on dirt, standing may cause your rear tire to lose its grip and spin out. Climbing requires traction. Stay seated as long as you can, and keep the rear tire digging into the ground. Ascending skyward may prove to be much easier in the saddle.

Lean forward. On very steep hills, the front end may feel unweighted and suddenly pop up. Slide forward on the saddle and lean over the handlebars. This will add more weight to the front wheel and should keep you grounded.

Keep pedaling. On rocky climbs, be sure to keep the pressure on, and don't let up on those pedals! The slower you go through rough trail sections, the harder you will work.

GOING DOWNHILL—*The Real Reason We Get Up in the Morning*

Shifting into the big chainring before a bumpy descent will help keep the chain from bouncing off. And should you crash or disengage your leg from the pedal, the chain will cover the teeth of the big ring so they don't bite into your leg.

Relax. Stay loose on the bike, and don't lock your elbows or clench your grip. Your elbows need to bend with the bumps and absorb the shock, while your hands should have a firm but controlled grip on the bars to keep things steady. Steer with your body, allowing your shoulders to guide you through each turn and around each obstacle.

Don't oversteer or lose control. Mountain biking is much like downhill skiing, since you must shift your weight from side to side down narrow, bumpy descents. Your bike will have the tendency to track in the direction you look and follow the slight shifts and leans of your body. You should not think so much about steering, but rather in what direction you wish to go.

Rise above the saddle. When racing down bumpy, technical descents, you should not be sitting on the saddle, but standing on the pedals, allowing your legs and knees to absorb the rocky trail instead of your rear.

Drop your saddle. For steep, technical descents, you may want to drop your saddle three or four inches. This lowers your center of gravity, giving you much more room to bounce around.

Keep your pedals parallel to the ground. The front pedal should be slightly higher so that it doesn't catch on small rocks or logs.

Stay focused. Many descents require your utmost concentration and focus just to reach the bottom. You must notice every groove, every root, every rock, every hole, every bump. You, the bike, and the trail should all become one as you seek singletrack nirvana on your way down the mountain. But if your thoughts wander, however, then so may your bike, and you may instead become one with the trees!

WATCH OUT!
Back-road Obstacles

Logs. When you want to hop a log, throw your body back, yank up on the handlebars, and pedal forward in one swift motion. This clears the front end of the bike. Then quickly scoot forward and pedal the rear wheel up and over. Keep the forward momentum until you've cleared the log, and by all means, don't hit the brakes, or you may do some interesting acrobatic maneuvers!

Rocks and Roots. Worse than highway potholes! Stay relaxed, let your elbows and knees absorb the shock, and always continue applying power to your pedals. Staying seated will keep the rear wheel weighted to prevent slipping, and a light front end will help you to respond quickly to each new obstacle. The slower you go, the more time your tires will have to get caught between the grooves.

Water. Before crossing a stream or puddle, be sure to first check the depth and bottom surface. There may be an unseen hole or large rock hidden under the water that could wash you up if you're not careful. After you're sure all is safe, hit the water at a good speed, pedal steadily, and allow the bike to steer you through. Once you're across, tap the breaks to squeegee the water off the rims.

Leaves. Be careful of wet leaves. These may look pretty, but a trail covered with leaves may cause your wheels to slip out from under you. Leaves are not nearly as unpredictable and dangerous as ice, but they do warrant your attention on a rainy day.

Mud. If you must ride through mud, hit it head on and keep pedaling. You want to part the ooze with your front wheel and get across before it swallows you up. Above all, don't leave the trail to go around the mud. This just widens the path even more and leads to increased trail erosion.

Vehicle Ruts. Either ride in them if they're wide enough or keep to the high ground above them. Get on the vertical wall of a deep rut and control skids away.

Urban Obstacles

Curbs are fun to jump, but like with logs, be careful.

Curbside Drains are typically not a problem for bikes. Just be careful not to get a wheel caught in the grate.

Dogs make great pets, but seem to have it in for bicyclists. If you think you can't out-run a dog that's chasing you, stop and walk your bike out of its territory. A loud yell to Get! or Go home! often works, as does a sharp squirt from your water bottle right between the eyes.

Cars are tremendously convenient when we're in them, but dodging irate motorists in big automobiles becomes a real hazard when riding a bike. As a cyclist, you must realize most drivers aren't expecting you to be there and often wish you weren't. Stay alert and ride carefully, clearly signaling all of your intentions.

Potholes, like grates and back-road canyons, should be avoided. Just because you're on an all-terrain bicycle doesn't mean you're inde-structible. Potholes regularly damage rims, pop tires, and sometimes lift unsuspecting cyclists into a spectacular swan dive over the handlebars.

LAST-MINUTE CHECKOVER

Before a ride, it's a good idea to give your bike a once-over to make sure everything is in working order. Begin by checking the air pressure in your tires before each ride to make sure they are properly inflated. Mountain bikes require about 45 to 55 pounds per square inch of air pressure. If your tires are underinflated, there is greater likelihood that the tubes may get pinched on a bump or rock, causing the tire to flat.

Looking over your bike to make sure everything is secure and in its place is the next step. Go through the following checklist before each ride.

- *Pinch the tires to feel for proper inflation.* They should give just a little on the sides, but feel very hard on the treads. If you have a pressure gauge, use that.
- *Check your brakes.* Squeeze the rear brake and roll your bike forward. The rear tire should skid. Next, squeeze the front brake and roll your bike forward. The rear wheel should lift into the air. If this doesn't happen, then your brakes are too loose. Make sure the brake levers don't touch the handlebars when squeezed with full force.
- *Check all quick releases on your bike.* Make sure they are all securely tightened.
- *Lube up.* If your chain squeaks, apply some lubricant.
- *Check your nuts and bolts.* Check the handlebars, saddle, cranks, and pedals to make sure that each is tight and securely fastened to your bike.
- *Check your wheels.* Spin each wheel to see that they spin through the frame and between brake pads freely.
- *Have you got everything?* Make sure you have your spare tube, tire irons patch kit, frame pump, tools, food, water, and guidebook.

HOW TO USE THESE MAPS

1 Area Locator Map

This thumbnail relief map at the beginning of each ride shows you where the ride is within the state. The ride area is indicated with a star.

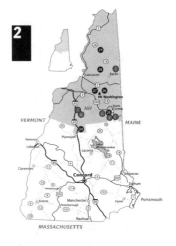

2 Regional Location Map

This map helps you find your way to the start of each ride from the nearest sizeable town or city. Coupled with the detailed directions at the beginning of the cue, this map should visually lead you to where you need to be for each ride.

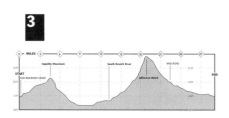

3 Profile Map

This helpful profile gives you a cross-sectional look at the ride's ups and downs. Elevation is labeled on the left, mileage is indicated on the top. Road and trail names are shown along the route with towns and points of interest labeled in bold.

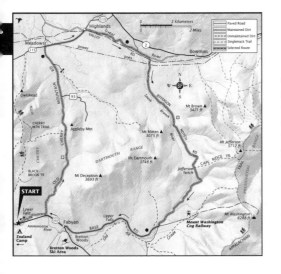

4 Route Map

This is your primary guide to each ride. It shows all of the accessible roads and trails, points of interest, water, towns, landmarks, and geographical features. It also distinguishes trails from roads, and paved roads from unpaved roads. The selected route is highlighted, and directional arrows point the way. Shaded topographic relief in the background gives you an accurate representation of the terrain and landscape in the ride area.

Ride Information (Included in each ride section)

🅠 Trail Contacts:

This is the direct number for the local land managers in charge of all the trails within the selected ride. Use this hotline to call ahead for trail access information, or after your visit if you see problems with trail erosion, damage, or misuse.

🕓 Schedule:

This tells you at what times trails open and close, if on private or park land.

🅢 Fees/Permits:

What money, if any, you may need to carry with you for park entrance fees or tolls.

🅝 Maps:

This is a list of other maps to supplement the maps in this book. They are listed in order from most detailed to most general.

Any other important or useful information will also be listed here such as local attractions, bike shops, nearby accommodations, etc.

THE MAPS — Map Legend

We don't want anyone, by any means, to feel restricted to just the roads and trails that are mapped here. We hope you will have an adventurous spirit and use this guide as a platform to dive into New Hampshire and Southern Maine's backcountry and discover new routes for yourself. One of the simplest ways to begin this is to just turn the map upside down and ride the course in reverse. The change in perspective is fantastic and the ride should feel quite different. With this in mind, it will be like getting two distinctly different rides on each map.

For your own purposes, you may wish to copy the directions for the course onto a small sheet to help you while riding, or photocopy the map and cue sheet to take with you. These pages can be folded into a bike bag, stuffed into a jersey pocket, or better still, used with the BarMap or BarMapOTG (see www.cycoactive.com for more info). Just remember to slow or even stop when you want to read the map.

5	Interstate Highway
8	U.S. Highway
3	State Road
CR 23	County Road
T 145	Township Road
FS 45	Forest Road
	Paved Road
	Paved Bike Lane
	Maintained Dirt Road
	Unmaintained Jeep Trail
	Singletrack Trail
	Highlighted Route
	Ntl Forest/County Boundaries
	State Boundaries
	Railroad Tracks
	Power Lines
	Special Trail
	Rivers or Streams
	Water and Lakes
	Marsh

✝	Airfield	⛳	Golf Course
✈	Airport	🚶	Hiking Trail
🚲	Bike Trail		Mine
🚫	No Bikes	🔭	Overlook
⛴	Boat Launch	⛩	Picnic
)(	Bridge	**P**	Parking
🚌	Bus Stop	✕	Quarry
▲	Campground	((A))	Radio Tower
⚑	Campsite		Rock Climbing
	Canoe Access		School
⊟	Cattle Guard		Shelter
†	Cemetery		Spring
⛪	Church		Swimming
🏠	Covered Bridge	🚉	Train Station
⤳	Direction Arrows	✶	Wildlife Refuge
🎿	Downhill Skiing	🍇	Vineyard
🎋	Fire Tower	◆◆	Most Difficult
	Forest HQ	◆	Difficult
	4WD Trail	□	Moderate
	Gate	●	Easy

MOUNTAIN BIKE NH/ME

The Rides

New Hampshire
1. Odiorne Point State Park
2. Newfields to Manchester Rail Trail
3. Foss Farm at UNH
4. Kingman Farm at UNH
5. Pawtuckaway State Park
6. Northwood Meadows State Park
7. Bear Brook State Park
8. Tower Hill Pond
9. Rockingham Rec Trail
10. Hopkinton-Everett Reservoir
11. Russell Abbott State Forest
12. Annett Wayside Park
13. Cheshire South
14. Pisgah State Park
15. Fox State Forest
16. Pillsbury State Park
17. Sugar River Trail
18. Hanover Rural Roads
19. Blue Job Mountain
20. Gunstock MTB Center
21. Green Mountain
22. Hemenway State Park
23. Sandwich Notch Road
24. Beebe River Ride
25. North Conway West
26. Great Glen Trails
27. Cherry Mountain
28. Phillips Brook Backcountry Recreation Area
29. Balsams Wilderness

Maine
30. Mount Agamenticus
31. Tatnic Hill Loop
32. Kennebunkport Bridal Path
33. Clifford Park
34. Ossipee Mountain Tour
35. Lake Arrowhead Dam Loop
36. Bradbury Mountain State Park
37. Summerhaven
38. Camden Snow Bowl
39. Camden Hills State Park
40. Acadia National Park

Honorable Mentions

New Hampshire
A. Henderson/Swazey and Oaklands Town Forests
B. Massabesic Lake
C. Litchfield State Forest
D. Gile State Forest
E. Conway Town Trails
F. Lower Nanamocomuck from Albany Covered Bridge
G. Sawyer River/Pond Trails Loop
H. East Branch River Loop
I. Franconia Notch Rec. Path
J. Success Pond Loop

Maine
K. University of Southern Maine Woods
L. Highwater Trail Along the Wild River
M. Turner Property
N. Jay to Farmington ATV Trail
O. Mount Blue State Park
P. Baxter State Park
Q. University Forest–Orono, ME
R. Lagrange to Medford ATV Trail
S. Carrabassett River Trail
T. Houlton to Phair Junction ATV Trail
U. Aroostook Valley Trails

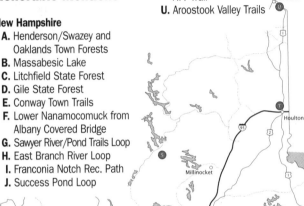

COURSES AT A GLANCE

1. Odiorne Point State Park

Length: 3-mile loop
Nearby: Portsmouth, NH
Time: 1 hour
Difficulty: Easy

2. Newfields to Manchester Rail Trail
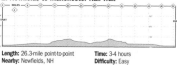
Length: 26.3-mile point-to-point
Nearby: Newfields, NH
Time: 3-4 hours
Difficulty: Easy

3. Foss Farm at UNH
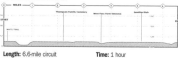
Length: 6.6-mile circuit
Nearby: Durham, NH
Time: 1 hour
Difficulty: Easy

4. Kingman Farm at UNH
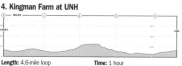
Length: 4.6-mile loop
Nearby: Madbury, NH
Time: 1 hour
Difficulty: Easy to Moderate

5. Pawtuckaway State Park

Length: 12.8-mile loop
Nearby: Raymond, NH
Time: 2-3 hours
Difficulty: Difficult

6. Northwood Meadows State Park

Length: 5.5-mile out-and-back
Nearby: Northwood, NH
Time: 1-2 hours
Difficulty: Easy to Moderate

7. Bear Brook State Park

Length: 10.1-mile loop
Nearby: Allenstown, NH
Time: 2 hours
Difficulty: Difficult

8. Tower Hill Pond
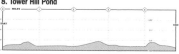
Length: 4.9-mile loop
Nearby: Manchester, NH
Time: 1 hour
Difficulty: Easy

9. Rockingham Rec Trail

Length: 19.4-mile point-to-point
Nearby: Windham, NH
Time: 2-3 hours
Difficulty: Easy

10. Hopkinton-Everett Reservoir
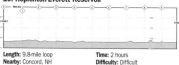
Length: 9.8-mile loop
Nearby: Concord, NH
Time: 2 hours
Difficulty: Difficult

11. Russell Abbott State Forest
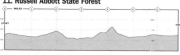
Length: 6.8-mile loop
Nearby: Greenville, NH
Time: 1 hour
Difficulty: Easy

12. Annett Wayside Park

Length: 7.8-mile loop
Nearby: Jaffrey, NH
Time: 1-2 hours
Difficulty: Moderate

13. Chesire South
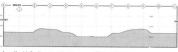
Length: 11.2-mile out-and-back
Nearby: Fitzwilliam, NH
Time: 1-2 hours
Difficulty: Easy

14. Pisgah State Park
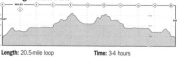
Length: 20.5-mile loop
Nearby: Winchester, NH
Time: 3-4 hours
Difficulty: Dificult

15. Fox State Forest

Length: 5.7-mile loop
Nearby: Hillsborough, NH
Time: 1-2 hours
Difficulty: Difficult

16. Pillsbury State Park

Length: 11-mile loop
Nearby: Washington, NH
Time: 2-3 hours
Difficulty: Difficult

Ride Profiles

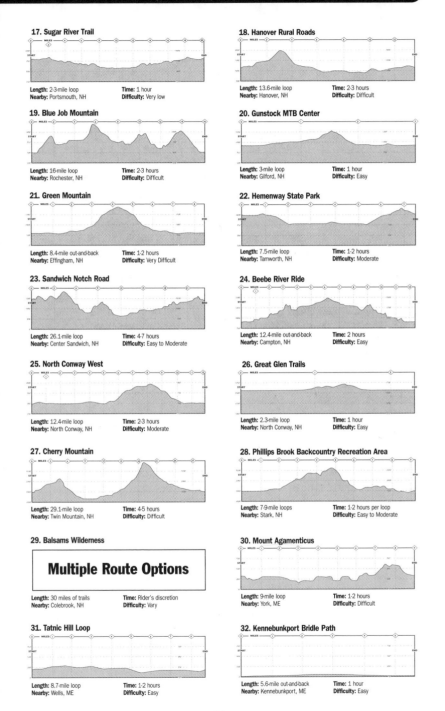

17. Sugar River Trail

Length: 2-3-mile loop
Nearby: Portsmouth, NH
Time: 1 hour
Difficulty: Very low

18. Hanover Rural Roads

Length: 13.6-mile loop
Nearby: Hanover, NH
Time: 2-3 hours
Difficulty: Difficult

19. Blue Job Mountain

Length: 16-mile loop
Nearby: Rochester, NH
Time: 2-3 hours
Difficulty: Difficult

20. Gunstock MTB Center

Length: 3-mile loop
Nearby: Gilford, NH
Time: 1 hour
Difficulty: Easy

21. Green Mountain

Length: 8.4-mile out-and-back
Nearby: Effingham, NH
Time: 1-2 hours
Difficulty: Very Difficult

22. Hemenway State Park

Length: 7.5-mile loop
Nearby: Tamworth, NH
Time: 1-2 hours
Difficulty: Moderate

23. Sandwich Notch Road

Length: 26.1-mile loop
Nearby: Center Sandwich, NH
Time: 4-7 hours
Difficulty: Easy to Moderate

24. Beebe River Ride

Length: 12.4-mile out-and-back
Nearby: Campton, NH
Time: 2 hours
Difficulty: Easy

25. North Conway West

Length: 12.4-mile loop
Nearby: North Conway, NH
Time: 2-3 hours
Difficulty: Moderate

26. Great Glen Trails

Length: 2.3-mile loop
Nearby: North Conway, NH
Time: 1 hour
Difficulty: Easy

27. Cherry Mountain

Length: 29.1-mile loop
Nearby: Twin Mountain, NH
Time: 4-5 hours
Difficulty: Difficult

28. Phillips Brook Backcountry Recreation Area

Length: 7-9-mile loops
Nearby: Stark, NH
Time: 1-2 hours per loop
Difficulty: Easy to Moderate

29. Balsams Wilderness

Multiple Route Options

Length: 30 miles of trails
Nearby: Colebrook, NH
Time: Rider's discretion
Difficulty: Vary

30. Mount Agamenticus

Length: 9-mile loop
Nearby: York, ME
Time: 1-2 hours
Difficulty: Difficult

31. Tatnic Hill Loop

Length: 8.7-mile loop
Nearby: Wells, ME
Time: 1-2 hours
Difficulty: Easy

32. Kennebunkport Bridle Path

Length: 5.6-mile out-and-back
Nearby: Kennebunkport, ME
Time: 1 hour
Difficulty: Easy

COURSES AT A GLANCE

33. Clifford Park In-town Loop

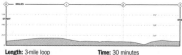

Length: 3-mile loop
Nearby: Biddeford, ME
Time: 30 minutes
Difficulty: Moderate

34. Ossipee Mountain Tour

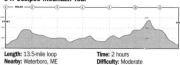

Length: 13.5-mile loop
Nearby: Waterboro, ME
Time: 2 hours
Difficulty: Moderate

35. Lake Arrowhead Dam Loop

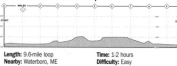

Length: 9.6-mile loop
Nearby: Waterboro, ME
Time: 1-2 hours
Difficulty: Easy

36. Bradbury Mountain State Park

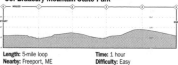

Length: 5-mile loop
Nearby: Freeport, ME
Time: 1 hour
Difficulty: Easy

37. Summerhaven

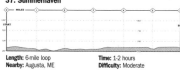

Length: 6-mile loop
Nearby: Augusta, ME
Time: 1-2 hours
Difficulty: Moderate

38. Camden Snow Bowl

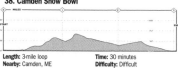

Length: 3-mile loop
Nearby: Camden, ME
Time: 30 minutes
Difficulty: Difficult

39. Camden Hills State Park

Length: 10-mile out-and-back
Nearby: Camden, ME
Time: 2-3 hours
Difficulty: Difficult

40. Acadia National Park

Length: 6.3-mile loop
Nearby: Bar Harbor, ME
Time: 1 hour
Difficulty: Easy

The Rides

Seacoast

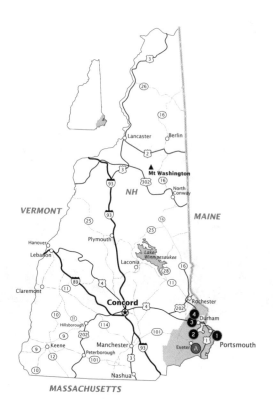

Region

Hampton

Great
Boars
Head

North
Beach

Atlantic

Seacoast Region

Typically flat topography dominates the New Hampshire Seacoast region. Though there are no large state parks or national forests in the area, the region offers the most to do when off the bike. There are many public beaches along the Atlantic Ocean, historic sites and popular watering holes throughout the riverside city of Portsmouth, and amusement attractions such as Water Country.

The University of New Hampshire (UNH) calls the Seacoast region home. Great mountain biking exists on various university properties, and two such rides are on the following pages. They are typical of the fun, accessible, meandering circuits that riders flock to in an area where much of the open land rests in private ownership or under protection as wildlife sanctuary.

The Seacoast offers a great link to the Merrimack Valley region via the Newfields to Manchester Rail Trail. Other bike friendly efforts include a bikeway-in-progress between Portsmouth and the University of New Hampshire, Durham. So whether you visit the Seacoast for vacation, go to school there, or live in the area, a good ride is surely close by.

North Hampton State Park

Rye Beach

Ocean

Odiorne Point State Park

Ride Summary

For a relaxed time alone, with a mate, or with youngsters on single-speed bikes, the smooth, flat terrain offers plenty of enjoyment. The day won't be spent entirely on the bicycle either, as there is a park museum and science center, picnic area, fields, and a playground.

Ride Specs

Start: From the Fort Dearborn Site parking lot for Odiorne Point State Park

Length: 3-mile loop

Approximate Riding Time: 40 minutes

Difficulty Rating: Very low difficulty due to limited obstacles and wide turns. Generally firm trails and no hills keep exertion low.

Trail Surface: Singletrack, doubletrack, woodland paths, and paved recreation path

Lay of the Land: Views of the rocky coastline of the Atlantic Ocean frame the eastern boundary of the ride. When out of view of the sea, trails travel through shrub forest. The northernmost point of the loop skirts the edge of a saltwater marsh.

Elevation Gain: 20 feet

Land Status: State park

Nearest Town: Portsmouth, NH

Other Trail Users: Walkers, joggers, picnickers, and cross-country skiers

Wheels: Fine for hybrids or kids on single-speeds. Trailer or baby seat fine for confident riders and passengers.

Getting There

From Portsmouth, NH: Drive south on NH 1A. At Foyes Corner in Rye, NH 1A makes a sharp left. The turn is posted and landmarked by Foyes Market. Continue south on NH 1A, passing the Odiorne Point State Park boat launch. Travel 0.5 miles beyond the boat launch and turn left into Odiorne Point State Park at the Fort Dearborn Site entrance.

DeLorme: New Hampshire Atlas & Gazetteer: Page 30, J-5

O diorne Point State Park's 332 acres preserve the largest undeveloped stretch of New Hampshire's 18 miles of ocean shoreline. Settled by Scottish fishermen in 1623, the community of Odiorne Point, New Hampshire's first European colony, missed becoming a major trading hub because it lacked the deep-water harbor found in nearby Portsmouth. Odiorne Point did, however, manage to develop into a thriving farm community. Following the American Civil War, the Point's rural seaside landscape attracted summer travelers and residents. Large homes and

grand hotels began springing up along the shoreline—remnants of this period remain in the outlines of formal gardens hidden among today's wild vegetation.

Odiorne Point's carefree and affluent times lasted through the 1930s. With Portsmouth and its naval shipyard under threat of attack during World War II, the country responded by establishing a series of coastal defense fortifications. The government purchased the land at Odiorne Point to build military bunkers for armaments and munitions. In the process of building up the fort's defense, all but one of the old homes (the Sugden House) were razed. For the next 20 years Odiorne Point was home to Fort Dearborn.

Bunkers are still scattered about, buried under a camouflage of dirt and vegetation. Battery Seaman is the largest of them— though it looks like little more than a low, oblong hill if viewed from above. Truck-sized openings penetrate its width. One can

WWII Army Bunker

stop midway through these tunnels to peer into the dark, cavernous belly of the bunker. Footpaths up the slopes of the Battery Seaman provide usually private views of the Atlantic and of Little Harbor—without the tension of expecting to see a German U-boat in the distance.

When it's time to ride, pick your route off the free site-map available at the park, or go with the planned loop here to catch many of the area's natural and historic offerings. For an asphalt extension to the day, a trip that runs past Wallis Sands Beach and the stately coastal homes of Rye and North Hampton, follow the park's paved bike path to its southern end at New Hampshire 1A. On both shoulders of the roadway, wide, marked bike lanes provide a buffer from traffic.

Whether you ride the paved recreation path, the main trails of the park, or explore the maze of interconnecting singletrack, go slowly. This is a popular area for walking and jogging. Though plenty of cyclists use the woods, you may not be expected at every bend. If you tire of pedaling and waving, take time off for the other diversions within the park. You can spend an hour or more at the Seacoast Science Center, which offers exhibits on the cultural and natural history of Odiorne Point and the seacoast of New Hampshire. In the Gulf of Maine tank, visitors can view deep-sea fish. The touch-tank at the Science Center will give the un-squeamish a true feel for tidal pool marine life.

The educational journey resumes once outdoors again in Nature's classroom. Hunt for treasures among the wrack on the rocky beaches, or seek out marshland for glimpses of heron and egrets. Interpretive panels along the woodland pathways invite the curious to learn about the area, its past and its natural habitats.

A boat launch at the north end of the park provides easy access to the Atlantic Ocean. On the southern end of the park, in sight of the Seacoast Science Center, there are shaded picnic areas cooled by sea breezes, a playground, and acres of open fields for games. Toilet facilities are available in this area, as is a section that can be rented for family gatherings or other functions.

Haven't found enough to do? Another great resource for learning about the local environment is the Urban Forestry Center, located three miles away in Portsmouth. The Forestry Center offers a network of nature trails and a schedule of programs on forest management, salt marsh ecology, tree and plant identification, and wildlife stewardship. Biking is allowed, but the terrain is limited, difficult in some sections, and can be popular with walkers.

If you decide to visit neighboring Portsmouth, check local listings for summer concerts and plays, many performed in the open-air venue of Prescott Park on the southern bank of the Piscataqua River. For a look into the lives and homes of Portsmouth's earliest residents, visit Strawberry Banke Museum, a restored historic preserve that keeps alive one of the city's earliest neighborhoods. Closer to Market Square, the center of Portsmouth, the streets are lined with art galleries, clothing boutiques, antique shops, book stores, natural foods stores, and home-brewing supply retailers. Perhaps the best thing about downtown Portsmouth after a workout at Odiorne Point is that every third door leads into a restaurant or a pub.

Off-road along the ocean

Ride Information

Trail Contacts:
Park Manager, Odiorne Point State Park, Rye, NH (603) 436-7406

Schedule:
The park is accessible all year, though facilities are only open from early May through late October. Call ahead, as rates and schedules may change.

Fees/Permits:
$2.50 per person

Local Information:
New Hampshire Division of Parks and Recreation Seacoast Region Office, Rye Beach, NH (603) 436-1552 • Greater Portsmouth Chamber of Commerce, Portsmouth, NH (603) 436-1118 or www.portcity.org

Local Events/Attractions:
Seacoast Science Center, Rye, NH (603) 436-8043 – open year-round, with the exception of Mondays during the winter. Cost $1. • Urban Forestry Center, Portsmouth, NH (603) 431-6774 • Strawberry Banke Museum, Portsmouth, NH (603) 433-1101 • Children's Museum of Portsmouth, Portsmouth, NH (603) 436-3853

Local Bike Shops:
Bicycle Bob's Bicycle Outlet, Portsmouth, NH (603) 431-3040 • Gus' International Bike Shop, Hampton, NH (603) 964-5445 or www.bicyclebobs.com • Banagans Cycling Company, Portsmouth, NH (603) 436-0660

Maps:
USGS maps: Kittery, ME-NH
Champion Map of Greater Portsmouth – available for purchase in many bookstores and at gas stations/convenience stores

MilesDirections

0.0 START from Fort Dearborn Site lot. Head to NH 1A and turn right on the bike path. Go one mile to the boat launch, turn in, and pass the tollhouse.

1.0 Take an immediate right after the tollhouse onto a singletrack trail along the marsh. The trail leads you to the ocean and then turns back into the woods, abreast the water. Watch for the Head-knocker—a large tree limb that curves over the trail. Veer right after the Head-knocker—a left here would bring you to a sandy beach, which though beautiful and hidden is not great for biking.

1.2 At the intersection with a grass path, turn right onto this wider track, which passes through the Heritage Garden area. Turn left once coming to the paved recreation path.

1.4 Turn left off the pavement onto the first wide pathway into the woods. This segment passes by Battery Seaman and continues on to the jetty at Frost Point.

1.8 Turn around in the circle by the jetty and retrace your tracks for a short distance. The trail splits three ways at Battery Seaman. The footpath (in the middle) leads to an abandoned lookout station and offers good views of the Atlantic and of Little Harbor. For the bike route, turn left and ride between the ocean and the bunker.

2.2 Merge left when the trail joins another wide dirt pathway. The pathway narrows before coming alongside the ocean and returning to the Seacoast Science Center.

2.5 Continue along the ocean to the opposite side of the science center. Turn left on the paved pathway beyond the picnic and play area and follow as it loops around clockwise.

3.0 Reach the parking lot. [For more riding, go back toward the boat launch and explore the maze of interconnecting singletrack.]

An Army bunker off the beaten path

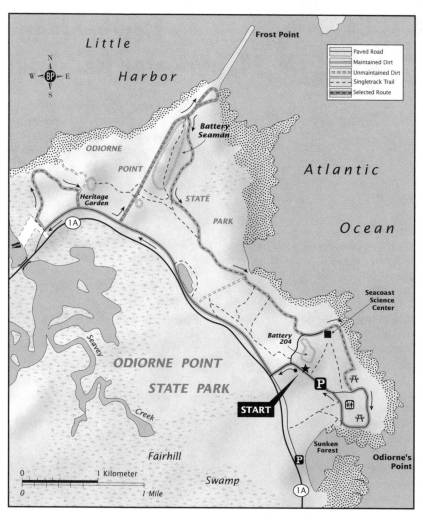

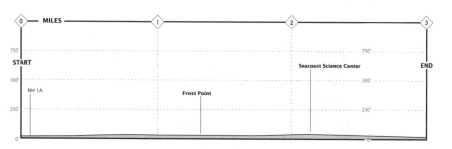

Newfields-to-Manchester Rail-Trail

Ride Summary

The Newfields-Manchester Rail-Trail offers the most casual way to explore Southern New Hampshire by mountain bike. You'll pass abandoned railroad stations that look about ready to fall in on themselves, as well as restored ones kept as showpieces of town history. Wide, packed trail surfaces invite group or family rides, while long stretches of solitude will please the single adventurer.

Ride Specs

Start: From the abandoned railroad depot just south of the Rockingham Country Club

Length: 26.3-mile point-to-point

Approximate Riding Time:
3-4 hours

Difficulty Rating:
Easy due to a wide, flat grade, with the only obstacles being seasonal wet spots and a number of roadway crossings. Signs warn of roadways in advance, and tunnels run under major routes. Generally hard-packed surface and no hills keep exertion low.

Trail Surface: Rail-bed cinder and gravel roads, with a number of traffic crossings

Lay of the Land: The trail passes along marshland on raised railroad bed, crosses old bridges, and passes through the backyards and forested acres of rural Southern New Hampshire.

Elevation Gain: 862 feet

Land Status:
State sponsored recreational trail

Nearest Town: Newfields, NH (starting point); Manchester, NH (shuttle point)

Other Trail Users: Hikers, joggers, cross-country skiers, and snowmobilers

Wheels: Fine for all mountain bikes. Kids on single speeds will have a blast, and hybrid riders or cyclists pulling child trailers will fare well on most sections.

Getting There

From Exeter, NH: Go north on NH 85 until its junction with NH 108 in Newfields. Turn left on NH 108 and travel 0.5 miles. Turn left onto un-posted Ash Swamp Road, which is across from the Great Bay Athletic Club. Pass the Rockingham Country Club and park at the abandoned train station across from the sharp right bend in the road. *DeLorme: New Hampshire Atlas & Gazetteer:* Page 29, J-14

Shuttle Point: From Exeter: Take NH 101 west toward Manchester to NH 28 Bypass south. Immediately, there will be a rotary at the junction with NH 121. Continue on NH 28 Bypass south for a few hundred yards past the rotary and turn left into the Massabesic Lake parking area. The Manchester trailhead is immediately north of the parking lot. *DeLorme: New Hampshire Atlas & Gazetteer:* Page 22, A-4

hether heading east or west through Southern New Hampshire, let your mountain bike take you to the horizon. Between Manchester and Portsmouth, two of the state's busiest and most populated areas, lies an off-road corridor that follows an old Boston & Maine rail line. The Newfields-to-Manchester Rail-Trail covers over 26 miles on its run from

Tunnel under Route 101

the Seacoast region to the eastern border of Manchester. Sightseers pass through everything from utterly secluded woods to residential development along the way. From the start at the derelict train station in Newfields to the restored Raymond Depot to trailside swimming holes complete with rope swings, this trail cuts through a wide cross-section of New Hampshire lifestyles.

Surrounded by attention-grabbing neighbors like Durham, Stratham (Strat-em), and Exeter, the small town of Newfields tends to operate at a slower pace. Almost forgotten, the town doesn't exactly leap to mind as a place for full days of mountain biking, but then, discovery is part of the sport. The discovery here might better be termed a re-discovery, of the calm that secluded paths create on a clear, warm day.

The village of Newfields grew along either side of a Squamscott Indian trail. In its early days, the town relied on the Squamscott River for shipping goods out through Great Bay, down the Piscataqua River, and eventually to Portsmouth or the sea. In 1775, a new bridge from Stratham over the Squamscott River let northern travelers and merchants bypass Newfields on their way to Exeter, the New Hampshire capital in Colonial times. The bridge effectively halted the growth of the village when it took it off the beaten path. And off the beaten path is still where you'll find Newfields.

Thanks to circumstance and modern zoning laws, Newfields has held at bay the spreading development of the Seacoast—though from time to time a contemporary house will rise from pastureland, usually in stark contrast to the century-old farmhouse next door. But largely the town center retains its village character. Colonial and Federal style homes line the main street (New Hampshire 85), and the Newfields Country Store still sells night crawlers. Across from the store are the steps of the town offices. The community church sits only a short walk away.

Starting from the old Newfields train station, this route is described in a point-to-point fashion, where distances and times must be doubled if you're interested in doing an out-and-back trip. A great thing about this trail is that you can do as few or as many miles as you want. You always have the option of turning around, and there are many access points along the way where you can drop off a shuttle car. In terms of technical terrain, nothing more severe than a mud puddle will hamper the typical trip, but be sure to use caution when approaching roadway intersections. You might emerge from the trail near a blind corner or at a busy traffic spot. And as for getting lost, the wide well maintained route is hard to lose.

Right from the start in Newfields, notice the orange trailside markers and "No Dig" symbols. After the Star Speedway in Epping, a sign for the Rockingham Recreational Trail appears. Unlike the Windham Depot-to-Epping portion of the Rockingham Recreational Trail [see Ride 9], ATV use is not allowed on the leg described in this chapter. As you ride farther west you encounter a mix of civilization and solitude. Homes and small farms appear off the trail, and stores, pizza parlors, or restaurants are at many of the roadway crossings. In between is woodland quiet, framed by the scenery of wetlands, lakes, and walls of granite ledge that were blasted through for the railroad many years ago. As you near Manchester, tunnels cross under major roadways. These are a convenience not encountered on other trails, but they can be disorientating when you ride through them.

The entire ride calls for many hours of pedaling. If you're interested, a one-day round trip is entirely possible—with a little effort. To do a weekend or marathon event, link together the Newfields-to-Manchester Rail-Trail with some connecting pavement and the Windham Depot-to-Epping portion of the Rockingham Recreational Trail [see Ride 9]. That roughly triangular loop covers over 60 miles. Schedule your trip in autumn to enjoy endless tree-lined corridors of orange, red, and yellow.

Near the railroad crossing

Ride Information

📞 Trail Contacts:
New Hampshire Division of Parks, Bureau of Trails, Concord, NH (603) 271-3254 • **Rails-to-Trails Conservancy**, National Headquarters, Washington, DC (202) 331-9696 or *www.railtrails.org*

🕐 Schedule:
Open year-round

❓ Local Information:
Exeter Area Chamber of Commerce, Exeter, NH (603) 772-2411 • **Manchester Chamber of Commerce**, Manchester, NH (603) 666-6600

🍴 Restaurants:
Ship to Shore Food and Spirits, Newfields, NH (603) 778-7898

💡 Organizations:
Friends of Massabesic Bicycling Association (FOMBA) (603) 483-2951 or *www.fomba.com* – they preserve trail use at the western trailhead at Lake Massabesic

🌳 Local Bike Shops:
Nault's Cyclery, Manchester, NH (603) 669-7993 or 1-888-640-7993 or *www.naults.com* • **Durham Bike**, Durham, NH (603) 868-5634 • **Exeter Cycles**, Exeter, NH (603) 778-2331 • **Wheel Power Bicycle Shop**, Exeter, NH (603) 772-6343

Ⓝ Maps:
USGS maps: Newmarket, NH; Epping, NH; Mount Pawtuckaway, NH; Candia, NH; Manchester North, NH

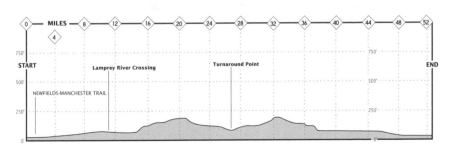

MilesDirections

0.0 START by heading west from the abandoned train station in Newfields.

5.7 Pass Star Speedway in Epping.

7.5 Cross NH 125 by Pam and Cheryl's Family Restaurant. The Windham-to-Epping leg of the Rockingham Recreational Trail joins in from the left by National Propane, but continue straight.

11.1 Cross the Lamprey River.

12.3 South of the junction of NH 27 and NH 156, pass through an area of feeding frenzy: Dunkin' Donuts, McDonald's, a pizza place, and food stores.

13.4 Pass the restored Raymond Depot, near downtown Raymond.

15.5 Ride along the shore of Onway Lake, past a beach.

25.7 Massabesic Lake comes into view to the left.

26.3 The ride ends at the NH 28 Bypass, but the trail continues past the ball field across from the Massabesic Lake parking lot.

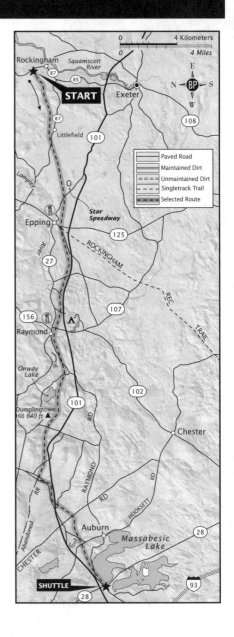

Foss Farm

Ride Summary

Woodland paths and a heart-pumping singletrack trail cut by members of the University of New Hampshire mountain bike club give variety to the off-road offerings at Foss Farm. This short loop is good for repeat efforts and is free of steep climbs. Beginner mountain bikers may appreciate that the ride layout brings them past the starting point before sending them off into the woods again in another direction for the last half of the mileage.

Ride Specs

Start: From Foss Farm Road
Length: 6.6-mile circuit
Approximate Riding Time: 1 hour
Difficulty Rating: Technically easy, with one difficult singletrack section that can be avoided (or repeated). Physically easy due to generally flat profile and wide trails.
Trail Surface: Forest roads and doubletrack over gravel, loam, and grass
Lay of the Land: Mostly early successional forest, with spatterings of wetland and open meadow
Elevation Gain: 127 feet
Land Status: State property, owned by the University of New Hampshire and used for research and public recreation
Nearest Town: Durham, NH
Other Trail Users: Walkers, woodlands researchers, cross-country skiers, and hunters (in season)
Wheels: Mountain bikes only

Getting There

From Portsmouth, NH: Take NH 16 North (Spaulding Turnpike) to U.S. 4 West to NH 108 South. Travel NH 108 (Dover Road) south into Durham. NH 108 turns left, by the Cumberland Farms convenience store and the county courthouse, but you'll want to bear right instead onto Main Street and into Durham center. Follow the one-way traffic pattern counterclockwise around downtown. As you complete three-quarters of the one-way loop around Durham center, turn right at the library sign onto Mill Road. Follow 0.6 miles and turn left onto Foss Farm Road, just before the railroad bridge. Park 0.3 miles farther on the right, across from the Stevens Way sign and before the doubletrack that leads onto East Foss Farm. (The University asks that no vehicles park down the doubletrack, as space is limited.) *DeLorme: New Hampshire Atlas & Gazetteer:* Page 29, G-14 (also see Page 59, D-9)

C ollege students, even the ones who go on to write mountain bike guides, tend to skip class now and again. As if blue skies on a warm day were not enough of a temptation to avoid the lecture hall, a handy mix of singletrack and doubletrack waits less than a mile away from the University of New Hampshire (UNH) in Durham. Trails so nearby could motivate even the laziest Bluto-wannabee out of the Delta house for a few hours of riding.

Though university owned, Foss Farm is open to everyone. Users from New Hampshire and beyond are welcome to experience nature on what was used to be

agricultural land, now grown mostly to woods. Half of the riding territory lies west of the railroad tracks on West Foss Farm. Slightly more rugged terrain lies east of the tracks on East Foss Farm. The split, East/West personality of the property traces its way back to 1841 when the Boston & Maine Railroad came through and separated the grazing pastures of Deacon Thompson's farm from his house and barns.

An overhaul of the East Foss Farm trail network was completed in 1997, thanks to the efforts of the UNH Cooperative Extension, the UNH Office of Woodlands and Natural Areas, student organizations like Club Tread, and others. The right-of-way onto East Foss Farm leads to the welcome board, which briefly describes the property and management efforts. Complimentary interpretive trail guides are available at the welcoming board—though they're sometimes out of stock. These guides inform sightseers about the natural and cultural history of the area. You're asked to return the guides to the box after your visit.

The first mini-loop of the ride follows along the White Trail (a.k.a. the Forest Management Trail). Points marked in the woods are referenced in the interpretive guide. Mature oaks, pines, and hickory trees fill the forest. In order to foster new growth and help older trees thrive, land managers conduct prescribed burns and make selective cuts. Near the finish of the first mini-loop, you'll pass an Adirondack log shelter set among a white pine stand.

The next mini-loop, of the four in this ride, follows the Blue Trail (a.k.a. the Wildlife Trail) and offers the toughest terrain of the day. You'll pass a pond on your right that was built as a fire control reservoir for prescribed burns. The initial doubletrack transitions into singletrack and becomes tight in sections. Expect to be scratched by underbrush. You emerge from the tree canopy into a clearing, only to feel that the forest is creeping in on you again. It is. You're witnessing the natural dynamic of forest succession.

Sights on the third mini-loop of the ride include the Thompson family cemetery, raised above the grade and cradled under tall pines. This area of East Foss Farm, nearest the railroad tracks, was the most recent to be used as grazing land and offers the most open space until you reach West Foss Farm. Once across the rail line and onto West Foss Farm, the biggest surprise of the day soon arrives. An abandoned satellite tracking dish, many antennas, and two trailers gathered in the middle of a meadow leave a rusting reminder of research abandoned many years ago.

The UNH Office of Woodlands and Natural Areas manages East and West Foss Farms, as well as the abutting Thompson Farm, which offers more doubletrack riding. They stress that you ride only on established trails, as a balance must be struck between use of the area and the sustainable health of the woods and waters. A carry-in/carry-out policy on trash applies, along with your acknowledgment that you assume your own risk when using UNH property. It's a fair trade for dirt under the wheels.

Once you're done with the ride, you might want to explore Durham or the UNH campus. Since 1893, Durham has developed on a different course than its sleepier neighbors Lee and Madbury. That year the New Hampshire College of Agriculture and the Mechanic Arts moved to town from Hanover. From this school which was created to prepare young men and women for service in farming and industry emerged the University of New Hampshire 30 years later. UNH now has a world-class mission: educate some 12,000 students a year in programs ranging from English Composition to Ocean Engineering.

Alien tracking station

Ride Information

📞 Trail Contacts:
Brendan Kelly, University of New Hampshire, Office of Woodlands and Natural Areas, Durham, NH (603) 862-3951 or *www.unh.edu/woodlands*

🕐 Schedule:
Year-round, though mud season should be avoided due to the multiple-use stress on the land

$ Fees/Permits:
No fees or permits required. [Important note: only foot traffic is allowed in UNH Natural Areas.]

❓ Local Information:
University of New Hampshire's web site: *www.unh.edu* • Town of Durham website: *www.durhamnhonline.com*

💡 Local Events/Attractions:
Paul Creative Arts Center, Durham, NH (603) 862-3038 – hosts performances by the UNH Department of Theatre and Dance and others • **The Whittemore Center,** Durham, NH (603) 862-4000 or *www.whit-center.com* – hosts concerts, UNH athletics, and other special events year-round

🏃 Organizations:
Club Tread (the UNH mountain bike club) or UNH Cycling Team, Campus Center, Durham, NH (603) 862-2031

🚲 Local Bike Shops:
Tony's Cyclery, Dover, NH (603) 742-0494 • **Durham Bike,** Durham, NH (603) 868-5634

Ⓝ Maps:
USGS maps: Dover West, NH; Newmarket, NH

MilesDirections

0.0 START down the doubletrack and bear left at the East Foss Farm sign onto the White Trail (the Forest Management Trail). Quickly, the trail branches into four trails—two of which are partially overgrown. Take the left-most option and ride bordering residential properties.

1.3 Circle the first mini-loop, which returns to the welcome sign. Go left and then quickly turn left again, between two large trees, onto the Blue Trail (a.k.a. the Wildlife Trail). This doubletrack becomes grassy, then narrows, and then transitions to a short, tight, downhill singletrack trail that heads to a "T" intersection at a beaver pond. Overshoot this "T" and you'll likely end up in the pond.

2.0 Go left at the beaver pond. Ride along a rusted sheep fence. The singletrack rolls and twists and eventually diverges from the fence.

2.4 At the "T" intersection (marking the return to the doubletrack Blue Trail) take a right. Turn left at the next "T" intersection and roll past the Thompson family cemetery. The doubletrack crosses under a power line and then travels along it.

3.0 Turn left at the "T" intersection and then right at the end of the singletrack. Ride past the gate and out to Foss Farm Road. Turn left

by the parking area and travel down Foss Farm Road to Mill Road.

3.6 Turn left at Mill Road and cross the railroad bridge. Take the immediate left and go down the gated access road to West Foss Farm.

4.1 Caution. After a power line crosses over the trail to a pole on the right, there is a metal bridge at the bottom of the slope that may require some cyclists to dismount. The bars of the bridge lay perpendicular to the trail and are many inches apart. (Never cross this type of obstacle at an angle. You're looking for a fast crash when the metal is wet.)

4.3 Pass the abandoned satellite-tracking dish, cross a culvert, and continue straight on doubletrack. Pass a shelter in the woods to the right and veer to the right. (The doubletrack to the left here leads off West Foss Farm onto UNH's Thompson Farm.)

5.5 Turn left at the "T" intersection and follow the doubletrack trail back past the satellite dish to Mill Road. Turn right on Mill Road, then go right again after the railroad bridge onto Foss Farm Road.

6.6 Class over. Go home to write a paper on why a ride is better than the lecture hall.

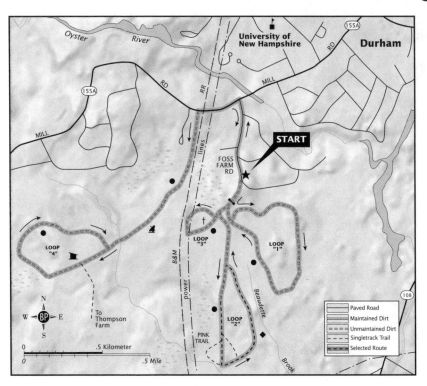

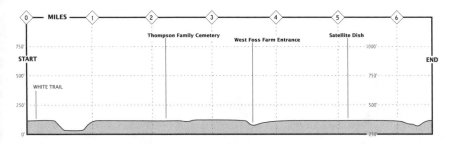

45

Kingman Farm

Ride Summary

University of New Hampshire mountain bikers ride from campus to Kingman Farm for an exceptional local mix of trails. They created superb new singletracks in the area of Hicks Hill, while the remainder of Kingman Farm already boasted well-used doubletracks. The ride crosses near wetlands and over tributaries as it eventually meanders to the bank of the Bellamy River before returning home.

Ride Specs

Start: From the Kingman Farm pasture gate off NH 155 (don't park at the Kingman Farm driveway)

Length: 4.6-mile circuit

Approximate Riding Time: 1 hour

Difficulty Rating: Technically easy, except in mud season. One moderate, avoidable climb in the middle of the loop. Physically moderate effort throughout, with one strenuous hill. Significant increase in effort during rainy periods.

Trail Surface: Loamy singletrack, doubletrack, and gravel roads

Lay of the Land: Open farmland planted for research. Easy grades—not quite rolling—on abandoned cart paths turned woodland trails.

Elevation Gain: 361 feet

Land Status: State property, owned by the University of New Hampshire and used for research and public recreation

Nearest Town: Madbury, NH

Other Trail Users: Walkers, cross-country skiers, agricultural and woodland researchers, hunters (in season). Groups of students from Moharimet Elementary School sometimes visit the white-blazed nature trail.

Wheels: Mountain bikes only

Getting There

From Portsmouth, NH: Take NH 16 (Spaulding Turnpike) north to Exit 8W (NH 155 South). Tracking mileage from the set of lights immediately off the highway, travel 2.4 miles on NH 155. Cross a bridge over railroad tracks. Immediately after the bridge, telephone lines cross over the roadway. Turn here onto the right shoulder of NH 155. Park so as not to block the gate. Do not park at the Kingman Farm administrative buildings.

DeLorme: New Hampshire Atlas & Gazetteer: Page 29, F-14

Owned and managed by the University of New Hampshire (UNH), the 335-acre Kingman Farm sits amidst the rural countryside north of Durham, in the town of Madbury. With over half of its 7,500 acres protected from development, the community of Madbury can expect to retain its rural character for some time to come. Corn fields and small dairy farms line the backroads, as do "Pick-your-

own blueberries" signs, which come December get replaced with plywood signs reading "Cut-your-own Christmas trees."

Though the acreage at Kingman Farm is small, the trails still satiate a wide variety of interests and ability levels. Novices and intermediates will find a home in these woods, particularly riders who are uninterested in the harder challenges of nearby areas like Blue Job Mountain [see Ride 19] or Mount Agamenticus [see Ride 30]. Kingman Farm is a favorite among UNH students, most of whom pedal the three miles north from Durham to test their skills on the terrain. The UNH Cycling Club runs a mid-week race series each spring on the property, and there is a fall series to raise money for the UNH Ski Team.

Students at nearby Moharimet Elementary School, in cooperation with the UNH, have established a nature walk through the farm's woods. The walk enhances children's understanding and appreciation for their natural environment. Trails lead right from the school to the farm to give pupils a safe and convenient corridor to their outdoor classroom.

The nature walk project involved clearing the existing trails on the farm and building passable routes over wet areas. Educational stations spread out along the route teach about the trees, the forest habitat, and the history of the area. Moharimet students also learn about the agricultural research and sustainable living projects going on at Kingman Farm. In the future, this cooperative effort may open up educational opportunities for other schools and the public at large.

The first stretch of this ride is just that, a stretch. There are no big challenges and the pace can be eased into. It may not seem like you're riding in a laboratory, but along the way you'll pass fields where plant growth and composting experiments are in progress. Once you pass the laboratory, the ride picks up part of the Moharimet Elementary School nature trail network. The surface roughens but doesn't cause too much trouble, unless it has recently rained.

After your brief foray of the woods on the first part of the nature trail, you return briefly to the research fields of the farm. It's back under the trees soon enough, though, for the climb up Hicks Hill—the highest elevation in Madbury at 331 feet. If the steepish climb isn't your idea of fun, look to the chapter map for the clear way to cut it off and continue on the ride. Once at the top of Hicks Hill, you descend on the East Coast singletrack equivalent of San Francisco's Lombard Street. The serpentine downhill trail, which cuts back and forth across a blocked doubletrack (formerly the only way up the grade), exemplifies conscientious erosion prevention management.

The terrain on the remainder of the ride stays sedate. Grass and soft, loamy surfaces can be expected for the most part. Another singletrack section comes up, but it's a flat one and all too short. The trip then runs to the Bellamy River before returning on doubletrack to the parking area.

Ride Information

Trail Contacts:
Brendan Kelly, University of New Hampshire, Office of Woodlands and Natural Areas, Durham, NH (603) 862-3951 or *www.unh.edu/woodlands*

Schedule:
Open year-round

Local Information:
University of New Hampshire's website: *www.unh.edu*

Local Events/ Attractions:
Contact the UNH Cycling Club for information on both the fall and spring midweek mountain bike race series at Kingman Farm.

Organizations:
Club Tread (the UNH mountain bike club) or UNH Cycling Club, Campus Recreation Center, Durham, NH (603) 862-2038

Local Bike Shops:
Tony's Cyclery, Dover, NH (603) 742-0494 • Durham Bike, Durham, NH (603) 868-5634

Maps:
USGS maps: Dover West, NH

MilesDirections

0.0 START by riding around the Kingman Farm pasture gate, which is usually closed so that cars don't enter. Bear left at the first intersection onto the farm vehicle path. Follow the farm vehicle path to the open expanse of fields and then turn right, traveling the beaten route along the woods' boundary.

0.6 At the "T" intersection with a gravel road, take a right. Pass loam and compost piles. Follow the gravel road straight to its end at the far corner of another research field. Continue onto a doubletrack trail that leads into the woods.

0.9 The doubletrack forks. Follow the right line.

1.4 Take a right at the "T" intersection and follow the white blazes.

1.7 Take a right at the intersection with the gravel road, then immediately turn left after the small gravel pit. Enter the woods on the white-blazed trail at the corner of the field.

1.9 Depart from the wide main trail onto a singletrack on the left, still following the white blazes. Begin the climb up Hicks Hill.

2.3 Cross a doubletrack trail at the crest of Hicks Hill. Slalom to the bottom of the hill on sweeping, singletrack turns.

2.7 Turn right at the "T" intersection with the gravel road. Make a left after the loam and compost piles onto the beaten route along the forest boundary. Cross through woods into a clearing and then ride to the left of an island of trees. At the corner of the clearing, cross through a narrow opening in the trees. Descend alongside a Christmas tree orchard.

3.3 Turn left at the four-way intersection with the gravel road. After the second of two backfilled culverts, turn left onto a worn singletrack trail.

3.5 Turn right onto doubletrack. Take a right at the bottom of the hill, by the Bellamy River. Take another right at the first intersection, a four-way.

4.1 Turn right and head uphill alongside the Christmas tree orchard. Pass through the narrow opening in the trees, and take a left once into the clearing. Turn left again at the gravel road, and roll right toward home.

4.6 Arrive back at the gate.

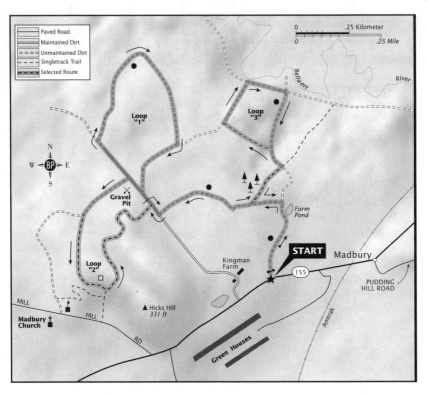

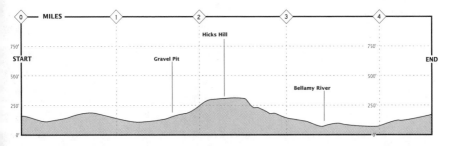

Honorable Mentions

Seacoast Region

Noted below is one of the great rides in the Seacoast region that didn't make the A-list this time around but deserves recognition nonetheless. Check it out and let us know what you think. You may decide that it deserves higher status in future editions or, perhaps, you may have a ride of your own that merits some attention.

Ⓐ Henderson/Swazey Town Forest and Oaklands Town Forest

These two town forests in Exeter, New Hampshire, are separated by state New Hampshire 101, but are joined by a walking and bicycling tunnel under the highway. Parking for Henderson/Swazey Town Forest is located on the west side of New Hampshire 85, before the railroad trestle a quarter-mile south of New Hampshire 101. Parking for Oaklands Town Forest is on the west side of New Hampshire 85, a quarter of a mile north of its junction with New Hampshire 101. Both areas offer great singletrack and doubletrack riding and are very popular with local mountain bikers. They are convenient to downtown Exeter. Wheel Power bike shop in Exeter runs group rides and has the info on these trails, (603) 772-6343. *DeLorme: New Hampshire Atlas & Gazetteer:* Page 23, A-14

Merrimack

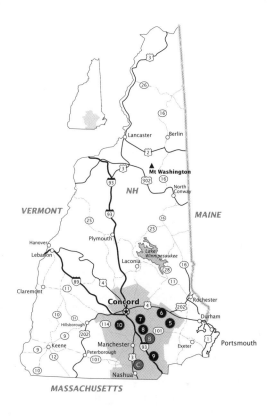

Valley

Mount
Pawtuckaway

ROCKY
RIDGE

South
Mountain

PAWTUCKAWAY STATE PARK

BIG
ISLAND

Pawtuckaway
Lake

Merrimack Valley Region

The heart of New Hampshire is home to the first-in-the-nation presidential primary, to the state's capital, and to its three largest cities. Those cities, Nashua, Manchester, and Concord, are linked by Interstate 3 and the Merrimack River. Through the Industrial Era, the river was the lifeblood of the region, which remains New Hampshire's most populated area.

Within 10 miles of any of the city centers one can find a dairy farm, or a cornfield, or state land full of great trails. The Merrimack Valley holds the most developed, maintained, and utilized trails in New Hampshire by open acreage. These trails roll over forested countryside full of rocks and loam, making for muddy spring conditions and speedway-fast singletracks come June. There are spots with hefty climbs and others that just ramble on rather flat courses, but the defining point in all of them is their accessibility from any place in the region, and the capacity of the forests to provide many hours of riding without covering the same trail twice.

Pawtuckaway State Park

Ride Summary

Symptoms of multiple-personality disorder show themselves on this ride. The early leg dishes out some fun technical challenges, but remains relatively tame. The challenge comes during the middle part of the ride, which is littered with rocks, steep grades, and long, twisty trails. The final, gradual climb to the parking lot gives time for the successes and failures of the day to sink in.

Ride Specs

Start: From the Pawtuckaway State Park administration building
Length: 12.8-mile loop
Approximate Riding Time: 2½–3 hours
Difficulty Rating: Technically difficult, with many water crossings and hike-a-bike sections along trails between the Boulder Fields and Fundy Trail. High effort expended due to overall length, jarring downhill sections, and repeated technical challenges, which require good pedaling and upper-body strength to negotiate.
Trail Surface: Rolling doubletrack and singletrack, with some steep grades and many natural obstacles, fire roads, and a paved park road
Lay of the Land: Three mountains dominate the center of the park. Rolling, forested terrain surrounds them, as well as wetland areas that encroach on trails and some roads during rainy times.
Elevation Gain: 778 feet

Land Status: State park
Nearest Town: Raymond, NH
Other Trail Users: Motorists, hikers, equestrians, campers, anglers, snowmobilers, cross-country skiers, and hunters (in season)

Getting There

From Manchester, NH: Follow NH 101 east until Exit 5. Turn north on NH 107. NH 107 turns left at its junction with NH 27. Make the left and follow NH 107 / 27 for a short distance. Turn right onto NH 156 North. Travel 1.3 miles to the sign for Pawtuckaway State Park, where you turn left onto Mountain Road. The park entrance is 2.1 miles ahead on the left. The parking lot and administration building are immediately on the right. Park here.
DeLorme: New Hampshire Atlas & Gazetteer: Page 29, I-9

T hings that start out simple can sometimes turn freakish. This loop through Pawtuckaway State Park demonstrates that point well. The route warms you up with a few miles of rolling doubletrack. But partway up the North Mountain Bypass, things get tricky. The ride begins weaving through boulders larger than most starter homes. Then all hell breaks loose. You enter a 2.7-mile stretch of singletrack and narrow doubletrack that runs over, through, or around rocks, granite ledges, trees, streams, and bogs. You'll come up against every imaginable obstacle found in Northeastern woods, so know this before you ride: the middle third of the loop is hard, not always rideable, and a long walk from the nearest anything.

Many riders are lured to "the place of the big buck"— the English translation of "pawtuckaway"—precisely because of this odd mixture of pain and pleasure. If you

stopped at any bike shop between the Atlantic Ocean and Interstate 93 asking for the best trails, you'd no doubt be steered here. Pawtuckaway offers a great diversity of terrain along its well-maintained trail network. The other attractions at Pawtuckaway only double the temptation to visit. Along with cool trails, the park offers a public beach, a picnic area, a lakeside campground, and three small mountains that are still plenty high enough to give views over the lawn you should be mowing or the job you called in sick to.

Within the park's 5,500 acres are marsh, woods, rivers, and mountains. Acquisition of the conservation preserve began in 1923 with the purchase of 60 acres on Middle Mountain. The following year, the widow of local farmer George W. Goodrich sold their homestead at the foot of South Mountain to the state. Later in 1924, the 450-acre Chase farm also became part of the reservation. As Pawtuckaway grew, so too did the need for a forest management plan, as well as a functional road network. The labor to accomplish this arrived with the Civilian Conservation Corps (CCC) during the Great Depression. The CCC planted timber to replace that harvested through the 1920s, improved roads ruined by logging, and cleared timbering debris from the slash lots.

Special sites to hit while visiting Pawtuckaway include the fire tower atop South Mountain, which offers views to the Atlantic Ocean on clear days. Tower Road takes cyclists near this spot, but you'll have to hike the short footpath to the tower. Similar vistas of the countryside from the elevations of Middle and North Mountain tend to be less crowded. A prime spot along the featured route to recuperate and soak in the view awaits at the marsh overlook near the end of North Mountain Bypass. It's 5.5 miles into the loop and a cool spot for a snack and a mouthful of water.

Soon after the marsh overlook are the Boulder Fields. Designated as a state Natural Area, the fields contain the largest collection of glacial erratics yet known. Geologists believe that the boulders were cut from North Mountain and deposited here by receding glaciers during the last Ice Age. Churchill Rock, "discovered" in 1870, takes honors as the king of Pawtuckaway's boulders. Measuring 62 feet long by 40 feet wide by 40 feet high, it weighs about 6,000 tons.

The Boulder Fields lead into the Boulder Trail before the ride crosses Round Pond Trail. Round Pond Trail is typical of the wide, gravel fire roads that loop through the western part of the park. These fire roads are the best bet for easy to moderate riding. North of Middle Mountain, expect rolling grades and some short, steep inclines on the roads. During the wet season, brief sections of these routes may flood under inches of water. You can find easier gravel travel south of Middle Mountain, on Reservation Road. For truly easy stuff, look into the Fundy Trail, which starts near the campground/beach area and makes up the last off-road leg of the featured ride. It runs 1.5 miles to the Fundy Cove boat launch.

New Hampshire allows mountain bikes on all Pawtuckaway State Park trails, but asks that Mountain Trail be avoided on summer weekends, as it's busy with day-hikers. State Snowmobile Corridor Trail 17 cuts through the park and extends northwest to Gilmanton, near Lake Winnipesaukee. Snowmobilers also utilize other Pawtuckaway trails, which means paths tend to be wide, with maintained bridges over running water.

Boulder Fields natural area

Make a copy of this chapter's map and stick it in a jersey pocket before heading out for any ride. You could keep a difficult loop from becoming gruesome by bringing it. Use the map for bailout options, should a fallen branch shoot through your spokes or should the doughnut you ate for breakfast erupt in your stomach. Markers at intersections in the woods correspond to reference numbers on the map. The official park map, found in the main parking area, charts an equally good overview of the trail network, but be wary if you've held onto a copy revised before 1993. On past issues, the 3s, 4s, 13s, and 14s were mislabeled.

Just 100 years ago, there were no state or federally owned forest lands in New Hampshire. Today, over 830,000 acres are in public possession. Nearly all of them are open to mountain bikers.

Ride Information

☏ Trail Contacts:
Park Manager, Pawtuckaway State Park, Raymond, NH (603) 895-3031

◴ Schedule:
The park is accessible year-round, but facilities are only open dawn to dusk, mid May through mid October.

⑤ Fees/Permits:
$2.50 per person. No cost from mid October through mid May, or at alternate starts. $14 to $20 per night for camping.

♀ Local Events/Attractions:
The Deerfield Fair, each fall, Deerfield, NH (603) 463-7421 – *one of the largest and most popular agricultural fairs in New England*

⊜ Accommodations:
Pawtuckaway State Park offers 193 tent sites.

⊕ Local Bike Shops:
Transition Performance, Raymond, NH (603) 895-6594 – custom road and mountain bike builders • **Exeter Cycles,** Exeter, NH (603) 778-2331 • **Wheel Power,** Exeter, NH (603) 772-6343 • **Nault's Cyclery,** Manchester, NH (603) 669-7993 or *www.naults.com* • **Nault's Cyclery,** Concord, NH (603) 228-3319 or *www.naults.com* **Benson's Ski & Sport Shop,** Derry, NH (603) 432-2531 • **Cycle City Inc.,** Plaistow, NH (603) 382-1820

Ⓝ Maps:
USGS maps: Mount Pawtuckaway, NH Pawtuckaway State Park Hiking Trails map – available at the park or in advance by calling (603) 895-3031

MilesDirections

0.0 START from the administration building parking lot and head right on State Park Road past the tollbooth ($2.50 per person). The downhill bottoms out at Mountain Pond, which lies on the left. Turn left after the pond onto Mountain Trail/Round Pond Trail. At the sign marking the trail split, bear left on Round Pond Trail.

1.8 Before leading onto private property, Round Pond Trail turns right at Marker 14 and passes through a stone wall. It comes parallel to a gravel road 0.2 miles later, where it makes an immediate left across the road. Round Pond Trail merges with a trail from the right.

2.2 Partway up a gradual climb, Round Pond Trail turns right off Snowmobile Corridor Trail 17. It descends and comes to a junction in an open area. Turn left here at Marker 13, then roll right following the white blazes. A wetland will be to the left through the trees.

2.6 Turn left on gravel Reservation Road.

3.2 Reservation Road bends left, uphill, where North Mountain Trail comes in from the right. Take North Mountain Trail and pass the sign for "No wheeled vehicles" (this applies to motorized vehicles).

3.7 Turn right at the trail junction, onto North Mountain Bypass. (This trail soon merges with another. Across the intersection, a short hiking path leads uphill to an open eastern view.) After a downhill, continue left, with the white blazes, rather than taking another doubletrack that branches right.

4.8 Stay on North Mountain Bypass as it splits left from the wider trail. A small arrow sign nailed to a tree points the way. (A missed turn will bring you over a wooden bridge and through a clearing.) North Mountain Bypass narrows into singletrack and climbs to a partial clearing that overlooks a marsh. Look for deer at the water's edge.

5.5 Soon after the marsh overlook, double white blazes and another small arrow sign nailed to a tree signal a 90-degree left turn. Turn here. The route switches back and drops downhill before a "T" intersection with a gravel road. A trail sign points to the Boulder Trail, among other trails. Turn left, as the sign directs.

5.7 Leave the gravel road at the sign for the Boulder Trail. Cross a stream and enter the Boulder Field, a den of giant rocks. Continue on the Boulder Trail, riding between a marsh and Rocky Ridge.

6.5 Exit the Boulder Trail at Round Pond. Turn right and immediately left along the shore on South Ridge Trail. Follow the white blazes.

7.0 At the intersection with the doubletrack Shaw Trail, turn left across the remains of a wooden bridge. There will be a number of wet

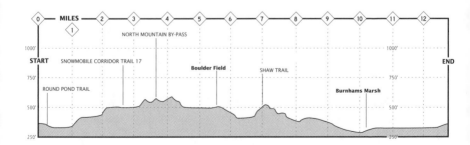

62

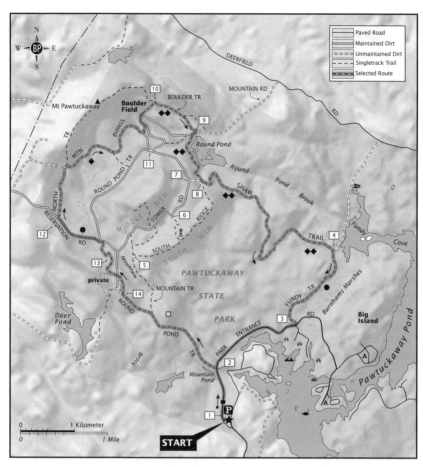

spots along Shaw Trail and one distinct wet-land 100 feet wide that in most seasons will require circumnavigation.

9.2 Shaw Trail crosses a large marsh, but a boat won't be necessary to continue the ride. Turn left on a primitive path along the shore, cross over rocks where the marsh comes to a point and the trail seems to end, and continue back to Shaw Trail by keeping the water to the right. A stream crossing by a washed-out bridge is followed by a knoll with a surprise drop to watch for on the other side.

10.2 Turn right at the "T" intersection with Fundy Trail (Marker 4). Immediately cross a

wooden bridge and come along Burnhams Marsh. One mile later, cross another bridge, and after an open area, turn right at an intersection with a dirt road.

11.2 Turn right on paved State Park Road. (Unless it's time for a swim at the state beach.)

12.8 Arrive at the parking lot.

Alternate Starts:

Reservation Road off NH 107 in Deerfield, or Mountain Road and the Fundy Cove Boat launch off Deerfield Road in Nottingham, provide trail access.

Northwood Meadows State Park

Ride Summary

Northwood Meadows State Park isn't the place to test one's brute pedaling strength, long distance endurance, or technical riding skills. But what it isn't makes it what it is—a quiet place to pedal alone, in a small group, or with family. Mostly local residents use Northwood Meadows for fishing and walking, but wide trails and good lines-of-sight make it ready for mountain bikers too.

Ride Specs

Start: From the Northwood Meadows State Park gate

Length: 5.5-mile out-and-back with a loop portion

Approximate Riding Time: 1-1½ hours

Difficulty Rating: Technically easy, with some loose surfaces to watch out for. Physically moderate overall, with one lengthy hill.

Trail Surface: Gravel roads and smooth woodland paths covered by pine needles

Lay of the Land: Rolling, forested acres surround Meadow Lake and adjacent low-lying wetlands. Trees provide shade cover for a portion of the loop, while the majority of the mileage offers open skies.

Elevation Gain: 437 feet

Land Status: State park

Nearest Town: Northwood, NH

Other Trail Users: Walkers, joggers, picnickers, wildlife viewers, anglers, and cross-country skiers

Wheels: Fine for hybrids. Gravel roads make child trailers with sling seats the least jarring option for toting little ones.

Getting There

From Concord, NH: Travel U.S. 4 east into Northwood. You'll pass Coe-Brown Academy. Northwood Meadows State Park is on the right one mile beyond the Academy and is marked by a large brown sign with gold lettering. **DeLorme: New Hampshire Atlas & Gazetteer:** Page 29, E-8

Northwood Meadows State Park's creators set out to provide the public with uninhibited access to both land and water. A group of local phone company workers, known then as the NYNEX Pioneers, led this ground breaking effort. Also out to help were employees from the New Hampshire Department of Parks and Recreation, as well as Northwood citizens and Conservation Commission members. The partnership's unlimited access goal was both novel and noble. Together they cleared, graded, and packed the path around the perimeter of Meadow Lake for wheelchair use. Wheel-chair friendly piers where also constructed along the shore for fishing or just for sitting in the quiet hollow.

The state acquired Northwood Meadows State Park's 600 acres of forest and water in 1991. A combination of pre-existing gravel roads and a smooth 1.5-mile path offer some of the easiest terrain available to New Hampshire mountain bikers. But if that sounds too lackluster for you, off the beaten path waits some very rough terrain to satisfy your needs.

Notice that the ride directions start at U.S. Route 4, but if the park gate is open—which it usually is—the first half-mile of the loop can be avoided by driving to the main parking area above the lake. From the main parking area drops a short downhill roll that levels out with views across Meadow Lake. In late afternoon, the sun turns the rippled surface golden. To the right of the shimmer, a small peninsula juts out from the land; while across the way, evergreens line the shore. Paths to the left lead along the water and to the rowboat and canoe launch, but this trip continues straight, adding a little distance to your ride before you return to the water by the earthen dam. This junction is a choice spot to enjoy unobstructed views before heading back into the woods.

Once over the dam, tread lightly on the trail, as wheelchair users rely on its smooth, packed surface. Turns and dips in the path keep things lively, and glimpses of the lake through the trees ensure that you're on the right course. When the wooden bridges come up, take care in crossing them if they're at all wet. Tires hold to wet wood only slightly better than they do to ice.

The New Hampshire Antiques Dealers Association lists 170 member shops in the state. No less than a dozen antique retailers line U.S. Route 4 in Northwood.

The excursion down the gravel road distances you from the parking area and the lake as you pedal additional quiet miles away from civilization. This stretch is not shaded, which is an important consideration on hot days. There is an initial descent, followed by a short climb, and punctuated by a longer, gradual climb before the road levels off. When followed to its end, the route passes over an embankment into the woods, where it intersects Old Mountain Road and opens up terrain much different from the easier trails conquered earlier. Some areas of Old Mountain Road are washed out and rocky, while others can be wet and muddy—especially in the spring. For those with the ambition, a right or left on Old Mountain Road forms the first leg of potential loops back to the park entrance off U.S. Route 4. This option to extend simply makes for a longer ride, but will also demand short travel on the shoulder of U.S. Route 4. Check out the map for the turns.

Thousands of people a day travel U.S. Route 4 between Portsmouth and Concord, passing right by the town Northwood and Northwood Meadows State Park. And yet they rarely stop. They simply don't know what they're missing. Someday on the commute home from work or while making your way across New Hampshire, pull off at the park entrance. Unload your bicycle, strap your bucket on your head, and pedal. Even with our hectic lives, a mountain bike ride is still that simple.

The Telephone Pioneers of America

The Telephone Pioneers of America make up "the largest industry sponsored volunteer community service organization in the world." They are employees and retirees from your local phone company who give their time and use their talents for the benefit of others. In 1996, over 100,000 Telephone Pioneers of America associated with what was then NYNEX gave 3 million hours of community service throughout New York and New England. Their contributions included work on the trails and piers at Northwood Meadows, assistance with the Special Olympics, and labor for Habitat for Humanity. Other places to find Pioneers lending a hand are at canned food drives, teaching Junior Achievement courses, or on a school playground, painting a map of the United States.

Ride Information

🕐 Trail Contacts:
New Hampshire Division of Parks and
Recreation, Concord, NH
(603) 271-3254

🕐 Schedule:
Users are welcome year-round, however,
the gate is locked through winter, and at
dusk from spring through fall.

🚲 Local Bike Shops:
Durham Bike, Durham, NH (603) 868-
5634 • Tony's Cyclery, Dover, NH
(603) 742-0494

Ⓝ Maps:
USGS maps: Northwood, NH

MilesDirections

0.0 START from the gate at the entrance off U.S. 4. Pedal down the gravel road into the park.

0.5 At the main parking area, turn right on the gravel road. Go down the hill and ride briefly along Meadow Lake. Pass by turns to the left and continue straight on the gravel road. After a modest climb and a gradual descent, the gravel road narrows and begins a tight left-hand turn that points back in the direction of Meadow Lake.

1.0 Just before coming alongside the water, turn right and head down a slope. Cross the earthen dam. The path turns to the right and heads up, travelling along a hillside before switching back toward the water. A number of access paths lead to the shore, but continue on the main trail by keeping the lake in sight on the left.

1.8 Exit the forest canopy briefly and then reenter on a path to the left (you've missed the turn if you come to the dirt road). There will be a smooth downhill with two tight turns to negotiate near the bottom. After that, you'll have two wooden bridges to cross.

2.0 Turn right and head uphill on the gravel road, away from Meadow Lake. Take another right at the hilltop. Pass the handicapped parking area and continue to the blockaded end of the gravel road.

3.5 Turn around at the embankment and retrace you tracks back to your vehicle.

5.5 Reach your vehicle.

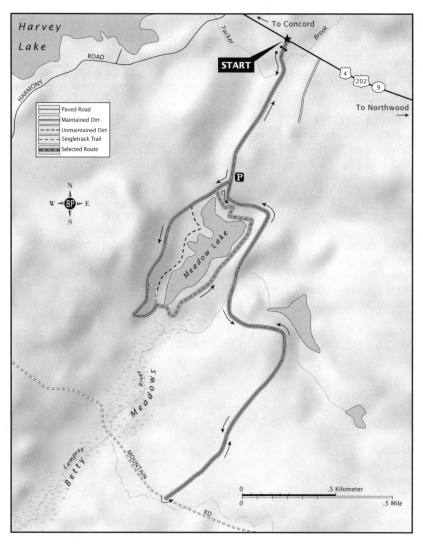

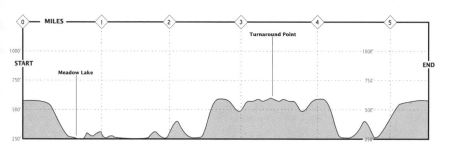

Bear Brook
State Park

Ride Summary

Bear Brook rocks. Any mountain biking regular from the central part of Southern New Hampshire will attest to that. It holds a great diversity of trail types, obstacles, and topography. The loop charted here gives a mixture of it all. So do it once, then come back another day with a free park map, or a friend knowledgeable of the area, and plan an epic ride.

Ride Specs

Start: From the mountain biker and hiker parking lot opposite the Bear Brook State Park winter office on Podunk Road
Length: 10.1-mile loop
Approximate Riding Time: 2 hours
Difficulty Rating: Technically difficult due to many rocky sections, loose surfaces, and sometimes muddy conditions. Extreme efforts will be needed on the many short climbs, and one extended ascent.
Trail Surface: Singletrack, doubletrack, and gravel roads
Lay of the Land: Distinct areas of contour-less topography, as well as hilly sections and extensive, bug-infested wetlands
Elevation Gain: 680 feet
Land Status: State park
Nearest Town: Allenstown, NH
Other Trail Users: Hikers, equestrians, campers, swimmers, anglers, archers, snowmobilers, cross-country skiers, and hunters (in season)
Wheels: Mountain bikes only. Front or full-suspension would lessen the punishment.

Getting There

From Manchester, NH: Follow U.S. 3 / NH 28 north toward Suncook. U.S. 3 and NH 28 split. Follow NH 28 north for 3 miles beyond the split. Turn right at the Bear Brook State Park sign onto Bear Brook Road. Follow to the tollbooth where park-use fees are charged in-season during the daytime. Continue past the tollbooth for 2.3 miles, then turn right onto Podunk Road. The parking lot is on the right 0.3 miles up Podunk Road and marked by a sign. *DeLorme: New Hampshire Atlas & Gazetteer:* Page 28, G-5

S ome 40 miles of trails run through Bear Brook State Park's 9,600 acres. Off-road routes over that much open land might be common in New Hampshire's North Country but not within a dozen miles of the state's two major cities and Interstate 93. And yet, there Bear Brook sits, midway between Manchester and Concord.

Promoted by the state as one of its top three forests for mountain biking, Bear Brook can fill the day or weekend of anyone who enjoys the outdoors. It would take years to fully understand the maze of trails. But do this ride and you're on your way to understanding. To help once you're on-site, park maps are available in boxes at the

mountain biker parking lot and at other places throughout the facility. In addition to all the riding available, ball fields, group shelters, picnicking areas, and a beach on Catamount Pond invite family gatherings. This is a good card to play when trying to rally the clan for a trip.

Expect a hard, maybe even extreme, workout when riding the charted loop. The first few miles mix flat sections with many ascents and descents. Typical obstacles like rocks and roots roughen the ride, but also pay attention in the logging areas. Though these spots are in the process of reclamation, the slash left behind from recent lumbering could quickly rip a spoke from its nipple or snap off a derailluer.

The shorter ascents along the beginning of the ride lead to an extended climb up Hall Mountain. Traction is good over the doubletrack of Hall Mountain Trail, but the relentless grade keeps the anaerobic pressure on. Just when you think you've reached the top, there's another descent before the final climb to salvation at the summit. You'll know you made it when you reach an area of exposed granite, which has been blown free of topsoil by the panting of those before you.

Since mountain bikes and water both adhere to the laws of gravity, the Hall Mountain descent brings the two together at the bottom. The trail stumbles over mud and exposed roots along the edge of a wetland before turning onto a dilapidated walking bridge. Beyond the bridge there's another mile of low-lying land that's often muddy. Once off Hall Mountain Trail and onto Podunk Road, the trip back runs mostly downhill along the maintained gravel surface. Watch for cars.

Atop a large, multi-level foundation.

After you've completed the loop and rested, explore other parts of Bear Brook. The many fishing holes at the park give anglers plenty of choices. Archery Pond, which is wheelchair accessible and stocked with trout, counts among the options. The second stocked pond is the Kids' Fishing Pond, which is for visitors younger than 12. It might just be enough to keep them away from the latest video game—when they're not riding, of course.

Archers can practice their skills at either of the two 15-target ranges, and a third range with four targets is wheelchair accessible. Signs clearly mark the archery range areas, so that users of the nature trails or the 1.25-mile fitness course have little chance of ending up like an arrow-headed Steve Martin in some stand-up act gone terribly wrong.

Ride Information

Trail Contacts:
Manager, Bear Brook State Park, Allenstown, NH (603) 485-9874

Schedule:
Bear Brook trails can be ridden year-round, except from snow-melt through the spring rains due to mud and erosion concerns. Camping and facilities are open mid May through mid October.

Fees/Permits:
$2.50 per person during the campground's open season

Local Events/Attractions:
New Hampshire State House, Concord, NH (603) 271-2154 • **The Christa McAuliffe Planetarium,** Concord, NH (603) 271-7827 • **Museum of New Hampshire History,** Concord, NH (603) 226-3189 • **The Conservation Center,** Concord, NH (603) 224-9945 • **The Deerfield Fair,** late September/early October, Deerfield, NH – contact the Deerfield Fair Association at (603) 463-7421 or visit the fair website at *www.deerfield-fair.com*

Accommodations:
Bear Brook State Park offers 93 tent sites. Call the state's central reservation line for Bear Brook and all other NH campgrounds, (603) 271-3628.

Group Rides:
Banagan's Cycling Company, Tuesdays at 6:30, Manchester, NH (603) 623-3330

Local Bike Shops:
Naults Cyclery, Manchester, NH (603) 669-7993 or 1-888-640-7993 or *www.naults.com* • **Naults Cyclery,** Concord, NH (603) 228-3319 or 1-888-499-3319 or *www.naults.com* • **S & W Sport Shop,** Concord, NH (603) 228-1441 • **Banagan's Cycling Company,** Manchester, NH (603) 623-3330 • **Banagan's Cycling Company,** Concord, NH (603) 225-3330 • **True Sport Inc.,** Concord, NH (603) 228-8411 • **Goodale's Bike & Ski Inc.,** Hooksett, NH (603) 644-2111 • **Waite Sports Specialists,** Concord, NH (603) 228-8621 • **Bike Doctor,** Manchester, NH (603) 627-5566 • **Bike Barn,** Manchester, NH (603) 668-6555 • **All Outdoors,** Manchester, NH (603) 624-1468 • **Alternative Bike Shop,** Manchester, NH (603) 666-4527 • **Hog Wild Bicycles,** Manchester, NH (603) 624-8703 • **Ski Market,** Manchester, NH (603) 647-1212

Maps:
USGS maps: Candia, NH; Gossville, NH; Manchester North, NH; Suncook, NH

If the promise of great riding and other physical pursuits sounds too exhausting, consider the Museum Complex just east of the park office. The buildings date to the 1930s, when recreation was far from the minds of most. They are what remains of the Civilian Conservation Corps Bear Brook Camp, one of the largest intact reminders of CCC camps in the country. The former Bear Brook CCC headquarters and bunkhouses now occupied by the museums are on the National Register of Historic Places.

The 4-H Center at the Museum Complex displays exhibits on the natural history of Bear Brook, and the park managers run interpretive programs through the summer. Adjacent to the 4-H Center is the Richard Diehl CCC Museum, which describes the hard work done in the building of park trails and facilities and provides a glimpse at the character of the men who built the park. Next in line to the 4-H Center, the Museum of Family Camping portrays the development of camping into its modern state. Next up is the New Hampshire Snowmobile Museum, dedicated to the history and sport of...well, isn't it obvious? Could the Museum of Fat Tire Revolution be far away?

The Deerfield Fair

Some weekend late in September, or one early in October depending on the year, continue past Bear Brook State Park to the Deerfield Fairgrounds. Off New Hampshire 43 in Deerfield, the acres burst to the colors of autumn. Crowds cheer and turf flies as oxen drag stoneboats from a dead-still to the finish line. In a nearby clearing, kids and parents watch the acrobatics of a high-wire team swinging amongst the trees. In another corner of the grounds, a local youth chases a muddy pig through the slop of the pig scramble ring. That last event sounds like an early spring mountain bike ride with a good friend.

The Deerfield Fair, which has been held yearly since 1876, is the largest and oldest "family fair" in New Hampshire. Today's event is no longer run just to show rural farmers the latest advances in animal husbandry and agricultural production. Though, sure enough, John Deere's representatives will be there to show their fancier and "bettah tractah." Parked right beside it will be a riding mower designed for cutting fairway-length lawns. There's irony in there somewhere.

Year after year, the Deerfield Fair reaffirms its reputation as a family event. It's also one where an entire town comes together as hosts and participants. On the Friday of fair weekend, Deerfield Community School takes the day off. Still, students and teachers inevitably cross paths on the way to the fair or waiting in line for cotton candy. Neighbors work together at the ticket booths and volunteer in the show buildings. At the same time, local farmers, bakers, and artisans wait anxiously as the judges award blue ribbons for livestock, produce, baked goods, and crafts.

Only during the annual 4-day run of the fair can the words "Deerfield" and "traffic jam" be used in the same sentence. Expect a packed event on Friday evening, and arrive early in the morning on Saturday and Sunday to beat the crowds. For more information watch the local papers near the end of harvest season, or contact the Deerfield Fair Association at (603) 463-7421 or visit the fair website www.deerfield-fair.com.

MilesDirections

0.0 START from the parking lot exit. Cross Podunk Road, traveling behind the administration building, onto the trail marked XC 1. Follow XC 1 to the left, as it soon departs from the old logging road.

0.5 Cross an access road and ride between a sand pit and the paved Campground Road.

0.8 Exit the woods at Archery Pond. Continue through the parking lot and turn left onto Campground Road.

1.4 Turn right at the sign for XC 4 onto Broken Boulder Trail.

1.8 Turn right at the trail junction. Turn left at the next intersection, and head away from Smith Pond Shelter. If you need to make a pit stop, there are outhouses at Smith Pond Shelter.

2.6 Turn left onto the gravel-surfaced Spruce Pond Road.

2.7 Make a right after the broken boulder and continue on Broken Boulder Trail.

3.7 Turn left onto Podunk Road.

4.5 At a small, open intersection with a tele-phone pole on the left, turn right onto Hall Mountain Trail. Immediately pass an old stone foundation on your left. Turn right at the next trail junction before beginning the climb to Hall Mountain.

5.6 Crest Hall Mountain and begin a steep descent. Stay straight and ignore trails that depart to the left. Cross a bridge after a swampy area and continue as Hall Mountain Trail becomes an abandoned road.

7.6 Turn right onto gravel-surfaced Bear Hill Road at the sign for Intersection 15.

7.7 The gravel road bends left, but continue straight around the boulder barricade onto a grassy track. Immediately pass into a playing field. Ride along the edge of the woods for about 150 yards. At the far corner of the field, turn right and pass the large boulder onto tight singletrack. Follow the yellow blazes out to Podunk Road.

8.6 Turn left onto Podunk Road.

10.1 After the gate, make a left into the parking lot.

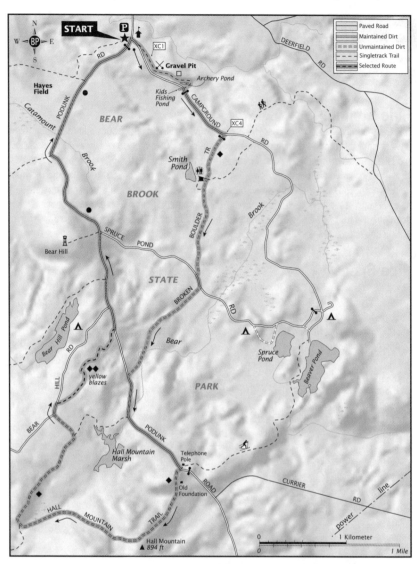

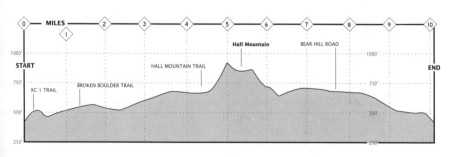

Tower Hill Pond Loop

Ride Summary

The trails around and about Tower Hill Pond give newer riders and groups with divergent talent a great spot to get the knobbies dirty. Even better, this user-friendly network of gravel service roads and rougher doubletrack is an easy reach from Manchester, New Hampshire's largest city. The loop travels around the Tower Hill Pond perimeter, providing water views from a number of vantagepoints. There are small hills to negotiate, but shallow grades and generally firm trail surfaces ease the way for the novice. For a greater challenge, explore the more difficult doubletracks that rise away from the pond, or try the extensive network of singletrack nearby at Massabesic Lake.

Ride Specs

Start: From the parking lot on Tower Hill Road
Length: 4.9-mile loop
Approximate Riding Time: 45 minutes
Difficulty Rating: Technically easy, though some spots puddle after rains. Physically easy, with gradual grades
Trail Surface: Gated service roads with loose gravel and puddles
Lay of the Land: Forested watershed area, with Tower Hill Pond at bottom of the drainage slope
Elevation Gain: 80 feet
Land Status: Public watershed land
Nearest Town: Manchester, NH
Other Trail Users: Hikers, joggers, snowmobilers, and occasional patrol and maintenance vehicles
Wheels: Mountain bikes are best, though kids' single-speeds, bike trailers, and hybrids will fair well in dry conditions

Getting There

From Manchester, NH: Follow NH 101 East, and take Exit 2. Turn south at the end of the off-ramp and travel 0.1 miles. Turn left onto Old Candia Road. Continue 0.4 miles and turn left again onto Tower Hill Road. Park to the right in the turnout immediately after the underpass. *DeLorme: New Hampshire Atlas & Gazetteer.* Page 28, J-5

The Fombanese do their work out in the open, though few will ever notice them at their task. They spend their time in the woods maintaining trails, building new trails, and doing whatever else is necessary to ensure the perpetuation of mountain biking privileges in the Massabesic Lake watershed. They are the members of the Friends of Massabesic Bicycling Association (FOMBA), and they have developed a laudatory relationship with the Manchester Water Works for cooperation between mountain bike advocates and resource managers.

FOMBA formed in 1995 to preserve mountain biking rights around Massabesic Lake. With the explosive popularity of the sport at that time, many existing trails were being damaged by excessive or insensitive use. Jack Chapman, the founding father of FOMBA, brought together the initial band of riders to ward off permanent mountain biking restrictions to the area.

When not tackling the trails the Fombanese revel in the social circuit. The Fombanese are not only trailrights advocates, but they are also social beasts. They host the Turkey Burner Fun Ride each year on the day after Thanksgiving. They throw Christmas parties at members' homes. And they basically get together for rides and post-ride fun whenever the mood arises. Each year they use the service roads around Tower Hill Pond to stage the Watershed Wahoo, an Eastern Fat Tire Association event with proceeds donated to the American Lung Association. FOMBA's selfless involvement earned them the 1998 Spirit of Manchester award, presented by Mayor Wieczorek, for their diligent and successful efforts at improving the quality of life for city residents.

While much of FOMBA's energy goes into the trails in and around Massabesic Lake, they also cooperate with the Manchester Water Works on mountain biking issues at Tower Hill Pond. The chapter loop is a result of their work with Manchester Water Works. It starts at the base of gravel Tower Hill Road and climbs for a third of a mile until a turn past a gate sends you into the woods. You pass over a mixed sur-face of gravel and broken pavement before descending to the signboard by Tower Hill

Pedaling alongside Tower Hill Pond

Ride Information

● Trail Contacts:
Manchester Water Works, Manchester, NH (603) 624-6483

● Schedule:
Open year-round

● Local Information:
Manchester Chamber of Commerce, Manchester, NH (603) 666-6600 or www.manchester-chamber.org

● Local Events/Attractions:
The Currier Gallery of Art, 201 Myrtle Way, Manchester, NH (603) 669-6144

● Organizations:
Friends of Massabesic Bicycling Association, Auburn, NH (603) 483-2951 or www.fomba.com

● Local Bike Shops:
Nault's Cyclery, Manchester, NH (603) 669-7993 or 1-888-640-7993 or www.naults.com

Banagan's Cycling Company, Manchester, NH (603) 623-3330 • **All Outdoors,** Manchester, NH (603) 624-1468 • **Alternative Bike Shop,** Manchester, NH (603) 666-4527 • **Haggetts Bicycle Shop,** Manchester, NH (603) 624-8362 • **Ski Market,** Manchester, NH (603) 647-1212 • **The Bike Barn,** Manchester, NH (603) 668-6555 • **The Squeaky Wheel,** Manchester, NH (603) 623-5828

● Maps:
USGS maps: Manchester North, NH; Candia, NH

Pond. Note that the pond, which fills your view, is a drinking water resource for the city of Manchester. The signboard lists activities that should be avoided, such as swimming in the reservoir.

The loop travels counter clockwise around the pond. Following along the eastern shore, neither hills nor difficult trail surfaces hamper your way. Rougher doubletracks run off to your right. To stay on the chapter's course, keep the water to your left. At the midpoint of the ride a buffer of forest blocks Tower Hill Pond from your sight. This is the only extended section where you will not catch an occasional glimpse of the water.

Maple Falls Brook passes under your wheels, and later, Snowmobile Corridor Trail 15 departs to the right. The return leg along Tower Hill Pond's western shore brings back views of the water, as well as introduces some grade changes. While the ascents are not extended or steep, be prepared to exert more effort. Brisk downhills over wide gravel surfaces will then restore your strength.

As you seal off your circumnavigation of Tower Hill Pond, you will cross successive earthen dams—both offer unobstructed views across the open water. Once you pass the signboard by the second dam, it's a quick return to Tower Hill Road. The ensuing descent to the parking area makes for a tidy finish to your trip.

As mentioned earlier, a second network of trails with a greater mix of singletrack has been laid out just south of Tower Hill Pond, at Massabesic Lake in Auburn, New Hampshire. Existing service roads access many miles of singletrack established and maintained by FOMBA through its partnership efforts with the Manchester Water Works. Talk with FOMBA to find the best places to explore at Massabesic Lake, or better yet, join them on a group ride.

Tower Hill Pond

MilesDirections

0.0 START uphill on Tower Hill Road. Continue to the third gated left—to include the gated doubletrack at the parking turnout.

0.3 Turn left off Tower Hill Road onto the gated service road. Signs instruct drivers not to obstruct the gate. The service road consists of a mixed surface of gravel and crumbled asphalt.

0.7 Pass the Tower Hill Pond signboard on your right. Ride counterclockwise around the pond, keeping the water to your left.

1.6 Pass the sign for the exit to the Southern New Hampshire Sno-Slickers Club.

2.1 Pass New Hampshire Snowmobile Corridor Trail 15.

3.6 Pass the "Bridge Ahead" sign. Cross over a backfilled culvert. Turn left onto a service road of gravel and broken pavement. Emerge at Tower Hill Pond and cross the first earthen dam.

4.1 Cross the second earthen dam. Turn right at the Tower Hill Pond signboard onto the service road that led you into the pond loop. Continue to the gate at Tower Hill Road and turn right.

4.9 Finish back at the turnout.

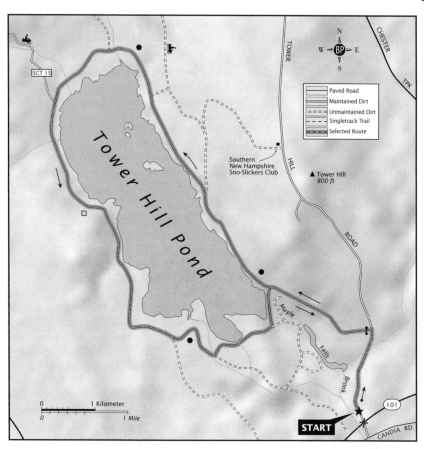

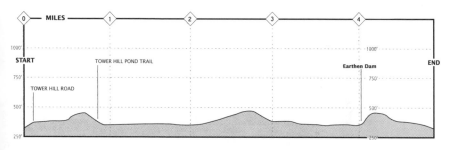

Rockingham Recreational Trail

Ride Summary

Abandoned rail lines invite yet another opportunity for easy mountain biking through Southern New Hampshire, the countryside that for so long inspired the poet Robert Frost. Steel and wood bridges remain to guide you over water, and the state has built a tunnel under NH 101 to keep your trip safe and fluid. Ready for groups and families, trail surfaces are generally firm, and long lines-of-sight keep even over-energized riders perceptibly near.

Ride Specs

Start: From Windham Depot
Length: 19.4-mile point-to-point
Approximate Riding Time: 2½–3 hours
Difficulty Rating: Technically easy, with the exception of the first four miles from Windham Depot, which has a loose surface that makes control difficult. Low effort due to the flat grade, though to ride the full length of the trail will require multi-hour endurance.
Trail Surface: Converted railroad bed: gravel and cinder
Lay of the Land: Flat, with areas of loose gravel and a series of small, rolling mounds
Elevation Gain: -156 feet
Land Status: State sponsored recreational trail
Nearest Town: Windham, NH
Other Trail Users: Walkers, joggers, cross-country skiers, ATVs, motorcyclists, and snowmobilers

Getting There

From Salem, NH: Travel north on NH 28 through Windham. Just over the town line from Windham into Derry, turn left (west) at the blinking light by the Over the Rainbow Preschool onto Windham Depot Road. Continue 1.3 miles to the intersection with Frost Road, and park in the area to the left, away from the buildings. A small brown sign marks the trailhead. *DeLorme: New Hampshire Atlas & Gazetteer:* Page 22, F-6

Shuttle Point: From Epping, NH: Travel south on NH 125 from its junction with NH 27. Take the first right onto Railroad Avenue, and then take the first left onto Main Street. Immediately, an abandoned rail line crosses the street. This trail runs east to Newfields, and west to Manchester (see Ride 2). It doesn't go to Windham. However, the obscured trail to Windham does intersect here. You'll find the Windham Trail by looking left toward National Propane. Ride southwest between the front of National Propane and NH 125 to get on the route. Quickly into the ride, you'll cross a tunnel under NH 101 to confirm you're on your way. *DeLorme: New Hampshire Atlas & Gazetteer:* Page 29, K-11

The starting point for this six-town rail-trail ramble lies just north of the Massachusetts border, only a hair east of Interstate 93. The first four miles of this multiple-use trail show wear from ATV traffic. Though ruts and erosion are not problems, many sections are sandy, soft, and can be a chore to pedal through. Once past the 4-mile mark, the surface firms up, but whoop-de-doos can still make for a roller

coaster ride. Near the transition to firm ground the trail passes on a raised bed through a wetland. Look for the turtle tracks across the path. Farther along, you might notice moose tracks alongside the knobby marks that you leave.

For the length of the ride, brown signs designating the trail and orange gates erected to keep 4x4s out will become familiar. Blue signs near road intersections point to restaurants and convenience stores, just like you'd encounter on a regular highway. Be aware that sources of nourishment are harder to come by in the first few miles, so pack plenty of water and edibles if an out-and-back trip is planned.

The mileage cues used for this route are laid out in a point-to-point fashion. A round trip is entirely doable, simply double your times and mileage. Another option would be to head west once you reach the Newfields-to-Manchester Rail Trail in Epping (see Ride 2). From the western terminus of the Newfields-to-Manchester Rail Trail, map a pavement route south to Windham Depot. This last option could give you over 50 miles of riding in one day.

A long ride that ends with a return to Windham might invite a side-trip to the Nutfield Brewery. Let the smell of wort boiling guide you to the refreshments. The microbrewery resurrected the colonial name for the area—a place long ago noted for its abundance of nut bearing trees.

In 1718, sixteen Irish and Scotch-Irish families emigrated with their minister, Reverend McGregor, from Derry, Ireland, to America. The settlers acquired 12

Restored Sandown Depot Station

square miles of territory from the state of Massachusetts, covering what would later become the towns of Windham, Londonderry, and Derry, as well as parts of Manchester and Salem. From a simple camp along West Running Brook, the town of Nutfield rose to prosperity.

The pioneers cleared farmland and built homes from the region's enormous supply of stone and wood. But there was the constant fear of Indian attack. To protect themselves, the settlers armed themselves and built two garrisons. But the attacks never came. The settler's good fortune had little to do with their guns and garrisons. It's believed that Nutfield was spared violence because Governor Vaudreuil of Canada, a college chum of Reverend McGregor's, spread word to the local tribes through French Catholic priests that Nutfield should be spared. And so it was.

Robert Frost Farm

If the countryside surrounding this ride inspires no more than the artistry of a perfect pedal stroke, you may be completely content. That would be quite less, though, than the impact the countryside had on Robert Frost, the classic American poet whose works reflected the rural New England scenes. Frost lived on his farm in Derry, New Hampshire, from 1900 to 1911, when he sold the property and moved with his family to England.

Four years later he returned to the United States, and in the meantime had published his first volumes of poetry, A Boy's Will (1913) and North of Boston (1914). Frost earned the Pulitzer Prize four times, and in 1961 read his poem "The Gift Outright" at John F. Kennedy's inauguration.

The poems of Frost gaze upon the beauty of Nature, yet often simultaneously reveal its destructive force. They reflect the spirit of individualism reared within New Englanders and their interplay with the landscape. Many, like "The Road not Taken," might even awaken memories of the hours you have spent in the woods.

Robert Frost Farm

Ride Information

📞 Trail Contacts:

New Hampshire Division of Parks, Bureau of Trails, Concord, NH (603) 271-3254 • **Rails to Trails Conservancy, National Headquarters,** Washington, DC (202) 331-9696 or www.railtrails.org

🕐 Schedule:

Open year-round

💡 Local Events/Attractions:

Robert Frost Farm State Historic Site, Derry, NH (603) 432-3091 • **Nutfield Brewery,** Derry, NH (603) 434-9678 or www.nutfield.com – tours available • **Canobie Lake Park**, Salem, NH (603) 893-3506 or www.canobie.com

🚲 Local Bike Shops:

Flyin' Wheels, Salem, NH (603) 893-0225 • **Cycles Etcetera of Salem Inc.,** Salem, NH (603) 890-3212 • **Buchika's Ski Shops,** Salem, NH (603) 893-5534

Hetzer's Bicycle Shop, Hudson, NH (603) 882-5566 • **Goodale's Bike & Ski Inc.,** Nashua, NH (603) 882-2111 or 1-800-291-2111 • **Benson Ski & Sport,** Merrimack, NH (603) 424-7641 • **Cycle City Inc.,** Plaistow, NH (603) 382-1820 or 1-800-750-2925 • **Merrimack Bicycle Shop,** Merrimack, NH (603) 424-7928 • **Nault's Cyclery,** Manchester, NH (603) 669-7993 or 1-888-640-7993 or www.naults.com • **Nault's Cyclery,** Nashua, NH (603) 886-5912 or 1-800-585-5912 or www.naults.com • **Banagan's Cycling Company,** Manchester, NH (603) 623-3330 • **Exeter Cycles,** Exeter, NH (603) 778-2331 • **Wheel Power Bicycle Shop,** Exeter, NH (603) 772-6343

Ⓝ Maps:

USGS maps: Derry, NH; Kingston, NH; Sandown, NH; Windham, NH; Epping, NH

In the summer of 1722, New Hampshire's General Court approved Nutfield's petition for township. The town changed its name to Londonderry, after Reverend McGregor's former home in Ireland. In 1742, Windham separated from Londonderry and was itself incorporated. Farming continued to be a way of life in the region. Later industries came to include linen making, large-scale farming (such as Harvey Hood's dairy farm), and eventually shoe making. As with many former mill towns in Southern New Hampshire, these old industries died by the latter part of the 20th Century. After many years of uncertainty, high-tech industry and the microbrewery have found their way into the area, leading to an economic revival.

Rockingham Rail-Trail

MilesDirections

0.0 START behind the garage and buildings. Immediately, take a left at the fork, where another rail trail runs straight ahead to Salem.

6.1 The trail appears to lead onto broken pavement, but instead bear right, rise over a knoll, and continue on the opposite side of the road.

6.4 Follow the trail left around a sandpit.

9.0 Pass the restored Sandown Depot on your left. There is a pizza shop within sight of this point.

14.1 Emerge from the tree canopy into the parking lot for Joe Bonis Memorial Park. Continue across the paved road, and then follow the trail left, between the dirt road and the pond.

18.5 The trail comes to a "T" intersection at a green fence by New Hampshire 101. Turn left and coast downhill, then cross through the tunnel under the highway.

19.4 Arrive at Epping, where you intersect with the Newfields-to-Manchester Trail (see Ride 2). Either connect with your shuttle car or turn around and head back to Windham Depot.

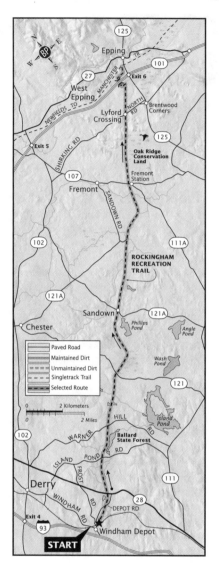

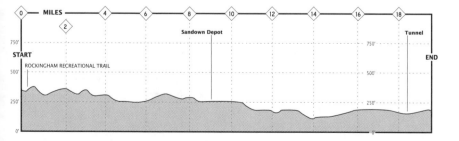

Hopkinton-Everett Reservoir

Ride Summary

Hopkinton-Everett Reservoir is a speedster's paradise. Steep berms let you rail through the corners, while rocks and roots keep you hopping around during the brief times that the singletrack straightens out. You'll find well-packed trail surfaces during the summer, and share the network with its predominant users, ATV pilots and enduro motorcycle riders.

Ride Specs

Start: From Stark Pond OHRV (Off-highway Recreational Vehicle) parking lot
Length: 9.8-mile loop
Approximate Riding Time: 2 hours
Difficulty Rating: Ruts, roots, rocks, and tight turns keep things technically difficult overall. Physically strenuous due to many short climbs and descents mixed between tight singletrack.
Trail Surface: Well-worn trails vary between sand, gravel, and loam. Muddy through the spring.
Lay of the Land: Wooded flood management area with rolling contours and multiple wetlands
Elevation Gain: 188 feet
Land Status: Designated State of New Hampshire OHRV riding area
Nearest Town: Concord, NH
Other Trail Users: Motorcyclists, ATVs, and snowmobilers
Wheels: Mountain bikes only on the chapter loop, but hybrids will manage well on the many gravel roads accessible from the START point

Getting There

From Concord, NH: Head north on I-89 and take Exit 2. Turn left onto NH 13 South. At the junction with NH 77, marked by a blinking light and signs for Clough State Park and Everett Dam, turn left and continue on NH 13. After 0.8 miles, turn right onto Winslow Road by the roadside store. Travel 0.6 miles, turn right at the sign for OHRV parking, and continue past the gate for one mile. The parking lot borders both sides of the road.
DeLorme: New Hampshire Atlas & Gazetteer: Page 27, G-12

E xperienced riders move to the front of the line. The multi-use trail system at Hopkinton-Everett Reservoir demands fitness and skill. You will find miles of singletrack that twists, climbs, and tilts violently downward in this hammerhead kingdom. Be warned though, an armament of rocks, roots, and trees may throw posers from their saddles to the dirt.

Over 20 miles of well traveled routes cut through the Hopkinton-Everett flood control area. Designed and developed by the United States Army Corp of Engineers in response to the destruction wreaked by the great storms of 1937 and 1938, Hopkinton-Everett Reservoir is a vital part of the Merrimack River Basin storm water management plan. It is a "dry" reservoir, as in it is not used for drinking water, but instead to control the flow of tributaries into the Merrimack.

Most anywhere at Hopkinton-Everett, you'll find yourself in the middle ring. You'll stay planted in it through the repetitive turns and short climbs, while firing off a thousand shifts between the middle cogs on the rear wheel. With all the quick descents and abrupt changes in direction, the brakes get a heavy workout. Before you ride, do a little cable tune-up on your bike if things aren't up to snuff.

The state of New Hampshire publicizes this area for ATV riding, enduro dirt biking, and mountain biking. Many loops are marked one-way for safety, though land managers may switch directional postings, so don't assume they'll be the same from visit to visit. If when following the chapter loop you see a sign that indicates you are going the wrong way, run the directional cues in reverse. Also, familiarize yourself with the warning symbols posted on the legend board at the parking area. Warning symbols are typically posted on trees near such danger spots as steep hills or trail merges.

Throughout the loop you'll cross plank bridges over soft spots, and you'll see chain-link fencing or interlocked concrete blocks buried in the hillsides to minimize erosion. You owe thanks for these resource management efforts to the Army Corps of Engineers, the New Hampshire Bureau of Trails, and the Merrimack Valley Trail

Riders. These groups have a long history of cooperation that enables Hopkinton-Everett to remain one of the best multi-use trail networks in New England.

Serious riding begins where the chapter loop transitions from the doubletrack of Sugar Hill Trail to a wide singletrack climb. The trail switches back on itself and descends before heading off on a snaking course over the hills and deeper into the woods. You pop out onto doubletrack for a short time before disappearing again between two stone walls.

The pedal-pressure eases when you emerge onto Bassett Mill Road, a flat gravel woods road. At the four-way intersection with Choate Brook Road, signs point the way to food stops and other trails. Forgoing those temptations, four miles of single-track await you. You'll roll over Hopkinton-Everett's characteristic short climbs and descents for the remainder of the ride. Just before the finish of the loop, trails widen and see two-way traffic again.

Though it may not seem likely, those bent on an easy off-road ride may take a shine to Hopkinton-Everett too. Anyone can set a recreational pace on the miles of smooth gravel roads such as Choate Brook Road, Bassett Mill Road, and Old Route 77. No matter your ability or how you choose to ride, take the double-dog dare to ride Hop-Ev.

Well-marked intersection at this ATV/MTB area

Ride Information

Trail Contacts:
New Hampshire Division of Parks and Recreation Bureau of Trails, Concord, NH (603) 271-3254

Schedule:
Open all year—however, it is best to stay off the trail in the spring during the mud season.

Local Information:
Greater Concord Chamber of Commerce, Concord, NH (603) 224-2508

Local Events/Attractions:
Clough State Park, Weare, NH (603) 529-7112 – swimming, fishing, boat rentals, and picnicking

Local Bike Shops:
Nault's Cyclery, Concord, NH (603) 228-3319 or www.naults.com • Wheelsuckers Bicycles, Weare, NH (603) 529-3372 • The Ped'ling Fool, Hillsborough, NH (603) 464-4439 • S&W Sport Shop, Concord, NH (603) 228-1441 • Cyclesmith, Henniker, NH (603) 428-8035 • Banagan's Cycling Company, Concord, NH (603) 225-3330 True Sport Inc, Concord, NH (603) 228-8411 • Waite Sports Specialists, Concord, NH (603) 228-8621

Maps:
USGS maps: Hopkinton, NH; Weare, NH

Stark Pond was named for General John Stark, the man who uttered the words that expressed the sentiment of the American Revolution: "Live free or die."

MilesDirections

0.0 START from the parking lot and head west on the road past the trail map board. Bear right immediately at the fork, then quickly turn off right again onto Sugar Hill Trail.

0.3 Turn left at the concrete barrier.

1.0 Cross a wooden bridge.

1.2 Turn right onto a fire road. Descend toward a field. Just before the field, turn left on the trail that runs between two stone walls.

2.0 Bike past the sign marking Horseshoe Hill. Continue for almost another mile and past the sign marking Shost Hill.

2.9 Cross over rock-fill in a wet area. Turn left onto the gravel surface of Bassett Mill Road.

3.8 Arrive at a clearly posted four-way intersection. Turn left toward the parking area, a sign marks the turn.

4.2 Turn right after crossing the wooden bridge over Choate Brook. Climb the immediate rise and turn left onto the BT Trail. Ride parallel to the gravel road you just departed.

4.8 Cross a stone wall and then turn right, away from the short outlet to the gravel road.

5.4 Ride parallel to the gravel road surface of Old Route 77, on your left. Follow the trail as it soon turns perpendicular to, and crosses, Old Route 77.

6.1 Turn left at the sandy "T" intersection. Turn right immediately after the "T" instead of continuing on the grassy track. Ride through the woods, between a marsh on the left and Old Route 77 on the right. At Intersection #8, turn left onto Hang Glider Hill Loop.

7.9 Turn left at the concrete barrier. Farther ahead, cross a number of wooden bridges.

8.2 Turn left at the "T" intersection, following the sign for OHRV parking.

9.4 Turn left at Intersection #1.

9.8 Finish back at the Stark Pond OHRV parking lot.

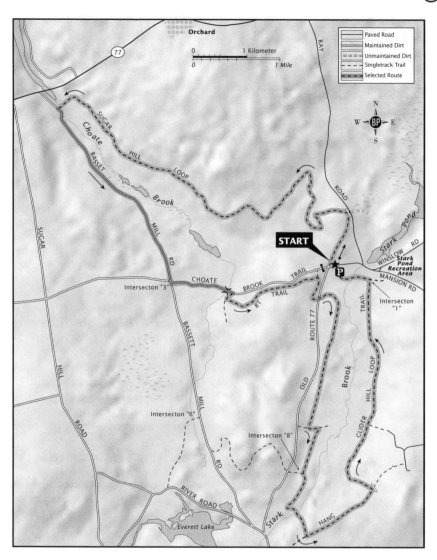

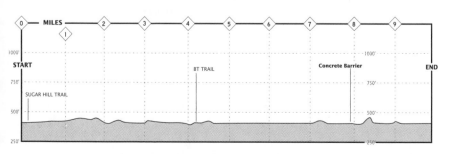

Merrimack Region

Compiled here is an index of great rides in the Merrimack Region that didn't make the A-list this time around but deserve recognition. Check them out and let us know what you think. You may decide that one or more of these rides deserves higher status in future editions or, perhaps, you may have a ride of your own that merits some attention.

Ⓑ Massabesic Lake

This area is mentioned in the Tower Hill Pond chapter. The Friends of Massabesic Bicycling Association (FOMBA) maintains trails and ensures mountain biking remains legal in this undeveloped watershed four miles east of New Hampshire's largest city, Manchester. The area offers varied challenge on dirt roads, woodland paths, and singletrack. The terrain is typically flat with some short grades, though don't be surprised if a climb pops up. Many available routes run along the shoreline of 2,500-acre Massabesic Lake. A perimeter loop via trails, dirt roads, and pavement covers over 12 miles and could take nearly two hours. A link to the Manchester to Newfields Rail-Trail is available from this area. Manchester Water Works owns the land and allows its use for walking, running, mountain biking, and hunting. Areas near Water Works facilities are posted as off-limits to all. Some dirt roads and all paved roads are open to motor vehicles. This area is convenient to Interstate 93. Parking is available across from the ball field south of the New Hampshire 28 Bypass traffic circle in Auburn, New Hampshire. Call FOMBA to join them for a group ride, (603) 483-2951, or visit *www.bit-net.com/~rath1/fomba*. *DeLorme: New Hampshire Atlas & Gazetteer:* Page 22, A-5

Ⓒ Litchfield State Forest

Uncomplicated off-road riding exists just over the Massachusetts border in Litchfield, New Hampshire. Though a small area with about four miles of double-track and woods roads through its 335 acres, Litchfield State Forest makes a restful place for an easy pedal. Forest trails are not technical and are smoothed by a pine-needle cover, while surrounding gravel roads can be used to add distance. All services are available in Nashua, including Tony's Cycles and Nault's Cyclery. Litchfield State Forest is half a mile east of New Hampshire 3A, off Albuquerque Road in Litchfield, New Hampshire. The New Hampshire Division of Forests and Lands administers the forest, (603) 271-2214. *DeLorme: New Hampshire Atlas & Gazetteer:* Page 22, F-2

Monadnock

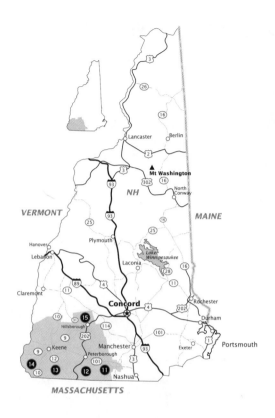

Region

Monadnock Region

Of all the places in New Hampshire that have weathered the passage of time and managed to hold on to the images and character of their past, the Monadnock Region seems to stand out. Covered bridges still cross rivers in many towns, rural roads remain unpaved, and white steepled churches still dominate small clusters of buildings in village centers. If the picture isn't yet clear, think of Yankee magazine and remember that it publishes from just north of Grand Monadnock Mountain in Dublin, New Hampshire.

Mount Monadnock
3,165 ft

MONADNOCK S

The word "Monadnock" comes from an Abnacki Native American word, which translates to "a mountain that stands alone." Mt. Monadnock was designated a National Natural Landmark in 1987. With its 5,000 acres and 40 miles of hiking trails, it is one of the most frequently climbed mountains in the world. A climb to the summit rewards a hiker with views of every state in New England.

Grand Monadnock is arguably the most hiked mountain in North America. But unlike the oft-trekked trails of Monadnock, the biking in the area remains a typically private and secluded experience. The region's topography is hilly, though rail-to-trail conversions make for a number of easy, level routes. The abundance of rural gravel roads let self-guided riders pick trips of minimal technical challenge, while New Hampshire's largest state park, Pisgah, throws out a true test on its rough, abandoned wagon tracks. Whatever your desire, so long as it isn't crowds or a rush of traffic on the trails, the Monadnock region can be your home.

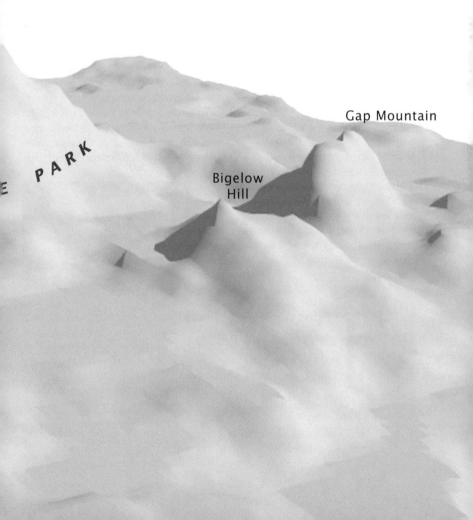

PARK

Gap Mountain

Bigelow
Hill

Russell-Abbott State Forest and the Greenville Rail-Trail

Ride Summary

Rural southern New Hampshire frames the setting for this lazy loop. The abandoned rail grade used in the ride can take you all the way to Massachusetts if you desire an out-and-back trip. Or stick to the chapter directions, which lead you on an easy ride overall, with one sketchy climb to contend with.

Ride Specs

Start: From the Pratt Pond parking lot
Length: 6.8 -mile loop
Approximate Riding Time: 1 hour
Difficulty Rating: Mostly easy abandoned rail grade and gravel road, with moderate technical challenge due to ruts and erosion on the one climb, which travels over abandoned road. Physically easy, with one taxing, avoidable climb and descent.
Trail Surface: Gravel and paved roads, abandoned rail bed, and abandoned road
Lay of the Land: Mildly contoured, forested terrain, with numerous ponds/wetlands, and an abundance of mountain laurel shrubs
Elevation Gain: 433 feet
Land Status: State forest, public rail-trail, and public roads
Nearest Town: Greenville, NH
Other Trail Users: Hikers, equestrians, motorists, cross-country skiers, snowmobilers, and hunters (in season)
Wheels: Mountain bikes only

Getting There

From Wilton, NH: Follow NH 101 / NH 31 west. Turn left on NH 31 by the Monadnock Spring Water plant. Turn left again immediately and cross the Souhegan River. Turn right onto Captain Clark Highway. In just over a mile the main road will turn left, but continue straight on Captain Clark Highway. The pavement transitions to maintained gravel. Continue onto Starch Mill Road, and take the first right onto the graveled Pratt Pond Road, just before a large farmhouse. Continue for 0.3 miles farther and turn right into the parking lot at Pratt Pond. *DeLorme: New Hampshire Atlas & Gazetteer:* Page 21, H-9

Three miles is no great distance by car or mountain bike, but over a century ago a trip of that distance made Greenville and Mason two distinct towns. Residents of the Greenville settlement grew tired of journeying to the meetinghouse in Mason and thus built themselves a Congregational Church closer to home. The settlers built a village around the new church and then sought and won township. The incorporation of Greenville in 1872 makes it the youngest town in Southern New Hampshire.

Nearly all of the early industries of Greenville have closed down and the abandoned buildings now house offices and apartments. The brick mills left behind after the closure of the Columbian Manufacturing Company still dominate Greenville's

Mountain Laurel abound in the area

downtown. Downriver from the refurbished buildings and the dismantled railroad trestle, the waters of the Souhegan River roar through The Gorge—the only Class V section of the river.

The chapter ride offers calm riding and with the exception of one hill, should not strain most. Around mid June, the green shores of the Pratt Pond blush with the pink of mountain laurel in bloom. These wild shrubs abound throughout the area and often fill both walls of the trail corridor. Less visible than the mountain laurel, but by no means less common to the area, are its quarries. Early into the ride, one can see the remains of Mason's granite industry in the form of rock debris and low ledges at trailside.

Past the power lines, the loop continues on its flat and easy course along the abandoned rail line. The only aberration is a dip down a sandy hill before crossing a snowmobile bridge and rising again to the railroad grade. Bike control on the sandy slope is difficult, and expect to jump off part way up the rise.

The intersection with Sand Pit Road signals the most demanding part of the loop, a half-mile climb over abandoned gravel road. The grade is moderate, but it will test the leg strength and stamina of anyone accustomed to riding flat surfaces. A break comes up less than a mile after the crest of the hill at an abandoned quarry, which is now filled with water. High cliffs line one edge of the quarry, while evergreens and birch ring the opposite shore. Leftover slabs of granite carved from the bedrock serve as picnic benches or a cool spot to rest.

Getting home from the quarry requires another trip on the rail trail before a smooth finish on the rural town roads of Mason. Mason's network of gravel and paved rural roads makes for a pleasant day of riding. One destination might be the center of town, a village dotted with Federal and Georgian homes. To reach downtown, continue straight at the 2.8-mile point where the trail turns left toward the quarry. Turn left again one mile later at the paved road, pass the First Meetinghouse monument, and soon you'll arrive downtown. If you reach a historical marker indicating the boyhood home of Samuel Wilson, better known as Uncle Sam, your excursion has taken you beyond the village limits.

For hard-charging riders looking for more variety than the sedate chapter loop might offer, a supreme singletrack option runs two miles through the hilly forest east of Pratt Pond. The trail begins on Pratt Pond Road about an eight of a mile before the parking area. The fairly hidden trailhead is distinguished by yellow blazes that mark the entire route. The track crosses below a dammed outlet to the pond before continuing into a number of steep hillsides which require carrying your steed when the traction and legs finally give out. The singletrack that remains is difficult but rideable, until it exits the woods at a power line beyond the blue-blazed forest boundary.

Ride northwest of Pratt Pond on the Greenville Rail Trail to its northern terminus to see the remains of stone foundations that once supported the highest train trestle in New Hampshire. The bridge spanned 600 feet across the Souhegan River, above a scenic section of rapids that led to the paddle wheels used years ago to power the mills of Greenville. Or, anytime you're looking for a longer ride, mix portions of the rail trail with the quiet rural roads surrounding Russell-Abbott State Forest.

Bike by abandoned quarry

Ride Information

Trail Contacts:
New Hampshire Division of Parks and Recreation, Concord, NH (603) 271-3254 • **Mason Conservation Commission,** Mason, NH (603) 878-2070

Schedule:
Open year-round

Local Information:
Milford-Amherst Chamber of Commerce, Milford, NH (603) 673-4360

Local Bike Shops:
Happy Day Cycle, Milford, NH (603) 673-5088 • **Absolutely Bicycles,** New Ipswich, NH (603) 878-4059 • **Sport Loft Ski Shop,** Amherst, NH (603) 889-4340 • **Eclectic Bicycle,** Peterborough, NH (603) 924-9797 • **Spokes & Slopes,** Peterborough, NH (603) 924-9961

Maps
USGS maps: Greenville, NH; Milford, NH; Townsend, MA

The area is loaded with debris from quarry work

MilesDirections

0.0 START by turning right out of the parking lot. Take the first left onto the gated Greenville Rail-Trail.

1.1 Cross the paved Wilton Road. After the next road intersection, the trail makes a sandy descent to a wooden bridge that crosses a pond outlet.

1.9 Reach the gravel Sand Pit Road, which is the third intersection along the rail-trail. To the right across Sand Pit Road, an abandoned road ascends away from the rail-trail. Take the abandoned road, travel uphill 0.5 miles, and descend.

2.8 Turn left onto doubletrack at the finish of the long descent.

3.2 Turn left after the quarry, and then roll right. Follow the trail back to the Greenville Rail-Trail.

3.5 Turn left at the intersection with the Greenville Rail-Trail.

5.3 Turn right at the third intersection onto Wilton Road, marked by an upright piece of granite by a tree across the way. Ride parallel to the right of the rail-trail for 200 yards.

6.3 Turn left at the junction with Starch Mill Road.

6.5 After passing the large farmhouse, turn left onto Pratt Pond Road.

6.8 Turn right into the parking lot.

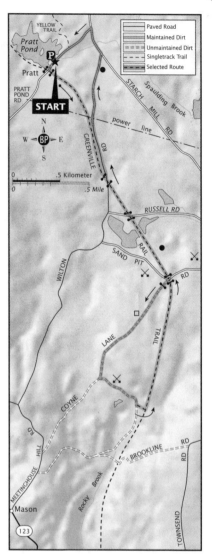

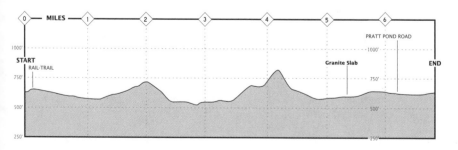

Annett Wayside Park

Ride Summary

A mountain bike ride through rural New Hampshire and a clean, quiet place to picnic afterward top the list of enviable ways to spend a sunny day. It's what you get though at Annett Wayside Park, a secluded picnic area in the midst of the Monadnock Region and surrounded by the 1,300-acre Annett State Forest. While there are miles of trails through the state forest, the chapter loop takes you around the perimeter of the property, using active town roads and unmaintained roads. Hills may challenge some riders, but trail surfaces generally will not, making the option for shorter excursions on the Annett State Forest trails a viable option for those wishing to explore on their own.

Ride Specs

Start: From the state picnic area off of Cathedral Road

Length: 7.8-mile loop

Approximate Riding Time: 1½ hours

Difficulty Rating: Moderate aerobic challenge due to hills, but trail surfaces are easy throughout

Trail Surface: Maintained and unmaintained gravel roads, and paved roads. Areas of unmaintained road will puddle in wet times, and minor erosion has impacted some slopes.

Lay of the Land: Hilly terrain through red pine woods and over rural countryside

Elevation Gain: 560 feet

Land Status: State forest

Nearest Town: Jaffrey, NH

Other Trail Users: Motorists, anglers, snowmobilers, and cross-country skiers

Getting There

From Jaffrey, NH: Follow NH 124 east for 2.2 miles (from its intersection with NH 202). Turn right onto Prescott Road, by the sign for Annett Picnic Area and Cathedral of the Pines. Travel one mile to the intersection with Squantum Road and continue left as the two roads become Cathedral Road. The park is 0.5 miles ahead on the left and marked by a large sign. *DeLorme: New Hampshire Atlas & Gazetteer:* Page 20, H-5

A secluded wayside picnic area in the hills of Southwestern New Hampshire serves as the staging ground for this ride. The start sits within a 1,300-acre state forest that straddles Cathedral Road. Industrialist Albert Annett donated the land to New Hampshire in 1922. During the Great Depression the Civilian Conservation Corps (CCC) used the field at the picnic area as its basecamp when reforesting the rolling hillsides with red pine. The CCC built fire roads and cut hiking trails on nearby Mount Monadnock. A short, smooth trip over old CCC roads leads to solitude on the quiet shore of Hubbard Pond, or, into a small network of cross-country ski trails west of Cathedral Road.

Cathedral of the Pines: Monument to women who made supreme sacrifice in defense of U.S.

Less than two miles beyond the entrance to Annett Wayside Park awaits Cathedral of the Pines, a national memorial to war veterans. This home of spiritual renewal welcomes people of all denominations into its sanctuary. The cathedral consists of simple wooden pews resting on pine-needle-covered ground. Mount Monadnock fills the view beyond the altar and an evergreen canopy shades visitors on warm summer days.

Cathedral of the Pines began as a tribute by Sibyl and Dr. Douglas Sloane to their son Sanderson who gave his life for freedom when shot down in Germany in 1944. Sanderson had chosen the site where the pews and altar now sit for his future home. After the Hurricane of 1938 Sanderson feared the uncommon beauty of the lot had been ruined by storm damage. On a cold day in the spring of 1939, Sanderson and his parents made their way through a maze of fallen branches, climbed over the trunks of downed tress, only to find that the storm, which had razed much of the countryside, spared the viewshed from the Cathedral knoll.

The short ride to Cathedral of the Pines from Annett Wayside Park can be done as a simple diversion from the chapter route. Near the end of the loop, simply make a left rather than a right on Cathedral Road. Cathedral of the Pines will be to the right once over the rise.

Though trail surfaces in and around Annett State Park are generally easy, the hills will challenge many. Fire roads, which leave from the parking area and also branch south from Annett Road, give a number of shorter options that might suit new mountain bikers or families. Also, across Cathedral Road the mix of cross-country ski trails already mentioned can give a spirited workout. The network is maintained by the nearby Woodbound Inn, which grooms and marks the trails for its winter guests. As with all New Hampshire state forests, blue blazes on the trees will signal the boundary between public and private land.

For the planned ride expect a good gravel surface once off the paved road until Annett Road becomes unmaintained after Black Reservoir. Any trails that leave past the blue blazes to the right enter Annett State Forest and are fine to explore despite the uninviting orange gates, which are meant to keep out 4x4s. When Annett Road crosses the Rindge/New Ipswich town line it becomes Hubbard Pond Road, but keep on pedaling. Along the way expect puddles after periods of rain and loose surfaces where the trail rises or falls.

The route transitions back to maintained gravel, then to pavement, soon after the turn onto Pine Road. The tar makes things smooth on this rural road, but the hills take away any thoughts of a free ride. Once out to Cathedral Road, the ride downhill to Annett Wayside Park lets the lasting impression of the rural countryside sink in. At the picnic area, unpack the cooler, eat guilt-free, and plan when to do it all again.

Cathedral of the Pines altar

Ride Information

Trail Contacts:
New Hampshire Division of Parks and
Recreation, Concord, NH
(603) 271-3254

Schedule:
Open year-round

Fees/Permits:
A small fee is charged to picnic at Annett
Wayside Park on summer weekends

Local Information:
Jaffrey Chamber of Commerce, Jaffrey,
NH (603) 532-4549

Local Events/Attractions:
Cathedral of the Pines, Rindge, NH
(603) 899-3300

Accommodations:
The Woodbound Inn, Rindge, NH
(603) 532-8341

Organizations:
Heart of New England Cycling Club,
Keene, NH (603) 756-9663 (call before
9:00 P.M.)

Local Bike Shops:
Absolutely Bicycles, New Ipswich, NH
(603) 878-4059 • Spokes and Slopes,
Peterborough, NH (603) 924-9961 •
Roy's Bike Shop, Jaffrey, NH (603) 532-
8800

Maps:
USGS maps: Peterborough South, NH

MilesDirections

0.0 START at the entrance to Annett Wayside Park and turn right on Cathedral Road. Travel on the pavement to the first right turn, the gravel Annett Road. Pass Black Reservoir, where beyond Annett Road deteriorates into an unmaintained route.

3.0 Annett Road changed its name to Hubbard Pond Road at some point in the woods. The unmaintained portion of Hubbard Pond Road transitions back onto a maintained gravel surface at the Annett State Forest boundary (marked by blue blazes on the trees).

3.6 Turn right just after the Woodland View condominiums, onto the gravel Pine Road. Descend past a small pond. (Pine Road changes its name to Old Ipswich Road when you cross the town line.)

6.1 Take a right at the intersection with Shaw Hill Road.

6.7 Take a right on Cathedral Road. [Side Trip. Cathedral of the Pines is 0.2 miles to the left at this intersection.]

7.8 Turn right into the finish at Annett Wayside Park.

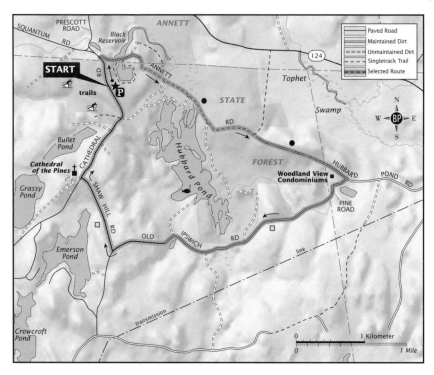

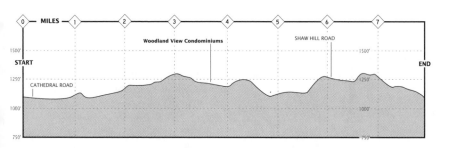

Cheshire South

Ride Summary

Mount Monadnock in Jaffrey, New Hampshire, draws thousands of hikers a year, while just south of it in Fitzwilliam, a converted railroad line gives cyclists similarly convenient access to the southwestern New Hampshire countryside. On the Cheshire South Trail, you'll be alone with your bike, your friends, or your family, for an easy tour through fall foliage or spring and summer blooms.

Ride Specs

Start: From the Fitzwilliam Depot, immediately south of the Depot General Store

Length: 11.2-mile out-and-back

Approximate Riding Time: 1½–2 hours

Difficulty Rating: Technically easy, with few trail obstacles other than puddles. Low exertion over flat, generally firm surfaces. A round trip ride will require multi-hour endurance.

Trail Surface: Flat, abandoned rail bed with some soft surfaces

Lay of the Land: Rural, forested acres frame the rail line, with an extended section past Rockwood Pond and adjacent wetlands

Elevation Gain: 319 feet

Land Status: State sponsored recreational trail

Nearest Town: Fitzwilliam, NH

Other Trail Users: Walkers, joggers, equestrians, cross-country skiers, and snowmobilers

Getting There

From Fitzwilliam, NH: Follow NH 119 west toward Fitzwilliam Depot. Soon after the marked road for Rhododendron State Park, NH 119 makes a 90-degree right turn at the Depot General Store. Don't take the turn! Continue straight past the store and park to the right in the gravel lot beyond the customer parking and across from the abandoned train station. *DeLorme: New Hampshire Atlas & Gazetteer:* Page 20, H-1

The Cheshire South trail departs from the old Fitzwilliam Depot, southwest of Fitzwilliam center. Built in 1849, the railway that became the trail supported the town of Fitzwilliam's once thriving granite industry. The chapter ride turns around in the village center of Troy, a town of about 2,200 people, where food and refreshments are available.

Paralleling New Hampshire 119 for the first leg, the ride runs a predictable course until a short, steep descent. The drop is immediately followed by a climb back to the rail grade where a train bridge once stood. You then twist through the woods for a very brief time before crossing New Hampshire 119 and picking up the rail-trail again. On the first part of route after the road, look for a small, water-filled granite quarry hidden away to the right. You might mark it for a rest spot on the way home.

At the next paved road, Rhododendron Road, a left turn will take you on a side trip to Rhododendron State Park, where you'll find the largest collection of

Rhododendron maximum north of the Allegheny Mountains. There is a 16-acre stand of the wild rhododendron within the 294-acre park. Explore the walking trails (bikes are prohibited) in early to mid July if you want to catch the blooms—they arrive a few weeks later than the blooms for the hybrid variety often found in home landscaping. Additional trails at Rhododendron State Park include a wildflower trail and a one-mile footpath up Little Monadnock Mountain.

If you forego the park, the Cheshire South Trail leads you on through quiet forests and moss-covered corridors of rock, where granite was blasted away years ago to allow trains to pass by. Midway to Troy, on the out-leg of the out-and-back ride, the trail travels on an earthen fill that partitions Rockwood Pond. Short footpaths lead to secluded fishing and swimming spots on the shore. Over the open water, and above the forested acres and small hills to the northeast, Mount Monadnock rises.

Steam whistles from ghost trains signal your approach to the abandoned passenger station in Troy. A short ride up paved Depot Street ends in the town center, across from Troy Common. If the sight of the cool lawn invites a rest, the general store has the refreshments to turn the stop into a mini-picnic. For history buffs who would rather explore than loaf about, the nearby town hall might interest you. Dating back to 1814, the building served as the original meeting house when Troy was incorporated in 1815.

Also near the village common, a short distance south on New Hampshire 12 and left on Monadnock Street, is the corporate headquarters of Troy Mills, Inc. Founded in 1865, Troy Mills has weathered the hard, post-industrial times that put so many New England mills out of business. Five generations of family leadership have taken the company from a regional maker of loom-woven horse blankets to its principle role today as a maker of fabrics for the automotive industry. A smaller aspect of Troy Mills' business is to supply the garment industry with fabric.

The day's ride isn't confined to the distance between Fitzwilliam Depot and Troy. The rail trail extends beyond the turnaround in Troy and can also be explored to the east of the parking area in Fitzwilliam. When you do finish your trip, the Depot General Store beckons you. Only 30 feet from the end of the ride, you can buy a hot dog there for just 25 cents. Divine intervention or a marriage of convenience? You decide.

Fitzwilliam Depot

Ride Information

Trail Contacts:
New Hampshire Division of Parks, Bureau of Trails, Concord, NH (603) 271-3254

Schedule:
Open year-round

Local Information:
Jaffrey Chamber of Commerce, Jaffrey, NH (603) 532-4549

Local Events/Attractions:
Rhododendron State Park, Fitzwilliam, NH (603) 823-7177

Organizations:
Heart of New England Cycling Club, Keene, NH (603) 756-9663 (call before 9:00 PM)

Local Bike Shops:
Roy's Bike Shop, Jaffrey, NH (603) 532-8800 • Banagan's Cycling Company, Keene, NH (603) 357-2331 • Norm's Ski & Bike Shop, Keene, NH (603) 352-1404 • Andy's Cycle Shop, Keene, NH (603) 352-3410 • Summers Backcountry Outfitters, Keene, NH (603) 357-5107 • Eclectic Bicycle, Peterborough, NH (603) 924-9797 • Spokes & Slopes, Peterborough, NH (603) 924-9961 • Joe Jones Ski & Sports, Keene, NH 03431 (603) 352-5266

Maps:
USGS maps: Monadnock Mountain, NH

Mt. Monadnock

MilesDirections

0.0 START by riding west on the Cheshire South Trail—away from the abandoned Fitzwilliam Depot station, rather than past it. NH 119 is to the right.

3.0 Rockwood Pond appears on your right.

5.6 Arrive in the village of Troy. Pedal up to the village green before turning around and retracing your tracks back to Fitzwilliam Depot.

11.2 Arrive at Fitzwilliam Depot.

Rockwood Pond

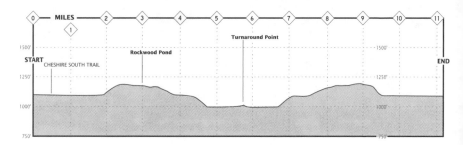

116

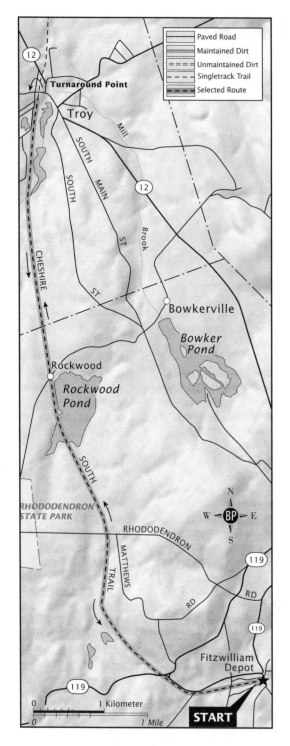

	Paved Road
	Maintained Dirt
	Unmaintained Dirt
	Singletrack Trail
	Selected Route

Turnaround Point

Troy

Bowkerville

Bowker Pond

Rockwood

Rockwood Pond

RHODODENDRON STATE PARK

RHODODENDRON

MATTHEWS TRAIL

Fitzwilliam Depot

START

0   1 Kilometer
0   1 Mile

Pisgah State Park

Ride Summary

Pisgah State Park offers hard terrain, but it also holds a network of maintained gravel roads through its center which can be targeted for easier riding. Thickly forested, with ponds, slow running streams, and large areas of wetland, Pisgah State Park really allows you to get away from it all. The sound of your bike and wildlife should be all you hear. This long tour provides challenging sections and sections where you can simply spin. And right in the middle of the ride is Chesterfield's village center, a wonderful spot to take a break.

Ride Specs

Start: From the Reservoir Trailhead
Length: 20.5-mile loop
Approximate Riding Time: 3–4 hours
Difficulty Rating: Technically difficult due to hilly, rocky terrain. Exceptional fitness is needed due to length of loop and extended technical sections.
Trail Surface: Doubletrack, abandoned roads, gravel roads, and paved roads
Lay of the Land: Abandoned cart paths enclosed by thick woods and slow streams. The hills surrounding Mount Pisgah rise to the west of the trail for much of the ride.
Elevation Gain: 1,290 feet
Land Status: State park and rural town roads
Nearest Town: Winchester, NH
Other Trail Users: Hikers, equestrians, ATVs, snowmobilers, cross-country skiers, and hunters (in season)
Wheels: The chapter loop demands a mountain bike, though gravel roads through the center of the park are suitable for hybrids and kid's bikes.

Getting There

Winchester, NH: Follow NH 119 west 3.2 miles from its departure from NH 10. Turn into the large, gravel Reservoir Trailhead parking lot on the right—just beyond a transformer station and the gated Reservoir Road.
DeLorme: New Hampshire Atlas & Gazetteer: Page 19, I-9

The early settlers of Southwestern New Hampshire borrowed the name of the mountain on which Moses stood to first behold the Promised Land because their mountain too commanded such an impressive view. Today, Mount Pisgah dominates the topography of New Hampshire's largest state park, Pisgah State Park. The massive 21-square-mile park draws in mountain ridges, streams, hiking trails, gravel roads, and seven ponds. Largely undeveloped in terms of campsites and other facilities, the park has concentrated trail growth around the periphery of the property, leaving only the old wagon routes through much of the interior.

Chesterfield Town Hall

Getting to the trailhead requires that you drive along the Ashuelot River. Impossible to miss on the short trip along New Hampshire 119 is the Ashuelot Bridge. The 169-foot covered bridge cost nearly $5,000 to build in 1864. In its day it was used to transport wood across the river to the railroad station in the village of Ashuelot. In the north part of Winchester, another covered bridge spans the river. The Coombs #2 Bridge can be found on Coombs Road, which is off New Hampshire 10 near the Swanzey and Winchester town line.

The loop featured in this chapter starts with a bang. The ride begins uphill, with the incline requiring some of the most difficult effort of the trip. The technical terrain continues on through the rolling South Link. After overcoming the challenge of the first mile, the pressure eases along Broad Brook Road. Soon, the first historical markers of the day appear. White signs to the side of the trail point out old mill sites, homesteads, and schoolhouses. In one cellar hole, a tree now grows from a pile of stone and brick that once made a chimney.

The Old Chesterfield Road section of the loop bisects the park on a diagonal from Winchester in the southeast to Chesterfield in the northwest. More markers along the way recognize the history of this once busy corridor. Old Chesterfield Road can be ridden independently, taking advantage of its smooth, packed gravel surface to see the bulk of the sights. The distances and terrain are suitable for an active family or groups with mixed abilities. Follow the signs from New Hampshire 119 in Winchester for the Old Chesterfield Road Trailhead to do the abbreviated ride.

Old Chesterfield Road degrades and climbs after the gate by the Chestnut Hill Trail parking area. The parking area is a good turnaround spot for those not looking for an exhausting ride. For those who continue, the loop emerges from the Pisgah State Park boundary to an area of hillside pasture by the home site of former Supreme Court Justice Harlan F. Stone.

After a downhill drop on pavement, the ride climbs to the village of Chesterfield at the midpoint of the trip. The slow pace of the village might seduce you to rest on the benches by the school or stretch out on the town hall lawn. While there, consider the fact that over all the hilly undulations, you have risen 450 feet. Gravity will be your friend on the way back.

Fat tires are welcome on dirt roads and most wagon tracks throughout the forest, but trails that lead to the summit of Mount Pisgah have hiking only restrictions. That should not stop the exploration though, as trails northeast of scenic Fullam Pond welcome knobbies.

One final word of advice for anyone planning a spring or summer trip to enjoy the 13,500 acres of Pisgah State Park: load up on bug repellent. The mosquitoes grow to the size of hummingbirds and could easily carry both body and bike away.

Post Office

Ride Information

📞 Trail Contacts:
Pisgah State Park Manager, Winchester, NH (603) 239-8153

🕐 Schedule:
Open year-round, though in spring bikes aren't welcome until after mud season, which is typically early May

💡 Local Events/Attractions:
Chesterfield Gorge Park and Picnic Area, off NH 9, Chesterfield, NH

💡 Organizations:
Friends of Pisgah, John Summers-Chair of Trail Committee, Summers Backcountry Sports, Keene NH (603) 352-0151 • **Heart of New England**

🚻 Cycling Club, Keene, NH (603) 756-9663 – call before 9:00 P.M.

🚲 Local Bike Shops:
Andy's Cycle Shop, Keene, NH (603) 352-3410 • **Banagan's Cycling Company,** Keene, NH (603) 357-2331 – runs a weekly off-road ride • **Brattleboro Bicycle Shop,** Brattleboro, VT (802) 254-8644 • **Summers Backcountry Sports,** Keene, NH (603) 357-5107 • **Joe Jones Ski & Sports,** Keene, NH (603) 352-5266 • **Norms Ski & Bike Shop,** Keene, NH (603) 352-1404 • **Bicycle Barn,** Northfield, MA (413) 498-2996

🅝 Maps:
USGS maps: Winchester, NH; Keene, NH

MilesDirections

0.0 START the ride by going uphill past the state park welcome board (maps available here). Cross under a power line and veer right at the next fork.

0.4 Turn right on Reservoir Road. Take the first left onto the South Link trail. Veer to the right at the split in South Link.

1.1 Turn left at the "T" intersection onto Broad Brook Road

4.2 Turn left on Old Chesterfield Road, a maintained gravel road.

5.8 Reach the junction with the access road to Fullam Pond. Stay left of the island of trees and ride toward the Chestnut Hill Trail parking area. Pass around the gate at the parking area into a climb up the abandoned portion of Old Chesterfield Road.

7.3 The trail splits high and low. Take the high route and soon pass Reservoir Trail, which is to the left.

7.8 Old Chesterfield Road runs dead into a swamp. Follow the primitive singletrack path to the right. The singletrack emerges onto abandoned Horseshoe Road. Continue on Horseshoe Road as it leaves Pisgah State Park, then transitions to a paved rural road.

9.8 Take a left at the stop sign.

10.0 Take a left on NH 63, by the Chesterfield post office and town hall.

10.5 Prior to starting downhill, turn left on Winchester Road. Continue on as the pavement transitions to abandoned road. Pass a gate back into Pisgah State Park. When the doubletrack forks, follow the more traveled left option onto Habitat Trail.

12.5 After climbing to its height, Habitat Trail descends and joins Horseshoe Road at an angle. Turn right at the junction. Come to a swamp. Follow the singletrack to the left and continue on abandoned Old Chesterfield Road.

16.2 Turn right onto Broad Brook Road, by the district schoolhouse historic marker.

19.4 After a yellow trail junction sign, turn right uphill on doubletrack toward Reservoir Road (this is actually South Link but it's marked as Broad Brook Link). Veer left at the fork.

20.1 Turn right onto Reservoir Road. Climb to the flat before turning left on doubletrack at the sign for NH 119 parking.

20.5 The rough ride is over.

Alternate Starts: The chapter loop can be entered from NH 63, and other trails can be accessed from roads around the perimeter of the park.

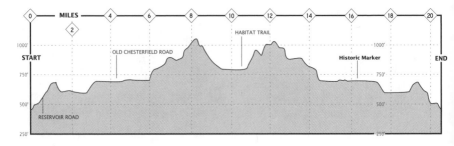

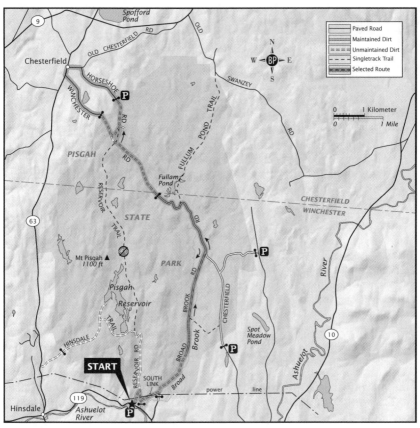

Fox State Park

Ride Summary

Fox State Forest balances an open user policy with a history of conservation. While the park boasts a well developed and mapped trail network available to nearly all types of recreationalists, it also protects such natural areas as Hemlock Ravine, one of New Hampshire's oldest hardwood tree stands. The riding on the chapter loop is as hard as the forest is precious, so please enjoy and appreciate both.

Ride Specs

Start: From Center Road, north of Hillsborough center
Length: 5.7-mile loop
Approximate Riding Time: 1½ hours
Difficulty Rating: Technically difficult—suited to good technical riders. Physically strenuous, with no extended climbs, but many short grunts.
Trail Surface: Fire roads and very technical singletrack
Lay of the Land: Rocky, root infested trails over rolling terrain, through thick forest, and past bogs and swamps
Elevation Gain: 287 feet
Land Status: State forest
Nearest Town: Hillsborough, NH
Other Trail Users: Hikers, cross-country skiers, snowmobilers, and hunters (in season)
Wheels: Mountain bikes only on this tough terrain

Getting There

From Concord, NH: Travel I-89 north to U.S. 202 / NH 9, heading west. When you enter downtown Hillsborough you'll pass a Cumberland Farms convenience store. Just before the traffic signal at the junction with NH 149, a small, brown road sign points to Fox State Forest. Turn right at the signal onto School Street and follow as School Street becomes Hillsborough Center Road. The forest is two miles from downtown, just past Intrepid Farm. ***DeLorme: New Hampshire Atlas and Gazetteer:*** Page 26, H-6

The town of Hillsborough has a reputation among New England mountain bikers for offering up the kind of gnarly terrain that breeds hardcore riders. That reputation developed around the Ped'ling Fool bike shop, which for years has supplied its cultists with the toys of the mountain bike game. From group rides out of the shop, to the annual Hillsborough Classic Cross-country Race, mountain biking has always been cool in Hillsborough.

Outside of the mountain bike world, Hillsborough holds a similarly rugged reputation as a classic New England village full of Yankee spirit—and when need be, spirited Yankees. Built along the Contoocook River that once fed thriving mills, Hillsborough has weathered economic hardship, land and roadway development that threatened the rural village, and the horror of being chosen as a potential dumpsite for high-level nuclear waste. Today it remains uniquely its own place, from the stone

Administration Building

arch bridges built by Scot settlers in the early 19th Century to the classic homes and shops of Hillsborough Upper Village. All the substance of small town New Hampshire remains, without the scrub and whitewash of a movie set image.

Like so many great tracts of preserved land, Fox State Forest came about through private donation. In 1922 Caroline A. Fox of Arlington, Massachusetts, donated her summer home (now the park headquarters), the surrounding 348 acres of lush forest, and a trust fund to maintain the property and promote conservation. Since then, Fox State Forest has been a great supporter of natural area research and conservation education. The forest has since grown to 1,445 acres, containing 22 miles of multi-use trails with enough vertical challenge to damage even the strongest mountain biker's ego.

Designated natural areas dot the landscape of Fox State Forest. Counted among these is Black Gum Swamp where ancient tupelo (black gum) trees grow— a rare sight in the Northeast. Hidden within the woods are timber-stand improvement areas, where competing trees are cleared to foster the growth of healthier crop trees. A boardwalk above Mud Pond Bog offers a close-up look at the bog habitat. The Henry I. Baldwin Environmental Center, built in 1972, rounds out the forest package.

The trail managers at Fox State Forest have done an excellent job of marking the otherwise complicated web of singletrack and fire roads throughout the forest. The trail markers, coupled with the chapter map or the park map (available at the head-quarters building), make a successful ride a snap.

White blazes with a red spot in the center mark the entire Ridge Trail. They appear frequently enough that if a wrong turn is made, their absence will become conspicuous. The ride starts on a gentle downhill roll before crossing a narrow wooden bridge and hitting the first of many short power-climbs. After turning off Hurricane Road for the first time, Vista Trail soon departs to the left. That optional short trip leads to an exposed granite porch, offering open southeasterly views.

After Vista Trail, the terrain tightens and stays difficult before emerging onto the doubletrack Chestnut Corner Road. Portions of Chestnut Corner, Hurricane, and Proctor Roads make up the next section of the Ridge Trail and give a rest from the narrow and bumpy stuff. You soon dive back under the tree canopy though, as the Ridge Trail follows along the forest's south boundary. The terrain gets very tight, so much so that even one fallen tree could quickly disguise the route. Keep your eyes open for the white blazes with the red dot to stay on course.

For riders just looking to get their tires dirty, the fire roads of Fox State Forest are well maintained. They are typically clear of the water crossings, protruding rocks, and other obstacles that make the singletrack riding so hairy. The grades on the headquarters building side of Center Road tend to be more difficult, but you can expect rolling terrain wherever you ride in Hillsborough.

Though Hillsborough does not lack hills, the credit for its name goes to Colonel John Hill who received a large land grant to settle the area.

Typical trail width

Ride Information

📞 Trail Contacts:
Fox State Forest Headquarters, Hillsborough, NH (603) 464-3453

🕐 Schedule:
Open year-round

❓ Local Information:
Hillsborough, NH at *www.conknet.com /~hillsboro* • **Hillsborough Chamber of Commerce,** Hillsborough, NH (603) 464-5858

💡 Local Events/Attractions:
The Franklin Pierce Homestead, Hillsborough, NH (603) 478-3165 – the boyhood home of the 14th President of the United States

👥 Organizations:
Eastern Fat Tire Association (EFTA), Hillsborough, NH (603) 529-3800

🚲 Local Bike Shops:
The Ped'ling Fool, Hillsborough, NH (603) 464-4439 • **Wheelsuckers Bicycles,** Weare, NH (603) 529-3372 • **Cyclesmith,** Henniker, NH (603) 428-8035

🅽 Maps:
USGS maps: Hillsborough, NH; Hillsborough Upper Village, NH

127

MilesDirections

0.0 START out on the Ridge Trail, on the opposite side of Hillsborough Center Road from the parking area. The loop follows white paint blazes with a red dot in the center. Turn left at the first "T" intersection, and then bear left after a stone wall. Cross a wooden bridge.

0.6 Turn left on doubletrack Hurricane Road. Climb to the top of rise then turn right, following Ridge Trail toward Black Gum Swamp.

1.1 Turn left at the "T" intersection with doubletrack Chestnut Corner Road.

1.5 Turn right at the "T" intersection with Hurricane Road.

1.9 Turn right, uphill, at the intersection with Proctor Road. Climb along a cemetery. At the trail split atop the hill, take the left most of the three options. Cross a wet area and roll left again at the next trail split.

2.4 Turn right off of the more worn track, still following Ridge Trail. (A missed turn will come out at a power line.)

2.9 Turn right on doubletrack Harvey Road. Just 100 feet farther, turn left for another long stretch of Ridge Trail singletrack.

3.9 Soon after the Bible Hill Trail junction, enter a technical downhill.

4.3 Cross a wet area of moss covered boulders. At the trail split on the far side of the boulder section, follow the white-and-red-blazed trail uphill.

4.4 Turn left at the "T" intersection with Harvey Road. Turn immediately left again onto White Cross Trail. A shallow descent transitions into a wet crossing at the border of a swamp.

4.8 Turn right, following Ridge Trail.

5.0 Turn right on doubletrack Hurricane Road.

5.2 Partway up a climb on Hurricane Road, turn left on Ridge Trail as it returns to the forest headquarters.

5.7 Sign the park guest book and call it a day.

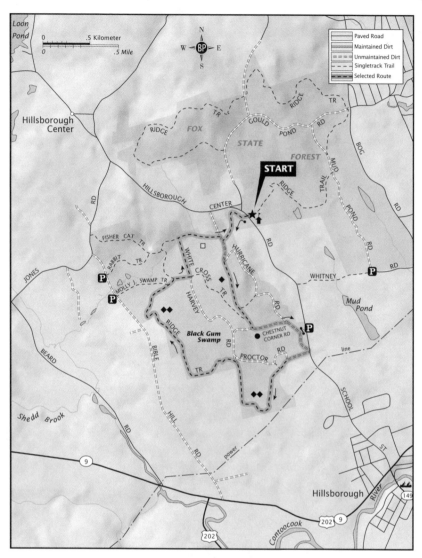

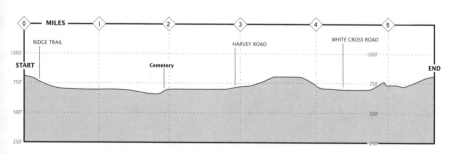

Dartmouth

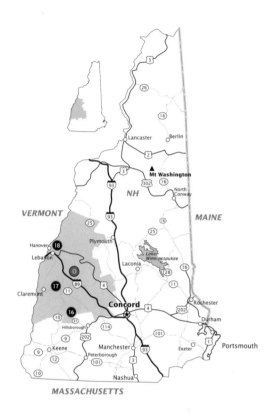

Lake
Sunapee

South Branch Sugar River
Bald Sunapee
Mount Sunapee
Page Hill
MT SUNAPEE STATE PARK
Bly Hill
Blueberry Mountain
Sunset Hill
Sunapee Lake

Dartmouth/Lake Sunapee Region

History, culture, and the great outdoors all mix in the Dartmouth-Lake Sunapee region. The history is supplied by such frontier sites as the Fort at Number 4. The cultural focal point of the region rests in Hanover, New Hampshire, home of Dartmouth College. The Ivy League university draws the brightest minds and most talented performers from around the world to awaken this otherwise quiet area of the state. And the outdoors, well it's all around, because this is a countryside characterized by its small towns and its secluded rural byways.

The Appalachian Trail runs through Hanover. Another of New Hampshire's major hiking trails, the Monadnock-Sunapee Greenway, crosses into the region to the top of Mount Sunapee. Though the Appalachian Trail is closed to bikes and the Greenway only hosts cycles across state lands, there is still plenty of off-road riding available. Much of the riding rests on abandoned roads, which are likely to bring up true challenges because of the erosion that tends to wear on them. The second variety of biking is on the miles of little-traveled gravel roads that abound. Whether searching out abandoned roads or spinning on the gravel ways, you'll be at the whim of the region's rolling countryside.

16 Pillsbury State Park

Ride Summary

Pillsbury State Park is one of those package deals familiar to New Hampshire outdoor enthusiasts. It offers a large, open-use forest with well-posted and mapped trails, and it gives visitors shoreline campsites to extend their stays. The Monadnock-Sunapee Greenway cuts through the park, allowing backpackers ready access to the 49-mile hiking corridor. The most difficult sections of the chapter loop use the Monadnock-Sunapee Greenway, while other park trails and forest roads lend variety to the ride.

Ride Specs

Start: From the Pillsbury State Park headquarters

Length: 11-mile loop

Approximate Riding Time: 2½ hours

Difficulty Rating: Technically difficult due tight, rocky trails with some loose surfaces. Physically strenuous due to rough trails, distance, and elevation changes.

Trail Surface: Park road, doubletrack, and rocky, hilly singletrack

Lay of the Land: Predominantly remote, rolling woodland, with sections of scrub growth from recent foresting

Elevation Gain: 1,056 feet

Land Status: State park

Nearest Town: Washington, NH

Other Trail Users: Hikers, cross-country skiers, snowshoers, snowmobilers, and hunters (in season)

Wheels: Mountain bikes only for the chapter route. Hybrids and kids bikes should be limited to Pillsbury State Park Road and Five Summers Trail.

Getting There

From Concord, NH: Follow I-89 north to U.S. 202 west, to NH 31 north. The Pillsbury State Park sign will appear off NH 31, 4.1 miles from the village center of Washington, NH. Turn onto Pillsbury State Park Road and unload at the headquarters building on the shore of May Pond.

From Newport, NH: Travel NH 10 south to NH 31 south. Look for the Pillsbury State Park sign about five miles from NH 10.

DeLorme: New Hampshire Atlas & Gazetteer: Page 26, D-1

M any of the old mills that once powered New Hampshire's economy now exist only as foundation holes whose stone walls have toppled and succumbed to the leaves of dozens of autumns. The stories of these mills are often bittersweet, with their era of prosperity tied to legacies of environmental damage. But the prosperity brought by the mills and the lessons learned have since helped to reestablish and preserve the woodlands of the Granite State for the future.

The waterpower for New Hampshire's great mills still flows down the undulating topography of a state shaped by glaciers. The drive along New Hampshire 31 to Pillsbury State Park, though perhaps not as dramatic as the high-elevation roads through the White Mountains, rolls and pitches with the countryside, foreshadowing what's to come along the bike ride ahead.

Pillsbury State Park rests in the area known decades ago as Cherry Valley. By the dawn of the 20th Century, local sawmills hungry for timber had left the land completely denuded. In 1905, successful mill owner Albert E. Pillsbury purchased much of the clearcut acreage. In 1920 he deeded 2,400 acres to the state for the establishment of a public forest. Today Pillsbury State Park encompasses over 5,000 acres of woods, ponds, and streams. Its campsites, which include hike-in and canoe-in sites, are among the most secluded in the state park system. The uncrowded trail network includes hiking paths to mountaintop overlooks, making the park an ideal place for solitary discovery.

Albert Pillsbury was also one of the founders of the Society for the Protection of New Hampshire Forests (SPNHF) *(see sidebar on page 136)*. Among its many projects, the SPNHF helps state officials and the Appalachian Mountain Club maintain the Monadnock-Sunapee Greenway, which is featured in this loop.

The loop begins with a lengthy, shallow climb on the gravel park road before things level out after entering the woods. The ride continues without major aerobic impact until the trail points up past Bear Pond. Loose, rutted surfaces, and possibly wetness, team together against progress. Farther along, the trail narrows as it steepens, leaving fewer lines to chose from, and seemingly more rocks to slink around or

Downtown Washington, four miles from the start of the ride

over. Bear Pond Trail sets the rhythm for what comes next on the Monadnock-Sunapee Greenway, one of the great technical singletracks in New Hampshire.

Be warned that the Monadnock-Sunapee Greenway was constructed for hikers, though it's open for biking within the state park. There are abrupt slopes and difficult obstacles to negotiate. The Greenway singletrack greets you with a climb over roots and around trees as it runs up the ridgeline separating the Connecticut and Merrimack river valleys. This flavor of tight, heaving terrain remains the norm for the next three miles. As you near the intersection with Five Summers Trail, repeated steep drops and ascents might make even the most skilled riders dismount. No shame; it's hard.

A quarter-mile beyond the junction of the Greenway and Five Summers Trail is Lucia's Lookout (elevation 2,493 feet). This short side-trip up the Greenway must be hiked due to the incline, but the pedestrian mode of travel rewards you with fine southerly views of Mount Monadnock. For the truly hearty, just over four miles north of Lucia's Lookout, still on the Greenway, waits the peak of Mount Sunapee. Here you'll find Mount Sunapee State Park and clear views over Lake Sunapee.

After turning off of the Greenway and onto Five Summers Trail, you're afforded a final blip of tight singletrack before joining onto a fire road. At the fire road intersection, you may notice that across the way the blue blazes of the Five Summers Trail continue down an eroded, overgrown slope. Don't follow the blazes here, as the trail cuts through a seasonal (probably four-seasonal) wetland. After the initial climb on the fire road, you pick up Five Summers Trail again at the base of the descent and follow its smooth, wide carpet back to the start. You'll enjoy a 300-foot elevation loss by the time you roll in.

The Society for the Protection of New Hampshire Forests

You can thank them for the preservation of Mount Monadnock. You can thank them for maintaining the grandeur of the White Mountain National Forest. You can thank them for helping defeat a proposed auto road over the Presidential Range. They are the Society for the Preservation of New Hampshire Forests (SPNHF), a driving force in the rebuilding and conservation of natural habitats in the state since 1901.

The SPNHF has preserved land through outright purchase, management of non-society forests and wetlands, public education, and lobbying at all levels of government. In their early years, they helped drive the passage of the Weeks Act, which among other things established the White Mountain National Forest. Today they own over 25,000 acres, with protective easements on over 54,000 acres. In all, they've protected 1,000,000 acres in their century of advocacy.

As with the preservation of Mount Monadnock and the White Mountains, the SPNHF played a major role in preserving Franconia Notch, the Old Man of the Mountain, Crawford Notch, and Mount Sunapee for generations to come. They have reintroduced wildlife to the state and lead by example in all areas green, from energy conservation and recycling, to warning about the damages brought by acid rain. Indeed, all who love the green countryside of New Hampshire owe much to the relentless vigilance of this organization.

Ride Information

Trail Contacts:
Pillsbury State Park Manager, Washington, NH (603) 863-2860

Schedule:
Trails are closed through mud season, which is typically early May.

Fees/Permits:
A day-use fee of $2.50 per person is charged.

Accommodations:
40 campsites are available at the park for $13 each per night. Call (603) 271-3628 for reservations.

Organizations:
Eastern Fat Tire Association (EFTA), Hillsborough, NH (603) 529-3800

Local Bike Shops:
Bob Skinner's Ski and Sports, Sunapee, NH (603) 763-2303 • The Ped'ling Fool, Hillsborough, NH (603) 464-4439 • Cyclesmith, Henniker, NH (603) 428-8035 • Outspokin' Bicycle and Sport Shop, Newbury, NH (603) 763-9500

Maps:
USGS maps: Lovewell Mountain, NH; Newport, NH

MilesDirections

0.0 START by turning right out of the park headquarters. Continue on Pillsbury State Park Road to its end at the swingset by Mill Pond.

1.0 Enter the campsite road to the left. Bear right at the next intersection onto the blue-blazed Five Summers Trail doubletrack.

1.5 Turn right at the fork onto Bear Pond Trail.

2.8 Bear Pond Trail and the Monadnock-Sunapee Greenway meet at a grassy inter-section marked by a large stump, trail signs, and a mailbox to the left containing a trail register. Turn left on the white-blazed Monadnock-Sunapee Greenway.

4.1 An overlook on the right allows open views east. To the left, a sign points toward Lucia's Lookout.

5.9 Turn left at the intersection with the Five Summers Trail. [**Side Trip**. Continue on the Monadnock-Sunapee Greenway for 0.25 miles to visit Lucia's Lookout, and an addi-tional four miles to reach Mount Sunapee.]

6.2 Five Summers Trail intersects with a grav-el fire road. Turn left on the road.

6.7 The blue-blazed Five Summers Trail rejoins from the right. Continue south with the blazes.

9.3 Bear Pond Trail comes in from the left. A gate soon comes up. Roll left after the gate down to the swingset by Mill Pond.

9.8 Turn right on the gravel Pillsbury State Park Road.

11.0 Declare victory.

Today, forest covers about 83 percent of New Hampshire. Just prior to the turn of the century, that figure stood closer to 17 percent.

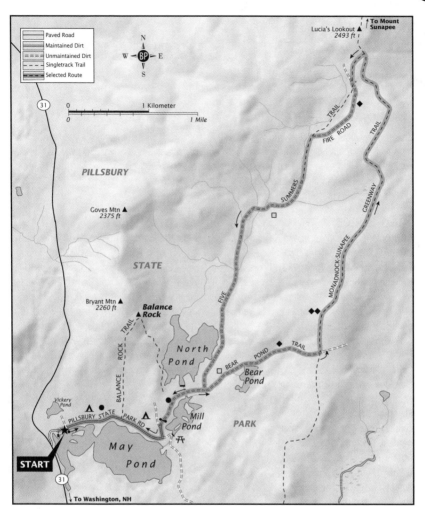

Legend:
- Paved Road
- Maintained Dirt
- Unmaintained Dirt
- Singletrack Trail
- Selected Route

N W E S

1 Kilometer
1 Mile

PILLSBURY

Goves Mtn ▲
2375 ft

STATE

Bryant Mtn ▲
2260 ft

Balance Rock ▲

North Pond

Vickery Pond

Mill Pond

May Pond

Bear Pond

PARK

BALANCE ROCK TRAIL

FIVE SUMMERS TRAIL

BEAR POND TRAIL

FIRE ROAD

MONADNOCK-SUNAPEE GREENWAY TRAIL

Lucia's Lookout
2493 ft

To Mount Sunapee

PILLSBURY STATE PARK RD

START

31

To Washington, NH

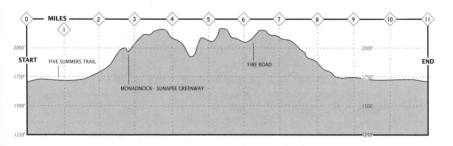

MILES 0 1 2 3 4 5 6 7 8 9 10 11

START
FIVE SUMMERS TRAIL
MONADNOCK - SUNAPEE GREENWAY
FIRE ROAD
END

2000'
1750'
1500'
1250'

Sugar River Trail

Ride Summary

This ride is about going slow and easy. You'll follow one of New Hampshire's premier rail-trails from Newport to its neighbor Claremont. The route crisscrosses the Sugar River via old steel railroad bridges, and even older covered wooden railroad bridges. While it remains close to civilization, the route stays quiet and secluded for its entire length.

Ride Specs

Start: From Belknap Avenue in Newport, NH
Length: 20.2-mile out-and-back
Approximate Riding Time: 2–3½ hours
Difficulty Rating: Technically easy, 'cause it's all flat, wide, and mostly well packed. Very low effort, though a full round-trip will require multi-hour stamina.
Trail Surface: Flat, smooth abandoned rail grade
Lay of the Land: Woods and homes frame one shoulder, while the slow moving Sugar River sits off the other.
Elevation Gain: 757 feet
Land Status: State recreational trail
Nearest Town: Newport, NH
Other Trail Users: Equestrians, ATVs, cross-country skiers, and snowmobilers
Wheels: Mountain bikes, hybrids, kid's single-speeders, and baby trailers will all fair well.

Getting There

From Concord, NH: Follow I-89 north to NH 11 South (Exit 12). Follow NH 11 into the town of Newport. Take a right onto NH 10 North (Main Street) and travel 0.25 miles. Turn left onto Belknap Avenue. Continue on Belknap Avenue 0.1 miles to the Sugar River Trail signboard on the right. *DeLorme: New Hampshire Atlas & Gazetteer:* Page 33, J-14

One's idea of perfection is always prone to change. Right now, the perfect trail might be hard but not too hard, while later on you might yearn for company and a quiet ride along a lazy river. The Sugar River Trail satisfies the latter. The trail travels over track wide enough for a group to pedal abreast—even a group with children. En route you'll find picnic spots along the water's edge and near the many old train bridges. Collect trailside poppies where the brambles break in Claremont, or do the trip in autumn for a wrapping of color on a woodland highway all your own.

The Sugar River Trail runs along a converted rail line. Though you're never far from civilization, there are no densely populated areas after you leave Newport. This keeps you very much in solitude for the 10 miles to Claremont. You come to the first bridge almost immediately into the ride, before crossing Oak Street onto a sandy sec-

tion of trail. Once beyond this loose section, a mile of quiet fills the distance to the next road crossing in a rural area where the river is popular for fishing.

At the first intersection of the Sugar River Trail and New Hampshire 11, the state has shown its concern for recreationalists by routing the trail under the highway bridge. You ride at the very edge of the river on wide gravel-fill before passing by a field on the way into the woods again. Soon come sights available only to those who explore the off-road byways of New Hampshire—two of the few remaining covered railroad bridges in the country, Pier Bridge and Wrights Bridge. Each bridge maintains the fine structural and aesthetic condition of its past.

At the western end of the line lies Claremont, a small city with a busy downtown. The ride stops a few miles east of the town center, but New Hampshire 11 can be followed in for food or refreshments. Otherwise, it's back home along the river, over the route thousands of railroad travelers took through the years.

The post-industrial centers of Newport and Claremont have revived aspects of their own history to feed economic development. The region has a fair number of covered roadway bridges. In fact, each autumn Newport holds its Covered Bridge Festival. Come winter, Newport puts on the longest running winter carnival of any town in America. It's been a popular event since 1916.

Among other attractions to the region are the 10-square-mile Lake Sunapee and Mount Sunapee State Park. Mount Sunapee State Park's 2,700 acres of forest, trails, beachfront, and lift-serviced mountain biking make it one of New Hampshire's most popular destinations. The Monadnock-Sunapee Greenway hiking trail travels 49 miles, from the state park to Mount Monadnock. Appalachian Mountain Club (AMC) President Allen Chamberlain conceived the trail in 1919. Today the AMC and the Society for Protection of New Hampshire Forests maintain it. To ride part of the Monadnock-Sunapee Greenway by mountain bike, return to the Pillsbury State Park chapter to learn more (chapter 16).

Underpass at Sugar River

The scenery and history along the Sugar River Trail combine to make it perhaps the most attractive multi-use rail line New Hampshire has to offer. Come winter, snowmobile use keeps the white surface packed firm for anyone out to prove that mountain biking is a year-round sport. So if January gets you down, look for crusty snow, no recent icing, and very cold weather for the best winter trail conditions.

Newport native Sarah Josepha Hale wrote the famous children's song "Mary Had A Little Lamb."

Ride Information

📞 Trail Contacts:
New Hampshire Division of Parks, Bureau of Trails, Concord, NH (603) 271-3254

🕐 Schedule:
Open year-round

❓ Local Information:
Claremont Chamber of Commerce, Claremont, NH (602) 543-1296 • Newport Chamber of Commerce, Newport, NH (603) 863-1510

💡 Local Events/Attractions:
Newport Opera House, Newport, NH (603) 863-2412 – holds town meetings as well as community stage productions • Claremont Opera House, Claremont, NH (603) 542-4433 – restored building

hosts performances year-round in its 800-seat theatre • Claremont Historical Society Museum, Claremont, NH (603) 543-1400 – open Sunday afternoons through the summer, with admission free

🚲 Local Bike Shops:
Claremont Cyclesport, Claremont, NH (603) 542-2453 • Bob Skinner's Ski and Sports, Sunapee, NH (603) 763-2303 • Outspokin' Bicycle and Sport Shop, Newbury, NH (603) 763-9500

Ⓝ Maps:
USGS maps: Newport, NH; Springfield, VT

One of two covered train bridges along the route

Sugar River trailside parking

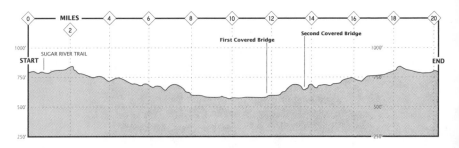

MilesDirections

0.0 START by riding to the trail entrance at the far end of the gravel lot. Pass around the orange gate, soon coming along the Sugar River.

2.7 Cross successive paved roads and travel over a number of bridges.

5.9 Come to Pier Bridge. At the intersection with the gravel road, turn right.

6.6 The gravel road bends left. Return onto the gated rail trail to the right. Cross Wrights Bridge.

10.1 Reach the trail end at NH 11 / NH 103. Turn around and retrace your tracks.

20.2 Last stop, Newport.

Alternate Start:

If you'd like to start from Claremont, begin your ride from the turn-off on the southern side of NH 11 / NH 103 in Claremont, across from the Pool Man supply store.

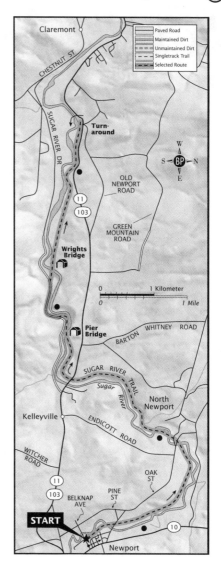

Hanover Rural Roads and Doubletrack

Ride Summary

Using the town of Hanover as your hub, ride in any direction to quickly find good trails. This loop mixes some of Hanover's maintained rural roads, with abandoned wagon tracks that have eroded into formidable challenges. Though it starts at Hanover Parade, nothing about the ride is a stroll. You could come home quite tired from the hills, and very soggy if there's been recent rain. It's a gritty excursion for sure.

Ride Specs

Start: From Hanover Parade, also known as Hanover Center
Length: 13.6-mile loop
Approximate Riding Time: 2½–3 hours
Difficulty Rating: Technically difficult due to rocky, eroded sections, and center-of-trail riding between water filled truck tire ruts. Physically strenuous, especially the steep climb and descent of Moose Mountain.
Trail Surface: Abandoned (sometimes overgrown) roads, gravel roads, and paved roads. Logging slash and rocky sections to watch for over Moose Mountain.
Lay of the Land: Hilly, forested countryside that's prone to wetness at lower elevations
Elevation Gain: 1,535 feet
Land Status: Abandoned town roads, gravel roads, and paved roads
Nearest Town: Hanover, NH
Other Trail Users: Hikers, motorists, equestrians, and hunters (in season)
Wheels: Mountain bikes only

Getting There

From Concord, NH: Travel north on I-89 to Lebanon. Take Exit 18. Turn right onto NH 120 north, toward Hanover. After 0.8 miles, turn right at the light onto Etna Road. Continue on Etna Road through the village of Etna, marked by the Etna General Store and the fire station. After Dogford Road passes on the left, the main road climbs uphill in a series of S-turns. At the hilltop pass a sign for Hanover Parade (Hanover Center). Immediately turn left onto the spur road between the parade (town common) and the cemetery to park. The entire trip from NH 89 to Hanover Parade runs 6.6 miles.
DeLorme: New Hampshire Atlas & Gazetteer. Page 32, I-4

Though miles away from the White Mountain National Forest and lacking a large state park, Hanover and its environs abound with mountain biking opportunities. Dirt roads crisscross the Vermont and New Hampshire countryside of the Upper Connecticut River Valley, an area which for New Hampshire holds the highest concentration of working farms in the state. Homes along these quiet routes predate the automobile, and even the bicycle. Cellar holes and abandoned cemeteries off of colonial wagon tracks truly turn back time.

Great opportunities in Hanover extend well beyond the trails. Phenomenal road cycling can be found on uncrowded two-lane highways, though perhaps the best opportunities are educational. Dartmouth College

fills downtown Hanover with bright young faces year-round and drives its cultural activity. It also drives local commerce, as evidenced on South Main Street by the number of coffeehouses, restaurants, and pubs. The college's sprawling campus, home to 5,000 students, extends mainly east from South Main Street and north across Dartmouth Green.

It was a Yale graduate, Reverend Eleazar Wheelock, who founded Dartmouth College. Difficulties with his effort to establish More's Indian Charity School in Connecticut, led Reverend Wheelock to New Hampshire, which held better prospects for land, governmental support, and candidates for enrollment. The move proved successful in 1769, when with the help of New Hampshire Governor John Wentworth, Dartmouth obtained its royal charter. Reverend Wheelock offered classes the next year from a single log cabin in Hanover. The first graduating class—all four students—matriculated with baccalaureate degrees in 1771.

Sixteen years after the first class graduated from the college, the Dartmouth Medical School formed under Dr. Nathan Smith, a renowned surgeon of the time. Today, the Medical School and its partners in the Dartmouth-Hitchcock Medical Center provide the rural people of the Upper Connecticut River Valley access to world-class healthcare. From cutting edge research to

Rural Humor

advanced treatments of disease, the Dartmouth-Hitchcock Medical Center improves the quality of life for its neighbors.

Not far from the medical center, nor from Hanover's popular downtown, sits a small hilltop common known both as Hanover Parade and Hanover Center. There's a church there and a group of homes, but a busy place it surely is not. Using this as the parking spot for the ride, you'll descend on Wolfeboro Road before climbing to a hilltop that offers clear southern views. A sign at the transition to abandoned road warns about the condition of the bridge. The warning is irrelevant since the bridge is no longer there. Take care over the stream crossing where the bridge used to be though, as the dip there makes a prime runway for a flight over the bars. The climb from the stream returns to the next maintained section of Wolfeboro Road.

The Appalachian Trail (AT) crosses the chapter loop at the base of Moose Mountain, though it isn't marked with the other trailside signs. Bikes are NOT welcome on the AT. The chapter loop heads up and over Moose Mountain via Clark Pond Loop Trail. Several runoff paths cross the climb, making the ascent a wet one after rainfall. Debris from logging also hampers upward progress—as well as downward progress on the eastern slope.

Once free of Moose Mountain a blip of smooth terrain appears on maintained gravel road. You'll then run a flat course over abandoned North Tunis Road, past the Hanover Town Forest. Riding difficulties after the exit from North Tunis Road onto Goose Pond Road will be mainly aerobic, as hills along the mixed gravel and pavement route back to Hanover Parade exact a toll on already tired legs. Save some energy for the final assault along the home stretch.

For another great ride just north of Hanover in Lyme, New Hampshire, check out Jen Mynter's *Mountain Bike America: Vermont*. Her route travels near the one in this chapter, using a similar mix of gravel roads, abandoned roads, and pavement. The rest of her book leads you through the great rides and the culture of the Green Mountain State.

Dartmouth Green

Ride Information

📞 Trail Contacts:
There are no trail contacts, as whole route follows town roads.

🕐 Schedule:
Open year-round

❓ Local Information:
Hanover Chamber of Commerce, Hanover, NH (603) 643-3115

🔄 Other Resources:
Mountain Bike America: Vermont, Jen Mynter, *www.outside-america.com*

💡 Local Events/Attractions:
Downtown Hanover — *Surrounded by* the campus of Dartmouth College, the downtown boasts dozens of shops and eateries. It's Ivy League atmosphere in the hills of New Hampshire.

🚲 Local Bike Shops:
Tom Mowatt Cycles, Lebanon, NH (603) 448-5556 or *www.sover.net/~tmc* — *Tom Mowatt Cycles has the latest information on group rides. The shop's website gives maps and directions for other local mountain bike rides.* • **Omer and Bob's Sport Shop,** Hanover, NH (603) 643-3525

🅝 Maps:
USGS maps: Canaan, NH; Lyme, NH

MilesDirections

0.0 START by taking an immediate right north of Hanover Parade onto Wolfeboro Road.

0.8 Continue on the grassy track where Wolfeboro Road becomes unmaintained. Watch for the drop-off into a seasonal stream at the bottom of the descent.

1.1 Pass to the left of the overgrowth and emerge over the dirt mound onto the maintained portion of Wolfeboro Road.

1.3 Turn left on gravel Three Mile Road.

1.7 Turn right back onto gravel Wolfeboro Road. A "Not A Through Street" sign opposite a group of mail and newspaper boxes marks the entrance.

2.3 Pass a trail junction marked with a number of trail names, among them Harris Trail and Clark Pond Loop. Continue straight after the signs, immediately beginning an extended climb up the doubletrack Clark Pond Loop. Cross a trail junction at the height of land and pass a maintained shelter on the left.

3.7 Cross Tunis Brook. Continue along its course downstream.

4.3 Emerge on maintained gravel. Pass a cemetery on the right.

4.9 Turn left at the intersection with Tunis Road. Pass the blue Hanover Town Forest sign. The road becomes abandoned and tracks through a low-lying area that will be very wet after rainy periods.

6.9 Turn left at the "T" intersection with Goose Pond Road. Ride past a number of horse farms.

9.7 Turn left at the stop sign, onto unposted Two Mile Road, and ride uphill on gravel. The road transitions to pavement by the crest of the hill. Continue straight as the road becomes Hanover Center Road and rolls back to Hanover Parade.

13.6 Arrive at Hanover Parade.

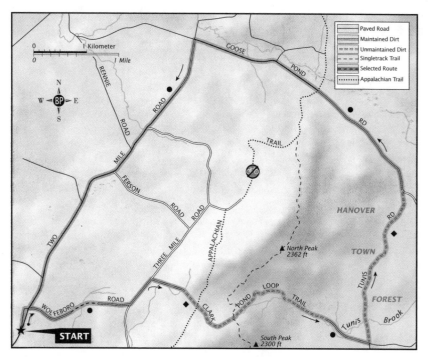

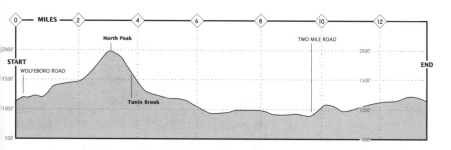

Honorable Mentions

Dartmouth Region

Noted below is one of the great rides in the Dartmouth region that didn't make the A-list this time around but deserves recognition nonetheless. Check it out and let us know what you think. You may decide that it deserves higher status in future editions or, perhaps, you may have a ride of your own that merits some attention.

D Gile State Forest

Springfield, New Hampshire's gravel roads, abandoned town roads, and single-track and doubletrack offer rides for a range of abilities. These routes run through and around Gile State Forest. Due to ruts and washouts, the abandoned roads require advanced skills. A 14-mile loop that includes crossings over wooden bridges and some pavement can be planned for advanced riders. An 11-mile beginner trip to Morgan Pond via pavement, dirt roads, and gated dirt roads can also be done. The cellar holes of Fowler Town and its small cemetery can be reached on the advanced loop. The pristine North Wilmont Church sits at a dirt crossroads that all can reach. Paved and ungated dirt roads are open to autos. Gile State Forest waits for you midway between Concord and Vermont. Park at Gardner Wayside Park, off New Hampshire 4A in Springfield, New Hampshire. For additional information, contact the New Hampshire Division of Forests and Lands, (603) 271-2214. *DeLorme: New Hampshire Atlas & Gazetteer: Page,* 34, E-4

Lakes

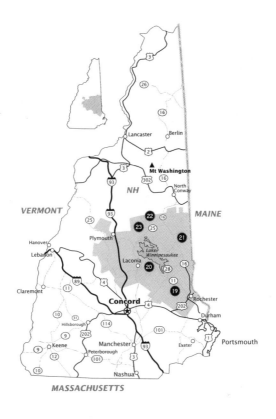

Region

Lakes Region

The Lakes Region spreads from the focal point of Lake Winnipesaukee. Because recreational activities and lifestyles often revolve around the many bodies of water in the area, the blessings of its rural countryside are too frequently overlooked. Gravel roads abound not far from most paved routes, and many of these roads lead on to rough abandoned tracks used mostly in the winter for snowmobiling.

Though the Lakes Region sits south of the White Mountains, it's better thought of as a warm-up for the steep stuff to the north. The topography rolls and pitches to only a slightly lesser extent than New Hampshire's truly mountainous land. In fact, the rides and riding areas written of in the Lakes Region section all contain chal-

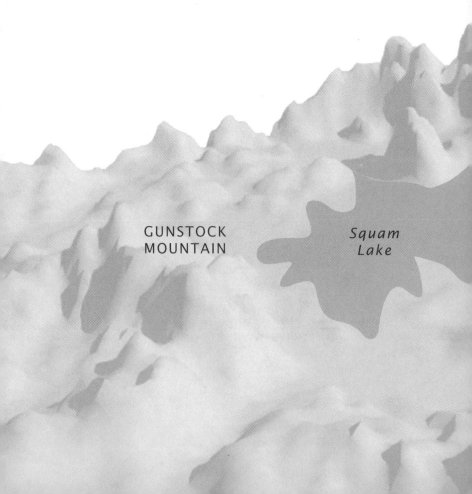

GUNSTOCK
MOUNTAIN

Squam
Lake

lenging grades. One of New Hampshire's hardest climbs can be made to the fire watchtower atop Green Mountain, while shallower grades such as those at Blue Job Mountain still bring on a fitness challenge.

The region is home to country shops filled with quilts and crafts, and more overtly commercial areas such as Weirs Beach with its mini-golf and waterslides. The large lakes of Winnipesaukee and Squam offer sight seeing cruises and pleasure boating to spare, while smaller water bodies serve as more private summer retreats.

)WICH RANGE

RED HILL

Lake Winnipesaukee

Blue Job Mountain Loop

Ride Summary

Blue Job Mountain serves up rugged terrain to those ready to mix abandoned roads with steep climbing. The route travels up the exposed, sometimes windswept granite surface of Little Blue Job, stopping in the midst of low bush blueberry fields. You'll have a climbing option to the top of Blue Job Mountain itself, and pass other spots of local renown, including Little Niagara and Barn Door Gap.

Ride Specs

Start: From the Rochester Reservoir, along Sheepboro Road
Length: 16-mile loop
Approximate Riding Time: 2½ hours
Difficulty Rating: Difficult due to eroded surfaces, trip length, and climbs
Trail Surface: Singletrack, doubletrack, 4WD roads, gravel roads, and pavement
Lay of the Land: Steep, forested hillsides; swamps and open fields; high elevation areas of exposed bedrock that provide panoramic views
Elevation Gain: 1,814 feet
Nearest Town: Rochester, NH
Other Trail Users: Motorists, hikers, and hunters (in season)
Wheels: Mountain bikes only on the chapter ride, though many of the rural roads around Blue Job Mountain have maintained gravel surfaces that are well-suited to hybrid bikes

Getting There

From Rochester, NH: Take Exit 13 off of the Spaulding Turnpike (NH 16 / U.S. 202) and travel two miles west on U.S. 202. Turn right at the blinking light onto Estes Road. Continue 1.4 miles to a stop sign. Cross NH 202A and continue on Meaderboro Road. Travel 2.7 miles to the pavement's end, just past Butternut Farm. At the four-way intersection, turn left onto the unpaved Cross Road. Travel 0.8 miles, and after passing Rochester Reservoir on the right, turn right at the four-way intersection onto unposted Sheepboro Road. Park to the side of Sheepboro Road, before the wooden bridge. **DeLorme: New Hampshire Atlas & Gazetteer.** Page 29, A-11

D on't be worried if the charred scent of a recent fire drifts into your nostrils midway into your ride. It's not your lungs roasting from the effort of the last climb—nor is it your rear tire breaking loose on New Hampshire's famous granite. It's the intentional cleansing of blueberry fields on Little Blue Job Mountain. (That's "Job" as in the Book of Job.) Each year, trained personnel from the New Hampshire Division of Forests and Lands and the Department of Fish and Game burn sections of the mountain in order to keep down competing brush and trees. This controlled process mimics the uncontrolled natural process and stimulates the growth of the low-lying bush blueberry.

At one point, the blueberry fields of Little Blue Job were in commercial production. Due to the lack of upkeep in later years, forest succession threatened to overtake the area. New Hampshire acquired the property in 1991 through the Land Conservation Investment Program, and in 1995 the state began the prescribed burn program. Due to the state's work, a special habitat is maintained and local wildlife continue to have a plentiful food source.

This trip includes a number of sketchy climbs and bone-jarring descents. It's kind of special like that. Erosion on many unmaintained roads puts a level of difficulty into things that will challenge all who ride here, and frustrate those out for an easy time. The start of the loop is deceptive. Initial climbs are short and can be tackled in the middle ring, but they keep coming. After one mile a driveway is passed on the right and brush creeps in on the road. The riding is grueling for the next half-mile, traveling over a series of steep, rocky washouts.

Past the red Cape Cod home, the joy of climbing soon births a streaking downhill trip scattered with rocks and waterbars. The route levels out and after a short flat section crosses a wooden bridge. Be cautious on your approach to the bridge as some boards may be loose or missing.

Meaderboro Road gives an extended stretch of smooth riding before the loop heads back into the woods. The climb to Little Blue Job soon begins and doesn't stop until the granny gear gets a hefty workout. The reward for this effort is a panoramic

view of the New Hampshire and Maine countryside, with the White Mountains to the northwest, and the ocean far off to the east. From mid July into August, you'll find ripe blueberries all around.

If your legs aren't toasted once atop Little Blue Job, there's an option for a steeper excursion departing briefly from the chapter ride. At the summit of nearby Blue Job Mountain, the closest higher land, there is a fire watchtower. Ride the half-mile ascent if you can. The path to the tower snakes through the stone wall on the opposite side of the nearby pond. The pond is tough to spot from Little Blue Job, but it sits in the low point on the line of sight to Blue Job Mountain. Return from the watchtower on the same route.

Whether climbing to the tower or descending the singletrack Candy Trail from Little Blue Job, be aware of hikers. Families love to visit this area, and in addition to children, unleashed dogs will be scampering about. One local clan is even known to take their goat with them on hikes.

The mix of climbing and descending over varied terrain continues for the remainder of the ride. Take particular care crossing the steel I-beams at the torn-out bridge—though the eight-foot drop to the river could be revitalizing. Stop for refreshment here by the cascade of water over Little Niagara, and then continue on to the gradual one-mile climb up the gravel road toward Barn Door Gap. Finish the loop, and then come back again to explore the side trails that open up dozens more miles of terrain.

Fresh Blueberry Crisp

6 cups fresh blueberries
1 teaspoon cinnamon (optional)
1 tablespoon water
1 teaspoon lemon juice
1 cup rolled oats
¾ cup all purpose flour
¾ cup firmly packed brown sugar
½ cup softened margarine or butter

Oven temperature: 375° F
Baking time: 25 to 35 minutes

Place blueberries into ungreased 2-quart casserole dish. Sprinkle with cinnamon, water, and lemon juice. In a large bowl combine oats, flour, sugar, and margarine; mix with a fork until crumbly. Spread oat mixture over blueberries. Bake until the fruit is bubbly and the topping is golden brown. Serve warm with vanilla ice cream.

Ride Information

🕿 Trail Contact:

New Hampshire Department of Forests and Lands, Concord, NH (603) 271-2214 – *Call here for the areas surrounding Blue Job Mountain and Little Blue Job. Other areas are simply abandoned town roads.*

🚴 Local Bike Shops:

Tony's Cyclery, Dover, NH (603) 742-0494 – *Call for group rides.* • **Tri-city Speedway and Mountain Bike,** Rochester, NH (603) 335-6440

Ⓝ Maps:

USGS maps: Baxter Lake, NH; Parker Mountain, NH

MilesDirections

0.0 START on Sheepboro Road and head toward the bridge. Begin a series of short, repetitive climbs for the next 1.6 miles. In the last 0.5 miles these climbs become steep and eroded.

1.6 Pass a red, cape-style home and follow the trail as it forks right, then bends right again. Surface conditions improve.

2.8 After a home, turn left at the gravel Meaderboro Road.

4.6 At the transition from dirt to pavement, turn left before a house onto Scruton Road. Descend to a marsh and begin another climb that levels as it approaches Scruton's Fields.

5.4 Immediately when the hayfields come into view, turn left up a gated doubletrack, past the "No Wheeled Vehicles" sign, if it's there—vandals periodically tear the sign down. It's intended to prohibit 4WDs, ATVs, and off-road motorcycles. Bicycles are allowed. Keep on with the uphill grunt. Follow to the right once the surface turns to uncovered ledge and climb to the height of land marked by a cairn built on a large, flat rock.

5.8 Continue across the rock surface as it transitions to a grass covered path. Descend to the doubletrack that parallels a small pond and turn right. About 250 feet after the pond, the singletrack Candy Trail branches left into the woods. Take it, crest a knoll, and begin a shallow, curvaceous descent through the trees.

6.4 The Candy Trail merges with a doubletrack and after a short, rocky descent reaches the Blue Job Mountain parking lot on the right. From the parking lot, turn right on paved First Crown Point Road.

7.9 Take the only left off First Crown Point Road. It's after a group of mailboxes. After the last home, the road passes through a low-lying area and becomes unmaintained.

8.8 Dismount at the boulders that block the trail. Portage by steel I-beams across the torn-out bridge, or cross lower over the rocks above Little Niagara, if the water isn't high.

9.2 Turn left on the gravel road.

10.8 At the end of the gravel road, turn left on the rocky, abandoned track through Barn Door Gap.

11.9 The abandoned track turns to maintained road where it passes a home. Take the immediate left after this home, up what looks like a driveway. Continue onto unmaintained road once past the last house.

12.5 Head left, uphill, on paved First Crown Point Road.

13.5 About 150 yards beyond the crest of the hill, turn right on an abandoned doubletrack between two homes. The doubletrack starts with a shallow, rocky climb and is just before the Blue Job Mountain parking lot. (Don't mistake it for the private way with the chain across it.)

14.3 Pass a steep, eroded downhill to the right. About 150 yards later, turn right at the intersection with unmaintained Sheepboro Road. Pass the red, cape-style home seen earlier.

16.0 Arrive at your vehicle.

Alternate Start:

From the Blue Job Mountain parking lot, just over the high elevation of First Crown Point Road.

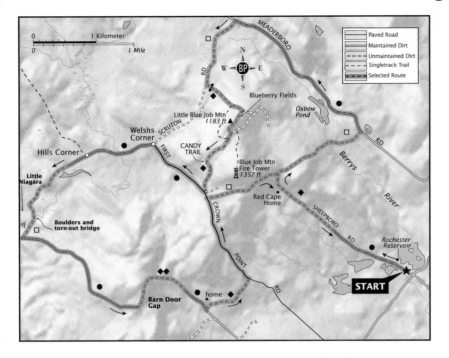

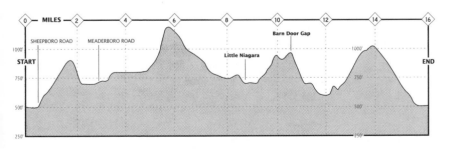

Gunstock

Ride Summary

Gunstock is a great mountain for family skiing and that atmosphere carries over to its summer camping and mountain biking. Miles of cross-country ski trails are turned over to fat-tire riders during the warm months. The chapter loop gives a warm-up option of minimal physical or technical challenge. Other trails along the network, which Gunstock rates for difficulty, can make for a full day of riding. There's even a terrain garden with obstacles intended to test your bike handling skills.

Ride Specs

Start: From the Gunstock Mountain Bike Center

Length: 3-mile loop

Approximate Riding Time: 40 minutes

Difficulty Rating: Technically easy. Wide trail surface, with few abrupt obstacles. Physically easy due to short length and relative flatness. Some brief climbs.

Trail Surface: Grass slopes, gravel roads, wide forest paths, and singletrack with rocks and roots.

Lay of the Land: Hilly forested terrain set against the backdrop of Gunstock Ski Area

Elevation Gain: 463 feet

Land Status: Belknap county property, used for skiing and summer recreation

Nearest Town: Gilford, NH

Other Trail Users: Equestrians (some trails posted horses only), hikers, cross-country skiers, and snowshoers

Wheels: Mountain bikes and kids' single speeds are fine on the chapter loop. Harder trails are for mountain bikes only.

Getting There

From Laconia, NH: Follow NH 11A east approximately seven miles into Gilford. Turn right at the sign for Gunstock. The Gunstock Mountain Bike Center is with the campground store. *DeLorme: New Hampshire Atlas & Gazetteer:* Page 36, D-5

Cumulus clouds speckle the day's open sky. Eyes lower to the evergreen peaks of the Sandwich and Ossipee ranges and follow down their slopes to the shore of Lake Winnipesaukee, the "Smile of the Great Spirit." Across the rippled water steams the M/S Mount Washington on its run from Weirs Beach to Alton. This is the northeastern viewshed from atop Gunstock Mountain.

The climb to Gunstock's summit is long and gains 1,400 feet, but in consolation you're afforded similarly spectacular views for a portion of the effort along the Ridge Trail. As a mid-summer bonus, the Ridge Trail is buffered in places by

blueberry bushes. Not everyone is a climber though, and the variety of terrain at Gunstock takes care of the gravity challenged. Most of the mountain bike paths follow the cross-country ski network at the base of the mountain. Flat trails with some short, tame grades meander through the forest, open spaces, and the wooded campground. These trails are typically wide with a good line of sight distance, so everyone in a group can stick together.

Signs posted at intersections in the woods, along with a copy of the Gunstock Mountain Bike Trail Map, ease any worries of getting lost. The map provides difficulty ratings and includes topographic contours so users can get a feel for the terrain ahead. Also, because of the efforts of the maintenance crew, fallen trees or erosion won't cut a great loop short.

The ride described in this chapter is a warm-up for the many more miles of trails available. The first part of its run along the west bank of Poorfarm Brook climbs gradually to the pace set by the flowing water. Once away from the brook, look for markers that identify yellow birch, oak, and evergreen trees. Also, look for other cyclists

Lake Winnipesaukee in the background

and give a nod of encouragement when you pass, for some of them may be haggard after having just finished the three-hour trip out to Round Pond and back.

The trail to the Round Pond is one of Gunstock's advanced offerings. For the rugged and fit, it mixes singletrack and doubletrack over technical terrain. The Ridge Trail, noted earlier, is another advanced torture test that will put a fiery burn into any rider's legs. In addition to the climbing, there are many steep, rough descents to shake things up.

With advanced routes like the Ridge Trail and Round Pond Trail, and easier paths closer to the Mountain Bike Center, it is plain to see that Gunstock offers a diversity of terrain and biking experiences. The staff understands that experienced riders are comfortable tackling whatever comes, while beginners and recreationalists may prefer a milder mix. On-site mountain bike rentals, guided tours by advance arrangement, and group rates for bands of 15 or more are a few of the ways Gunstock tries to put everyone off-road.

Family camping at Gunstock makes it easy for the whole clan to explore the region on mountain bikes. There are 220 tent sites and another 80 spots for the RV set. While not all amenities for campers are available to day-users of the trails, the crucial ones are: the snack store, the bathhouse showers, and the swimming pool.

The list of non-biking activities in New Hampshire's Lakes Region is a long one, so check with local chambers of commerce or the Lakes Region Association for a complete rundown. A trinity of nearby favorites includes the hiking trails at Mount Major, the amusements at Weirs Beach, and Castle in the Clouds. Mount Major is off New Hampshire 11, west of Alton Bay. Yearly, thousands make the short hike to the open summit. It's a popular trip with families and chaperoned youth groups. Weirs Beach is the inland cousin of New Hampshire's ocean beaches, offering the cool water of Lake Winnipesaukee, a boardwalk, water slides, a summer schedule of fireworks, and enough sand to pacify the sunbathing crowd. Castle in the Clouds, in Moultonborough, sits high in the Ossipee Mountains. Tours of the grounds, horseback riding, hiking, and wide-open views are some of the surprises to be found here.

Ride Information

🌑 Trail Contact:
Gunstock Mountain Bike Center, Gilford, NH 1-800-GUNSTOCK or *www.gunstock.com*

🕐 Schedule:
Memorial Day weekend to Columbus Day Weekend, 8 A.M. to 6 P.M.

💲 Fees/Permits:
One-day trail pass: $4 for ages six and older. County resident season pass: $40. Non-resident season pass: $50. Riders 65 and older and five and younger, as well as campers, pedal for free. Bike rentals are available on site.

❓ Local Information:
Greater Laconia-Weirs Beach Chamber of Commerce, Laconia, NH (603) 524-5531 or 1-800-531-2347 • **The Lakes Region Association,** Center Harbor, NH 1-800-605-2537 or (603) 253-8555 or *www.lakesregion.org*

💡 Local Events/Attractions:
Gunstock Crafts Festival, Octoberfest, Brewfest, Country Jamboree, and other celebrations, Gilford, NH 1-800-GUN-STOCK (486-7862) or *www.gunstock.com* • **Motorcycle Week,** typically runs the week before Father's Day, Laconia/Loudon/Weirs Beach, NH area – *This event brings two-wheeled racing to New Hampshire International Speedway [(603) 783-493] and a grid-locked boulevard of customized Harley-Davidsons to Weirs Beach.* • **Mount Major, Alton, NH** • **Weirs Beach, NH** – *Call Laconia-Weirs Beach Chamber of Commerce at (603) 524-5531 or 1-800-531-2347 for information.* • **Castle in the Clouds,** Moultonborough, NH (603) 476-2352 or 1-800-729-2468

🚴 Local Bike Shops:
Gunstock Mountain Bike Center rental/repair shop, Gilford, NH 1-800-GUNSTOCK (486-7862) or *www.gunstock.com* • **Boot 'N Wheel,** Laconia, NH (603) 524 -7665 • **Piche's Ski and Sport,** Gilford, NH (603) 524-2068

🅝 Maps:
USGS maps: Laconia, NH; West Alton, NH • **Gunstock Mountain Bike Trail Map** – available on-site or in advance by calling the mountain at 1-800-GUNSTOCK (486-7862)

MilesDirections

0.0 START across the road from the Mountain Bike Center. Turn left along Cobble Mountain Trail (Trail 5 on the Gunstock map). Follow as it turns into the woods along Poorfarm Brook.

1.3 Turn right at the "T" intersection to continue on Cobble Mountain Trail.

2.0 A descent ends alongside a brown maintenance garage. Turn right opposite the garage, and head up the small rise. Continue along Cobble Mountain Trail. At the first fork turn right onto Long Bow (Trail 2). Long Bow merges with Quiver (Trail 6).

2.7 Just before the intersection with Cobble Mountain Trail, Quiver switches back to the left and heads to Technical Difficulties, a collection of skill-improvement obstacles. Follow the switchback and continue onto Technical Difficulties. Pass through Technical Difficulties and to Cobble Mountain Trail on the opposite side. A left onto Cobble Mountain Trail returns you to the Mountain Bike Center.

3.0 Warm-up over.

Looking up the ski jump

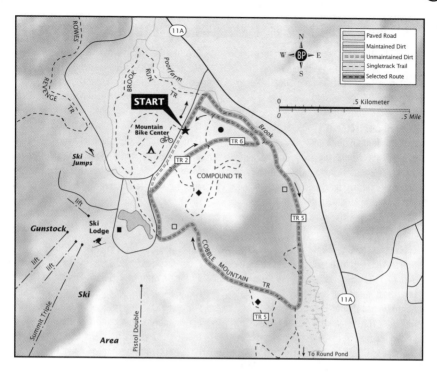

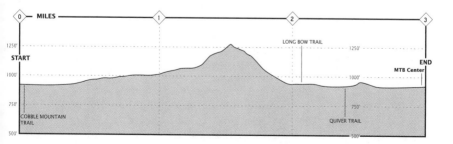

Green Mountain Climb

Ride Summary

Green Mountain promises mountain bikers what is arguably the hardest climb in New Hampshire to clean. Its steep pitch and loose trail surface demand both power and bike handling skills. A few miles of rural, unpaved road give ample warm-up before things really tilt to the sky. Once you dispatch the ascent, and perhaps lunch, you can climb the fire watchtower to really feel on top of the world.

Ride Specs

Start: From Hobbs Road, at the First Normal School of New Hampshire
Length: 8.4-mile out-and-back
Approximate Riding Time: 1½ hours
Difficulty Rating: Very difficult to maintain traction along the loose, rocky climb and descent of Green Mountain. Extremely strenuous due to an 1,160-foot, technical climb
Trail Surface: Rural gravel road, abandoned road, doubletrack, and fire watchtower access
Lay of the Land: Thickly wooded, rural countryside, with "small" mountains surrounded by rolling terrain
Elevation Gain: 1,636 feet
Land Status: Town roads and state forest
Nearest Town: Effingham, NH
Other Trail Users: Motorists, equestrians, hikers, and snowmobilers
Wheels: Mountain bikes only

Getting There

From Ossipee, NH: Travel north on NH 16. Turn right onto NH 25 east. Follow NH 25 for 6.6 miles. Turn right onto NH 153 South along the Ossipee River. Pass the Effingham Fire station on the right and a cemetery on the left 3.2 miles from NH 25. Immediately after the cemetery, at the historical marker for the First Normal School of New Hampshire, turn right onto the gravel Hobbs Road. Park to the side of Hobbs Road. *DeLorme: New Hampshire Atlas & Gazetteer.* Page 41, H-13

For a ride that starts at the First Normal School of New Hampshire, this trip should draw a fairly abnormal bunch. Not that abnormality makes climb-lovers bad. It just means those that would enjoy this ride may not find too many friends among the downhill mountain bikers in the lift line at a typical ski resort.

James W. Bradbury, former United States Senator from Maine, established the First Normal School of New Hampshire in 1830, for the training of new teachers. The Effingham Union Academy building, site of the First Normal School,

View from the firetower atop Green Mountain

remains a pristine estate, though its teacher training role ended long ago. It is one of many early 19th Century structures in the Lord's Hill Historic District of Effingham. A few hundred feet away—at the bend in New Hampshire 153—is the village common, complete with shade trees, town green, and bandstand. A white clapboard country church along with the Honor Role of Effingham citizens whom fought for American freedom complete the rural setting.

Dirt roads abound in this town on the New Hampshire and Maine border. Recreational riders could link these with Effingham's rural paved roads to create a smooth ride through quiet countryside. The chapter loop, however, is for those with advanced skills and fitness. It includes a sleepy beginning on gravel Hobbs Road, followed by some warm-up efforts once Hobbs Road becomes unmaintained. These warm-up sections prepare the hearty for an uninterrupted 1,160-foot climb to the fire watchtower atop Green Mountain.

The relentless ascent begins gradually up the tower access road, then steepens and roughens beyond a home on the left. Once into the climb, speeds might creep to four miles per hour, but don't count on it. Do count on dabbing some sections or pushing them, particularly midway through the assault. An overgrown doubletrack rolls off to the right where the access road switches back near the mountaintop. Avoid the temptation to capitulate to gravity. Continue climbing on the access road to the 1,884-foot summit.

A sign at the base of the fire watchtower provides an overview map of the countryside's mountains, lakes, and rivers. Signs also mark Dearborn Trail and High Watch Trail, two insanely difficult singletracks that depart from the Green Mountain summit. The Ice Storm of 1998 did major damage to each, dropping beech trees and other hardwoods in an impenetrable blockade. The local rangers have begun clear-

ing the routes, but limited resources have slowed progress, which can only be made on Class II and lesser fire danger days. During dry forest conditions, the rangers must remain on watch in the tower.

Dearborn Trail drops into the woods east of the tower. The singletrack—tight, steep, potentially dangerous, but a blast when clear—descends for two miles back to Hobbs Road. The route is marked with white blazes on the trees. Some sections are grassy and hide nasty endo-makers like rocks or roots. Other sections demand to be ridden off the back of the saddle. The alternative choice, High Watch Trail, brings similar risks with steep walking sections. It deposits you on the opposite side of the mountain from the start, with more pavement than dirt to traverse on the way home.

The chapter route returns straight back down the access road on a rough descent equal in challenge to the climb. For a respite and an odd surprise once out to the maintained section of Hobbs Road, catch the Woodland Cemetery. After passing a large white barn to the right at the roadside, turn left opposite the small cemetery just beyond it. Follow the dirt driveway until the woods open to a field with views of the surrounding mountains.

Riders set on the panorama of the New Hampshire and Maine countryside offered by the Green Mountain fire watchtower, but who are daunted by the thought of biking up the trail, can easily pedal from the parking area to the base of the Dearborn Trail. The trailhead is to the right, about a half-mile onto the unmaintained portion of Hobbs Road. A small white sign across a clearing marks the entrance. It's a two-mile hike from the entrance.

Ride Information

🍥 Trail Contacts:
New Hampshire Department of Forests and Lands, Concord, NH
(603) 271-2214

☉ Schedule:
Anytime after the spring rains

❓ Local Information:
Greater Ossipee Area Chamber of Commerce, West Ossipee, NH
(603) 539-6201 or 1-800-382-2371

🍄 Local Bike Shops:
Piche's Ski and Sport Shop, Wolfeboro, NH (603) 569-8234 • Joe Jones Ski and Sports, North Conway Village, NH (603) 356-9411 or www.joejonessports.com • The Bike Shop, North Conway, NH (603) 356-6089 • The Nordic Skier, Wolfeboro, NH (603) 569-3151

Ⓝ Maps:
USGS maps: Freedom, NH; Kezar Falls, ME

MilesDirections

0.0 START on Hobbs Road. Pass a sparse mix of old homes and newer houses until Hobbs Road becomes unmaintained.

1.7 Emerge briefly onto a maintained section of road at the intersection with Old Pound Road. Continue straight onto an unmaintained section again.

2.3 On the right is a green gate barring motor vehicles from the access road to Green Mountain. Turn right here.

4.2 Reach the top of Green Mountain. Turn around and retrace your route.

6.1 Turn left after the gate. Stay straight on the abandoned route that led into the ride. Continue straight once out the maintained section of Hobbs Road.

8.4 Reach your vehicle.

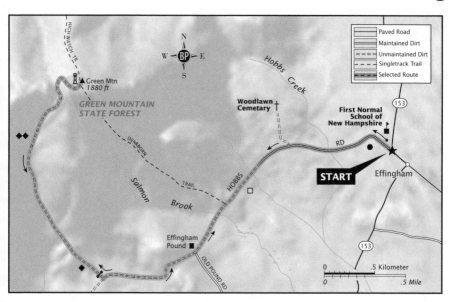

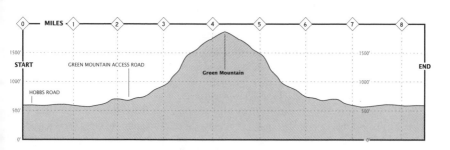

Hemenway State Forest

Ride Summary

Hemenway State Forest offers a little extra seclusion in an area dominated by Lake Winnipesaukee to the south and the White Mountain National Forest to the north. Trails are wide and the challenges varied along the chapter loop. Two highlights include the long, flat trip beside Paugus Brook and the views from the fire watchtower atop Great Hill.

Ride Specs

Start: Intersection of Hemenway Road and Great Hill Road

Length: 7.5-mile loop

Approximate Riding Time: 1½ hours

Difficulty Rating: Technically moderate overall, with difficult sections along loose, eroded climbs and descents. Physically moderate, though the climbs from New Hampshire 113A to Hemenway Road and to the Great Hill fire tower are legitimate efforts

Trail Surface: Doubletrack and secluded gravel roads

Lay of the Land: Hilly, forestland split by Paugus Brook and the Swift River

Elevation Gain: 590 feet

Land Status: State property

Nearest Town: Tamworth, NH

Other Trail Users: Snowmobilers, equestrians, motorists, and cross-country skiers

Wheels: Mountain bikes only, though hybrids will fair well along gravel roads and Paugus Brook

Getting There

From Tamworth, NH: Follow Cleveland Hill Road west from the junction of NH 113 and NH 113A. Immediately cross the Swift River. Take the right turn after The Barnstormers Summer Theater, onto Great Hill Road. Follow for 2.6 miles to the parking by the Hemenway State Forest signboard, at the intersection with Hemenway Road. *DeLorme: New Hampshire Atlas & Gazetteer.* Page 40, D-6

Cradled between the Ossipee Mountains and the Sandwich Range, Tamworth sits near the gateway to the Mount Washington Valley. It's home to great mountain bike riding on rural dirt roads and borders the southern trailheads of Mount Chocorua. Away from the major byways and well traveled roads, Tamworth maintains its rural character and quiet downtown. Vacationers to the area might consider making Tamworth their base for easy access to Lake Winnipesaukee, North Conway, or the trails of the White Mountains.

The drive to Hemenway State Forest brings you through Tamworth Village, a classic mix of well kept homes, businesses, and community buildings. The eclectic

Other Store, Remick's Country Store, Cook Memorial Library, and the white clapboard Tamworth Congregational Church are all found within the village. Just beyond these attractions you will see the Remick Country Doctor Museum and Working Farm.

A fixture of Tamworth Village commerce since its construction in 1833, the Tamworth Inn sets the standard for country lodging and dining in the area. The Tamworth Inn abuts the Swift River and has a library, a pub, fine gardens, and spectacular views of the mountains. From the dining room, one has only to walk across the street for an evening show at New Hampshire's oldest professional theatre, The Barnstormers.

The drive out of Tamworth Village to the start of the ride passes through more rural countryside. As befits all routes that lead to great mountain bike discoveries, civilization soon fades behind you in a cloud of dust. When you spot blue blazes on the roadside trees, you've entered the state forest boundary. Finish your bagel and gulp down the rest of your coffee, the day starts soon.

The beginning of the ride utilizes cross-country ski trails maintained by the Tamworth Outing Club. The first doubletrack, the Duck Pond Loop Trail, passes

View of Mt. Chocurua

through a low-lying area near the western shore of Duck Pond. Often slippery with mud and thick with bugs, this greasy section is the hardest to handle of the ride. Bear with it though, as the technical stuff ends quickly at Middle Road.

Side-trips to Duck Pond are best made from Hemenway Road. Waterfowl will surely be seen, and maybe even the ripples of a beaver's wake as it swims away from the shore. Forgoing Duck Pond, the loop takes you on a kind descent from Hemenway Road to the Swift River. A swim downstream would lead through Tamworth Village and into the Bearcamp River that flows from Sandwich Notch, but you will ride upstream on a very shallow grade.

Once across New Hampshire 113A, you'll soon divert from the Swift River to ride along Paugus Brook. Paugus Brook accompanies your pedal until you cross the water via the snowmobile bridge, built by the Ossipee Valley Snowmobile Club. The leg from the bridge to Fowler's Mill Road passes through a former Civilian Conservation Corps camp. Fowler's Mill Road allows a rest before you cross back over New Hampshire 113A to climb the hill that originally brought you down to the Swift River. The ascent seems steeper and longer than the descent.

Francis Cleveland, the son of President Grover Cleveland, founded the Barnstormers summer theatre in 1931.

Ride Information

Trail Contact:
New Hampshire Department of Forests and Lands, Concord, NH (603) 271-2214

Schedule:
Open year-round

Local Information:
Greater Ossipee Area Chamber of Commerce, Ossipee, NH (603) 539-6201 or 1-800-382-2371

Local Events/Attractions:
The Barnstormers professional summer theater, Tamworth Village, NH (603) 323-8500

Accommodations:
The Tamworth Inn, Tamworth Village, NH (603) 323-7721 or www.tamworth.com

Restaurants:
Chequers Villa Restaurant, Tamworth, NH (603) 323-8686– pasta, pizza, steak, and seafood

Organizations:
Tamworth Outing Club, Tamworth, NH (603) 323-8687

Local Bike Shops:
The Nordic Skier, Wolfeboro, NH (603) 569-3151 • Piche's Ski and Sport Shop, Wolfeboro, NH (603) 569-8234 • Ski Works, West Ossipee, NH (603) 539-2246 • The Bike Shop, North Conway, NH (603) 356-6089 • Joe Jones Ski and Sports, North Conway Village, NH (603) 356-9411 or www.joe-jonessports.com

Maps:
USGS maps: Tamworth, NH; Mount Chocorua, NH

Another short break on gravel road sets you on the trip to the fire tower atop Great Hill. Pedaling Great Hill will challenge but not break you. From the observation deck of the tower you'll have unobstructed views of Mount Passaconaway, Mount Paugus, and Mount Chocorua to the north, and Tamworth Village to the south.

MilesDirections

0.0 START west on Great Hill Road, with the face of the signboard mapping Hemenway State Forest trails at your back.

0.2 Turn right up a gravel track at the Huckins Parking sign. Continue left of the signboard onto Duck Pond Loop. At the clearing, pass to the right of the protruding boulder. Continue straight across the field to an opening in the woods. Roll downhill on doubletrack with a stone wall to the right and two birch trees dead ahead. At times, Duck Pond will be visible to the right. Cross a wet area of moss covered rocks.

1.0 Turn right onto the woods road Middle Road.

1.2 Emerge onto gravel Hemenway Road and turn right.

1.5 Turn left at the orange gated snowmobile trail. Continue through a clearing before descending to the Swift River.

2.8 Turn right onto New Hampshire 113A. Cross the Swift River and immediately turn left. Follow the river trail, the left-most woods road, upstream along the bank.

3.8 Turn left at the wooden snowmobile bridge, toward Wonalancet. Turn right atop the short climb. Bear right at the next intersection and notice the CCC Camp Amphitheater to your right.

4.2 Take a left onto gravel Fowler's Mill Road.

4.9 Turn left onto New Hampshire 113A. The bridge over the Swift River will be in sight. Before the river, turn right at the orange gate onto the doubletrack that leads to the river section of the loop.

6.1 Turn left onto gravel Hemenway Road

6.4 Turn left at the parking lot onto the gated tower access road.

6.7 Climb to a flat section of trail and turn left. Turn right when the cabin comes into view, onto Fire Tower Road. Climb to the fire tower.

7.0 Return to the parking lot by the same route you climbed to the fire tower.

7.5 Ride ends at the parking lot.

Mount Chocorua

The exposed pink-granite horn of Mount Chocorua rising above Chocorua Lake makes it perhaps the most recognizable peak in New Hampshire. It is also one of the most photographed and hiked mountains in the world. A half-dozen trails lead to Chocorua's summit, including the Liberty Trail and Brook Trail which can be reached from Fowler's Mill Road in Tamworth.

Many other peaks in the White Mountains surpass Mount Chocorua's 3,475 feet, but the trailheads of Chocorua leave from low elevations, making hikes more strenuous than may be expected. Sections of rock face, particularly near the summit, make it no walk around the neighborhood. Still, families with children regularly take to the mountain, and crowds manage to reach the top each warm summer day.

Conflicting legends of the Pequaket sachem Chocorua fill local lore. The most romantic tale holds that Chocorua jumped to his death from the mountain's cliffs after being chased to the top by settlers bent on revenge. The simplest version holds that he perished after he fell from the rocks while hunting. Other tales fit in between these, but most of them agree he died on the summit.

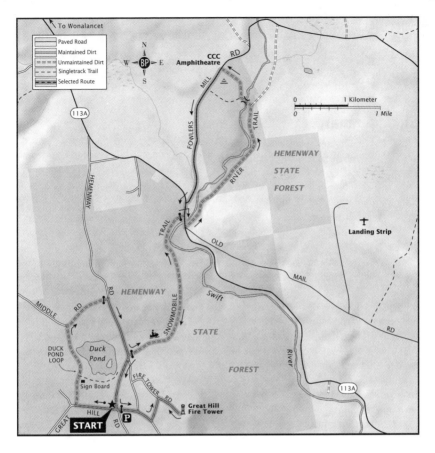

Paved Road
Maintained Dirt
Unmainained Dirt
Singletrack Trail
Selected Route

To Wonalancet

CCC
Amphitheatre

HEMENWAY
STATE
FOREST

Landing Strip

HEMENWAY

STATE

FOREST

Swift

River

MILL RD

FOWLERS

RIVER TRAIL

TRAIL

OLD

MAIL

RD

SNOWMOBILE

MIDDLE RD

RD

HEMENWAY

DUCK
POND
LOOP

Duck
Pond

Sign Board

FIRE TOWER RD

Great Hill
Fire Tower

GREAT HILL RD

START

P

113A

113A

0   1 Kilometer
0   1 Mile

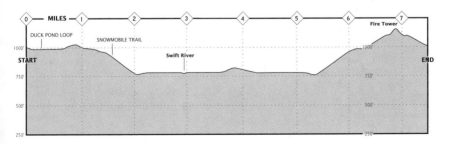

MILES

START

DUCK POND LOOP

SNOWMOBILE TRAIL

Swift River

Fire Tower

END

1000'

750'

500'

250'

1000'

750'

500'

250'

Sandwich Notch Road

Ride Summary

While this loop offers little challenge to bike handling skills, a full circle trip demands both stamina and leg strength. Groups should be of comparable fitness so that neither harmony nor temper are lost late into the ride. You'll climb up through historic Sandwich Notch, descend its northern side, and enjoy a gradual rise along the meandering Beebe River. Mountain bikers will enjoy the hours away, and the trip is a good choice for roadies who seek just a taste of unpaved satisfaction.

Ride Specs

Start: From Beede Falls/Bearcamp River/Cow Cave parking lot off Sandwich Notch Road

Length: 26.1-mile loop

Approximate Riding Time: 4–7 hours

Difficulty Rating: Low technical difficulty due to use of gravel roads. Excellent fitness needed due to duration and multiple long climbs.

Trail Surface: Dirt roads, logging roads, and paved roads

Lay of the Land: Mountainous terrain, mostly forested though logging has cleared some sections

Elevation Gain: 2,981 feet

Land Status: Town roads, national forest land, and private logging road

Nearest Town: Center Sandwich, NH

Other Trail Users: Motorists, walkers, cross-country skiers, and loggers along Beebe River

Wheels: Mountain bikes, though in a pinch a low-geared hybrid with knobby tires will do

Getting There

From Moultonborough, NH: Follow NH 109 north toward Center Sandwich, NH. Continue straight a short distance on NH 113 west as it bears left. Bear right immediately across from A.G. Burrows country store, onto Grove Street. After 0.4 miles bear left again onto Diamond Ledge Road. At 2.1 miles the road forks, bear left onto Sandwich Notch Road. Parking is on the right, 0.8 miles up at the Beede Falls/Bearcamp River/Cow Cave lot. *DeLorme: New Hampshire Atlas & Gazetteer:* Page 40, F-2

A winding road leads away from the white clapboard buildings of Center Sandwich, turning to dirt as the homes fade away. It makes a nine-mile run through the Squam Mountains and dead over a gap in the Sandwich Range. Nineteenth Century farmers urged the construction of Sandwich Notch Road to give them an alternative to toll routes and the Connecticut River. It gave them a direct and cost-free means to reach coastal cities like Portsmouth, and allowed them to bring home sugar, salt, fabrics, and other imported products.

The cliff behind Pulpit Rock

What started as a cart path became Sandwich Notch Road in 1801. Plans for the route had been talked of since 1795, but detractors believed a road through their township would benefit passers-through more than citizens. In the end, these skeptics were proven wrong. Life in Sandwich Notch became even more prosperous, as evidenced by the building of homes, schools, a sawmill, and a gristmill.

The imprint of Notch settlers remains in the names of the rivers and the land today. Daniel Beede, one of the first Europeans to reach the Notch, brought his name to Beede Falls, which is a 150-foot walk from the parking area. His expeditions also brought about the naming of Bearcamp River, after a bear raided his camp and supplies while he and the five other original Notch settlers hunted a mile downstream from the falls.

This ride requires multiple-hour stamina. Pavement covers about a third of the run, but singletrack hounds can take the ad-lib option and hit other trails along the way, like Ridgepole or Flat Mountain Pond. Each of these is within three miles from the start and bust open dozens of miles of much harder track. Don't underestimate the loop described, though. Many of its ascents go on for over a mile, making the descents seem all too short. A warning: reckless hairball downhill runs on Sandwich Notch Road could end in the grill of a car chugging up from below. Watch out for braking bumps and potholes too.

On the steepest grades of Sandwich Notch Road, pavement has been laid down to prevent erosion. The trip starts up one of these sections and soon passes onto White Mountain National Forest land. To the right a few tenths of a mile beyond the Ridgepole Trail entrance, and before the second of three successive bridges over the Bearcamp River, is Pulpit Rock. In the early 19th Century the Quaker Pastor Meader gave his sermons here to folk from up and down the Notch. They came to listen to a man who taught, not preached, one who lived as they lived and coped with the triumphs and tragedies of a settler's life.

In its day, farms and fields covered much of the Notch. One of the few clearings that remain is along the flat stretch of road at Mount Delight. A Forest Service sign can be seen nailed to a tree across the open field. Beyond the sign is a small cemetery that might invite the curious. Otherwise, Sandwich Notch Road continues on a downhill run to the Mead, Guinea Pond, and Flat Mountain Pond trails at mile 2.5 before it crosses a bridge over the Beebe River.

Among The Hills

*Through Sandwich Notch the west wind sang
Good Morrow to the cotter;
And once again Chocorua's horn
Of shadow pierced the water*

—John Greenleaf Whittier
Among the Hills

The second extended climb is the one through the Sandwich Range. The Notch Road then makes a long descent before passing homes and leveling as it leaves the forest. The next few miles are on pavement, but pavement means civilization and the opportunity for pizza. Drinks, pizza, and snacks are available at the Family Store at the intersection of Winter Brook Road and New Hampshire 175. Once stuffed and on your way again, you'll travel about 2.4 miles on New Hampshire 175—so be wary of frequent car traffic. The loop heads next toward the Beebe River, where there may be logging activity. For detailed information on this leg of the trip, see Ride 24: Beebe River.

During the summer, activities on nearby Lake Winnipesaukee and Squam Lake draw visitors from all over. Movie buffs will recognize Squam Lake as the setting for the film *On Golden Pond*. For mountain bikers who also enjoy leaf peeping, Sandwich Notch Road provides one of the best opportunities to view the fall foliage. Other months, the draw to the area may be Center Sandwich for its handcrafted goods shops, lunch at the Corner House Inn, or a leap back in time at the Sandwich Historical Society museums.

Ride Information

Trail Contact:
USDA Forest Service, Pemigewasset Ranger Station, Plymouth, NH (603) 536-1310

Local Information:
Lakes Region Association, Center Harbor, NH 1-800-605-2537 or www.lakesregion.org • **Greater Ossipee Area Chamber of Commerce,** Ossipee, NH (603) 539-6201 or 1-800-382-2371 • **Waterville Valley Region Chamber of Commerce,** Waterville Valley, NH 1-800-237-2307

Local Events/Attractions:
Sandwich Fair, Columbus Day weekend, Sandwich, NH (603) 284-7062 – the last traditional country fair of the season

Local Bike Shops:
The Greasy Wheel, Plymouth, NH (603) 536-3655 • **Ski Fanatics,** Campton, NH (603) 726-4327 • **Piche's Ski and Sport Shop,** Wolfeboro, NH (603) 569-8234 • **Riverside Cycles,** Ashland, NH (603) 968-9676

Maps:
USGS maps: Squam Mountains, NH; Center Sandwich, NH; Plymouth, NH; Waterville Valley, NH • **Appalachian Mountain Club,** White Mountain Guide – *available at bookstores and outdoor outfitters* • **White Mountain National Forest Mountain Bike Map,** Pemigewasset District – *available for purchase at USDA Forest Service Ranger Stations or by calling (603) 536-1310*

MilesDirections

0.0 START from the Beede Falls lot, turn uphill and begin to climb. Battles with elevation changes continue for much of the remainder of Sandwich Notch Road.

7.8 Turn left onto New Hampshire 49 in Thornton. Then take the first left onto Chickenboro Road.

8.5 At the Waterville Estates sign, bear right onto Goose Hollow Road. Begin a pavement climb of over a mile.

10.1 At the stop sign by Waterville Estates Sales and Rental Office, turn left onto Winter Brook Road. Climb again, then tuck the long descent to the Family Store at New Hampshire 175 in Campton, New Hampshire.

12.5 Turn left onto New Hampshire 175.

14.9 Two successive 90-degree turns mark Campton Hollow. Continue straight at the second turn, past a gift shop, onto Perch Pond Road. Continue onto Eastern Corners Road one-half of a mile later, at the 90-degree right in Perch Pond Road. Follow as Eastern Corners Road turns to pavement, then again to dirt, then descends on a deteriorated gravel road.

17.4 Turn left at the intersection before the bridges over the Beebe River. The long gradual climb along the Beebe River to Sandwich Notch Road begins. Continue past the gate, Outside America has obtained permission from the landmanager to use this dirt road. Please be cautious of logging activity, and note that during spring runoff and wet spells the trail may be flooded but rideable.

23.6 At the 4-way intersection, turn right onto Sandwich Notch Road. Immediately cross a wooden bridge and pass the Guinea Pond trailhead. Ascend again before descending to the parking lot, on the left shortly after leaving national forest land.

26.1 Arrive back at Beede Falls.

Alternate Starts:

Exit 28 off Interstate 93 North puts you on New Hampshire 49, which gives access to various points along the loop. The Smarts Brook Trail parking lot, off New Hampshire 49, 5.5 miles east of Interstate 93, is convenient. There is also parking off Sandwich Notch Road, at the bridge over the Beebe River. Roadside parking is available at other automobile accessible points, so consult the map for the your best option.

Cow Cave got its name from the story of the lost heifer that sheltered there for a winter. Lore says that the cow survived on the brouse that grew nearby and moisture from the surface of the rock.

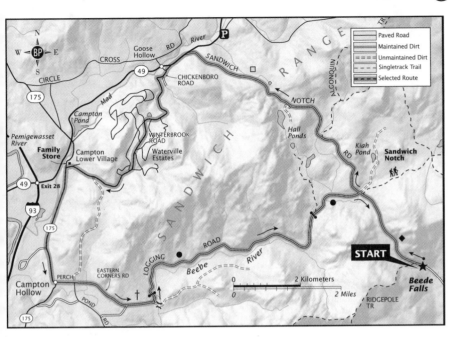

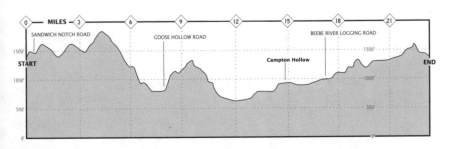

White

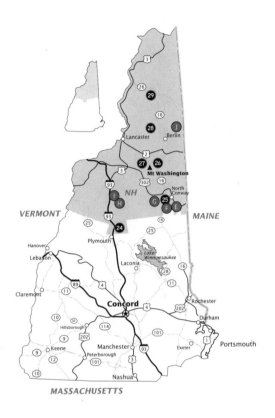

Mountains

White Mountains Region

Mount Clay

Mount Washington
6,288 ft

Mount Monroe

PRESIDENTIAL RANGE

TUCKERMAN RAVINE

WHITE MOUNTAIN NATIONAL FOREST

White Mountains Region

The White Mountain National Forest protects 780,000 acres in New Hampshire and western Maine. Hiking trails crisscross the slopes and valleys, and with the exception of designated wilderness areas and the Appalachian Trail, mountain bikes are welcome on all. You'll have to be hearty, though, and ready for anything if you just go out with ambition but no foreknowledge of the terrain, because the White Mountain National Forest can hold dangerous challenges.

The highest and most dramatic mountains in New Hampshire make this region the most ruggedly beautiful. Sheer cliffs line the road through Franconia Notch and frame the western view from the outlet center of North Conway. The area's high elevations make mountain streams and rivers run white and fast during spring snowmelt, but come summer they turn to quiet brooks.

Beyond the White Mountain National Forest rests the region known for years as the North Country, but now more modernly known as the Great North Woods. This is where New Hampshire's most remote country will be found, where the moose population runs high, and where timbering and pulp mills dominate the working lifestyle. Two of the most unique and dissimilar spots to ride reside in the North Country. The first is Phillip's Brook Backcountry Recreation Area, where over 24,000 acres wait for you to ride and rough it in a tent, yurt, or rustic lodge. The second is The Balsams Grand Resort, which offers mountain biking and luxury accommodations during the "summer social season."

24

Beebe River Ride

Ride Summary

The quiet flow of the Beebe River guides you most of the way to secluded Kiah Pond. The ride climbs gently upstream along the Beebe's riverbank using a smooth gravel road that is closed to public traffic but remains open for logging trucks. It's a fine choice for groups of riders looking to enjoy each other's company without the worries of riding a technical trail with partners of unmatched fitness or skill levels.

Ride Specs

Start: From Eastern Corners Road in Campton, near the Beebe River
Length: 12.4-mile out-and-back
Approximate Riding Time: 2 hours
Difficulty Rating: Easy, with no overly steep grades
Trail Surface: Maintained logging roads and fire roads
Lay of the Land: A mountainous area, with gently rising terrain along the chapter loop. The wide, slow-running Beebe River frames the ride's southern border.
Elevation Gain: 1,257 feet
Land Status: Mix of White Mountain National Forest public land and private timber land with permission granted for non-impacting recreational use
Nearest Town: Campton, NH
Other Trail Users: Logging trucks, hikers, cross-country skiers, snowmobilers, and hunters (in season)
Wheels: Mountain bikes, hybrids, kid's single-speeds, and bike trailers

Getting There

From Plymouth, NH: Take I-93 North to Exit 27 (Blair, NH). Turn right at the stop sign. Continue through the next stop sign and across the Blair Covered Bridge. Turn left at the "T" intersection with NH 175. Continue 1.4 miles north, passing the Campton Grange Hall and crossing over the Beebe River. Turn right onto Perch Pond Road where NH 175 North makes a sharp left. Within half a mile, Perch Pond Road will make a 90-degree right turn. Continue straight here onto gravel Eastern Corners Road. Travel 1.5 farther until the road begins to degrade past the last house. Park at the old cemetery on the left. *DeLorme: New Hampshire Atlas & Gazetteer.* Page 39, F-13

The Blair Covered Bridge had to be rebuilt in 1869 after God prompted a local arsonist to burn it.

The White Mountains dish out some of New England's most challenging terrain, and yet the riding doesn't always have to be that tough. The Beebe River Trail requires very little technical expertise, allowing you time to enjoy the surroundings and observe the wildlife—a true amble through the woods. This ride is one of good but not exhausting length along the northern bank of the Beebe River. It rises on a shallow, almost imperceptible grade to secluded Kiah Pond, while the return trip meanders gently downhill.

Beebe River

From the start at the cemetery, a downhill roll on gravel road brings you to the riverbank. A summertime ride will be greeted by quiet, slow-moving water, but the Beebe River betrays signs of its power at peak runoff as you pedal upstream. Erosion has carved mid-channel islands, while continuing to undercut the remaining land. Toppled trees with driftwood in their branches form natural dams, bridging the space between shore and island.

Smoothed-over granite outcrops and rounded riverbed rocks show more signs of the river's age. The trail has been washed away in places by spring's high water and rebuilt with stones and gravel. These few sections get bumpy, but are not terrible to negotiate. The only other challenge might be mud and puddles if doing the ride during wet periods, as the Beebe River and the low-lying land around it drain the surrounding mountains out to the Pemigewasset River. Take note also that the route is an active logging road. Truck traffic may vary from sporadic to non-existent, but should be considered just the same.

The Beebe River (to the right) and a power line (to the left) frame the outer leg of the trip. Both will migrate in and out of view, but you won't cross either until the final approach to Kiah Pond. This last mile is the most challenging due to its short hills, but the difficulty is only relative to the overall ease of the loop.

For something harder than the trip to Kiah Pond, you might want to explore Guinea Pond Trail. The Guinea Pond trailhead sits off Sandwich Notch Road, right across the bridge from the Notch road's intersection with the chapter route. You'll follow doubletrack on a mild climb, later intercepting Flat Mountain Pond Trail. From there the trail gets progressively harder going toward the Flat Mountain Ponds. The distance to the Flat Mountain Ponds from Sandwich Notch Road is about eight miles, or about 14 miles from the start of the Beebe River Ride.

Options for other mountain bike rides are plentiful in the region. For a fee, the Waterville Valley Resort offers its cross-country ski network and a lift-serviced mountain full of downhill terrain. The resort also boasts golfing, reasonable rates on summer accommodations, and arrangements with the local sports center (which offers to swimming, racquetball, and other fitness activities).

The area bike shops are staffed by enthusiasts knowledgeable of local trails, changing conditions, and loops tailored to any adventure a customer desires. Most shops offer bike rentals, which can vary from rigid models to plush, full-suspension mounts from top name makers.

Campton's trio of historic covered bridges may interest you. If you follow this particular ride's "Getting There" directions, you'll cross Blair Bridge. It spans the Pemigewasset River. On Bump Road, which you'll pass on the way to the ride's starting point, is the Bump Bridge, built in 1972 using traditional techniques. The third local bridge is Turkey Jim's Bridge at the Branch Brook Campground. Its odd name came about in typical rural fashion; it happened to be near "Turkey" Jim Cummings' turkey farm.

Beebe River

Taking a break next to Kiah Pond

Ride Information

🕻 Trail Contacts:
USDA Forest Service, Pemigewasset Ranger Station, Plymouth, NH (603) 536-1310

🕐 Schedule:
Open year-round

❓ Local Information:
Waterville Valley Region Chamber of Commerce, Waterville Valley, NH 1-800-237-2307

💡 Local Events/Attractions:
The Pemi Valley Bluegrass Festival, Campton, NH (603) 726-3471 — musical festival that takes place each summer • **Waterville Valley Resort,** Waterville Valley, NH 1-800-468-2553 or *www.waterville.com*

🕴 Organizations:
White Mountain Mudskippers, Campton, NH (603) 744-2998

🌴 Local Bike Shops:
The Greasy Wheel, Plymouth, NH (603) 536-3655 • **Ski Fanatics,** Campton, NH (603) 726-4327 — rentals available • **Joe Jones Ski and Sports,** Campton, NH (603) 726-3000 — rentals available • **Waterville Valley Base Camp,** Waterville Valley, NH (603) 236-4666 — rentals available

Ⓝ Maps:
USGS maps: Squam Mountains, NH; Waterville Valley, NH

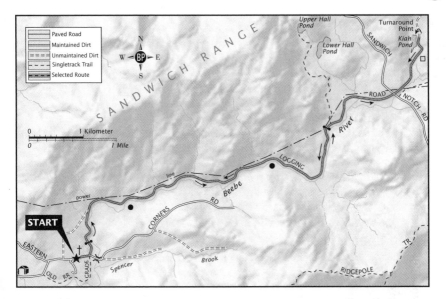

MilesDirections

0.0 START by descending past the cemetery. Turn left at the bottom of the hill, and do not cross Beebe River. Pass a gate, which will either be open or shut, depending on logging activity.

3.5 Cross a bridge over a tributary to the Beebe River.

4.3 Bear left away from the logging truck bridge that crosses the river. Later, pass another gate and signs that announce your entry into the White Mountain National Forest.

5.7 Cross Sandwich Notch Road, onto the fire road directly opposite.

6.2 Arrive at Kiah Pond. Turn around and return on the same route.

12.4 Turn right, uphill, away from the Beebe River. Climb to the cemetery where the ride ends.

Alternate Start: Kiah Pond trailhead parking lot, off Sandwich Notch Road at the Beebe River bridge.

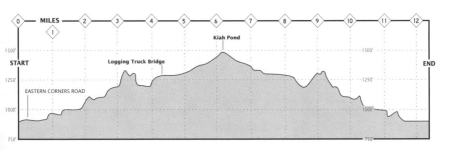

North Conway, West of the Ledges Loop

Ride Summary

This ride throws some very hard terrain at you, but still gives only a sampling of what the White Mountains have to offer. Utilizing fire roads and primitive singletrack full of rocks and roots, you'll negotiate a bit of everything. Before popping out of the woods for the last time, you'll pass Diana's Baths, a series of waterfalls popular for viewing and for wading in when Lucy Brook is running slow. Nearer the finish, you'll pass the access road to Cathedral Ledge, a popular spot high above North Conway that offers views over the town and countryside.

Ride Specs

Start: Gravel lot adjacent to Echo Lake State Park, North Conway
Length: 12.4-mile loop
Approximate Riding Time: 2-2½ hours
Difficulty Rating: Moderate, with very difficult sections on the Red Ridge Trail
Trail Surface: Singletrack, doubletrack, gravel fire roads, and paved roads, with constant elevation changes on the middle third of the loop
Lay of the Land: Flat valley floor with Saco River running through, framed by forested mountains
Elevation Gain: 589 feet
Land Status: State park, national forest, and sections of town road
Nearest City: North Conway, NH
Other Trail Users: Hikers
Wheels: Mountain bikes only

Getting There

From North Conway, NH: Travel north on NH 16 / U.S. 302 out of downtown North Conway. Turn left onto River Road at the light. Continue 1.4 miles to the left turn for Cathedral Ledge and Echo Lake. Turn here and bear left immediately onto Old West Side Road, toward Echo Lake. Continue 0.8 miles to the gravel parking lot, straight past the right turn for Echo Lake State Park. *DeLorme: New Hampshire Atlas & Gazetteer:* Page 45, I-9 and Page 72, G-1, H-2

G rand hotels and picturesque bed and breakfasts dot the Mount Washington Valley. Also built against the backdrop of the White Mountains are restaurants, outlet shops, and other vacation attractions. Cars and cyclists share the byways, and along the roadsides hikers re-entering from a week in the woods trek back to whichever trailhead they started from.

The wilderness has always drawn visitors to North Conway. For two centuries the town has offered a northern haven for Easterners bent on escape from urban and suburban lifestyles. They come in the winter for skiing; in the spring and summer for hiking, canoeing, and biking; and in the fall for a peep at the autumn foliage.

The character of the North Conway, West of the Ledges Loop is best considered in thirds. The first and last segments are quite similar, while the middle seg-

In front of Diana's Baths

ment is something else entirely. Smooth riding greets you upon departure from the parking area. The terrain gets even smoother for the short pavement stint down the West Side Road bike lane.

Once into the woods again at Cedar Creek development, fire road transport awaits you. The fire road section is not without amusement though. Puddles and mud appear after rainy periods, and about 1.5 miles off of West Side Road, the route travels below the grade of a marsh containment. Water flows across the road here in the summer, so be prepared for flooding of several inches or more through late spring.

Once past the second Forest Service gate, a trail to the left leads to an abandoned mineral mining site. The chapter loop heads straight though, uphill at a challenging but manageable grade. Red Ridge appears through the tree-lined corridor when the flat is reached, before disappearing for good after you hit the middle third of the loop.

The Red Ridge Trail offers up a bumpy challenge to all riders. The rough singletrack is littered with rocks, exposed roots, and ruts ready to catch a tire or throw you off the saddle. You may find yourself walking your bike along sections of this trail. If you manage to stay in the pedals the whole way, congratulations. However,

Diana was the Roman goddess of hunting, the moon, and virginity. She was also the protector of springs and streams.

once on Moat Mountain Trail you will have to walk. The Forest Service has posted "Foot Travel Only" signs for the short, popular descent to Diana's Baths.

A stop at Diana's Baths exposes you to one of the best-known natural sites in the region. A thrill to behold during spring run-off, the spot can be equally appreciated in the summer, when comparably meager flows allow access across the smooth granite of the streambed. Getting up close reveals eroded channels through the rock and spots where flow reverses uphill before quickly turning downstream again.

From Diana's Baths, one last section of singletrack takes you out to the paved road for the trip home. Take care on this singletrack, as it's usually full of people during weekends and through the tourist season. Children, the elderly, and city-folk unaccustomed to walks in the woods may be unsteady over the rough ground. Watch out too for the occasional unleashed dog.

The final turn toward Echo Lake provides a good opportunity to climb the access road to the top of Cathedral Ledge. Once atop the ledge, enjoy wide-open views of North Conway. If you skip the ascent up the access road, continue to Echo Lake State Park for a swim under the shadow of White Horse Ledge.

The AMC *White Mountain Hiking Guide* contains comprehensive maps of trails throughout this region. USGS topographic maps also do a good job of laying out the terrain, and typical road maps will show how to get around on the pavement. Once on your bike though, things change quickly. Old dirt roads have been paved, logging roads can spring up almost overnight, and forgotten paths and double-tracks spin off with abandon. This is not a warning that the loop is hard to follow, for landmarks abound. It's only to point out that changes come over time and that the White Mountain National Forest offers opportunities for extended adventures, whether those adventures are intended or not.

White Horse Ledge and Cathedral Ledge

In a state filled with amazing natural landscapes, two of New Hampshire's great geological features, White Horse Ledge and Cathedral Ledge, rise before you on the way to the start of the loop. Cathedral Ledge sits to the north and springs 700 feet from the forest floor. Its name was drawn from a feature in its shear face that reminded visitors of a cathedral. Below the Cathedral cavity is a similar feature, Devil's Den.

Look into White Horse Ledge for the spirit of the great horse that rides across it. If you can't make out the horse's silhouette, perhaps you can see the rock climbers who dot the towering wall of granite on any given weekend.

Ride Information

🕓 Trail Contacts:
Saco Ranger Station, Conway, NH (603) 447-5448 or (603) 447-1989

🕐 Schedule:
Unrideable during snow-melt/spring rains due to flooding and high rivers

❓ Local Information:
Mount Washington Valley Chamber of Commerce, North Conway, NH 1-800-367-3364 or www.4seasonresort.com • Conway Village Chamber of Commerce, Conway, NH (603) 447-2639

💡 Local Events/Attractions:
At the turn onto Old West Side Road is the access road to **Cathedral Ledge,** North Conway, NH (603) 356-2672 • **Outlet shopping** in Conway and North Conway. • **Echo Lake,** Echo Lake State Park, North Conway, NH (603) 356-2672 — has public swimming ($2.50)

🚶 Organizations:
White Mountain Wheel People, Jackson, NH (603) 383-4660

🌳 Local Bike Shops:
Red Jersey Cyclery, Glen, NH (603) 383-4660 or www.redjersey.com • **Boardertown**, Glen, NH (603) 383-8981 or www.mwv.org/bt — rentals available • **Joe Jones Ski and Sports,** North Conway Village, NH (603) 356-9411 or www.joejonessports.com • **The Bike Shop,** North Conway, NH (603) 356-6089 • **Sports Outlet,** North Conway, NH (603) 356-3133

🚌 Intercity Bus Service:
Concord Trailways, First Stop Deli, Conway, NH 1-800-639-3317 or www.concordtrailways.com

Ⓝ Maps:
USGS maps: North Conway West, NH

Painted roof

MilesDirections

0.0 START by riding away from the road and onto the doubletrack to the right at the end of the parking lot. Continue on the main trail by choosing the left option each time there is a split into two equally worn paths.

0.4 Turn left at the paved roadway. Cross Elm Brook.

0.9 Turn right onto the West Side Road bike lane.

2.9 Make a right turn into the Cedar Creek development. Follow the abandoned town road that enters the woods immediately to the right, marked by an obscured but visible "No Parking" sign. The abandoned road travels behind condominiums. It merges with another road at the corner of a field before continuing past a Forest Service gate. Remain on the fire road once past the gate.

5.3 Pass another Forest Service gate and the "FR" marker to the right beyond it designating the fire road. Begin a gradual climb.

6.8 Cross the rocky bed of Moat Brook, which will be dry in a typical summer. Immediately cross a wooden bridge. Just beyond the bridge, turn right onto the Red Ridge Trail, which cuts across the fire road. Climb a knoll and stay to the right on the yellow-blazed trail where another trail leaves to the left. At one point Red Ridge Link joins the Red Ridge Trail downhill from the right.

8.4 Continue across Lucy Brook onto Moat Mountain Trail. Obey the "Foot Travel Only" signs by becoming a pedestrian for the short walk downstream to Diana's Baths. Diana's Baths will be to the right as the trail opens to gravel road. There will also be a signpost in the middle of the trail. Turn left at the signpost onto the singletrack to the Diana's Baths parking area.

10.8 Pass through the parking area and turn right on paved River Road.

11.6 At the sign for Cathedral Ledge and Echo Lake, turn right onto Old West Side Road toward Echo Lake.

12.4 Arrive at your vehicle and enjoy a swim at Echo Lake State Park.

Not all are riding...

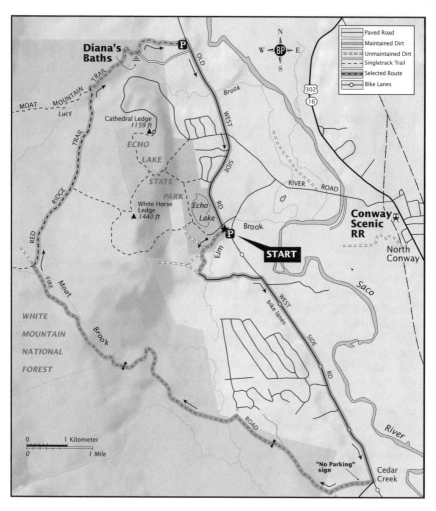

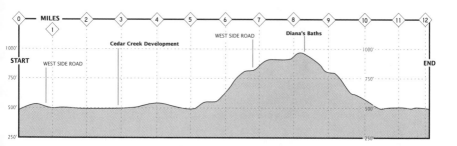

203

Great Glen Trails

Ride Summary

Don't get tricked by the ride directions for the chapter ride, which lay out a short warm-up loop at Great Glen Trails. There are many more miles of smooth gravel paths, or rough singletrack, to pick from. This superbly maintained facility in the heart of New Hampshire's White Mountains scores high marks with families and groups with more ambition to share the experience than bounce off rocks and trees. Wander down Great Glen Trails to find Great Angel Station, a yurt with a picnicking deck secluded in the forest high above the West Branch Peabody River.

Ride Specs

Start: From Great Glen Trails lodge and mountain bike center
Length: 2.3-mile loop
Approximate Riding Time: 40 minutes
Difficulty Rating: Easy trail surfaces, with grade changes adding short, moderate challenges
Trail Surface: Packed gravel paths modeled after the carriage trails of Acadia National Park in Maine
Lay of the Land: Hilly, forested terrain set amidst New Hampshire's tallest mountains. Mountain rivers and flat meadowland as well.
Elevation Gain: 135 feet
Land Status: Private property, open to public for a trail use fee
Nearest Town: North Conway, NH
Other Trail Users: Walkers, joggers, cross-country skiers, snowshoers, and anglers
Wheels: Mountain bikes, kids' single-speeds, trailers, and low-geared hybrids

Getting There

From North Conway, NH: Follow NH 16 North through Pinkham Notch to Great Glen Trails, which is clearly marked by signs. Great Glen Trails is on the left and at the base of the Mount Washington Auto Road. *DeLorme: New Hampshire Atlas & Gazetteer:* Page 45, A-8

Mount Washington is renowned for its unpredictable weather, its early fall frosts, and its snow-capped summit that lingers well into spring. Peaking above its neighbors in the Presidential Range into the paths of three major storm tracks, temperatures atop the 6,288-foot Mount Washington average 26.5 degrees Fahrenheit annually. Winter temperatures of 40 degrees below zero are not unheard of—and neither is snow, with an average snowfall of about 21 feet. Next, factor in the wind. On April 12, 1934, the fastest recorded wind in history swept across the exposed mica-schist of "The Rock Pile": 231 mph. Now that's extreme.

Great Glen Trails lies 4,600 feet below all the wicked weather. This outdoor recreation park offers activities for every season. Proper winter footwear should include either cross-country ski boots, snowshoes, or ice skates—but come summertime anything from biking shoes to hot pink Chuck Taylor's will be fine.

Great Glen's trails wind you through meadows and forest. Kids in trailers or baby seats won't get jostled here because the paths are graded and packed regularly to provide a firm surface. Superb trail conditions help maintain the karma, too, among pairs or groups of riders with unequal off-road skills. Not only are the routes well maintained, they're also clearly and accurately identified with ratings from easy to difficult. Excluding singletrack, riding tougher loops will mean repeated short climbs and descents, although surface conditions do not vary. Follow the green "Easier" signs posted along the paths to keep exertion down. Or face off with riders tackling the steep grades on the "More Difficult" and "Most Difficult" trails. Believe "Most Difficult" signs, as a few inclines on these routes tip past 20 percent.

Because of other cyclists on the network and at the nearby lodge, you can ride through the woods without the usual worries and fears that accompany biking in remote areas. Fellow riders pass every few minutes, but not so frequently as to crowd the trails. The pace you set will be your own and if the track followed takes you by Great Angel Station, put away any thoughts of pedaling past. An idyllic spot for snacking or lunch, the Station sits high above the eastern bank of the fast moving West Branch Peabody River. The rush of the water, with views through the evergreens to the peaks of the Northern Presidential Range, could make even an energy bar taste good. Great Angel Station has picnic tables on its deck, and the yurt provides shelter in case bugs or a surprise sun-shower threaten a good feast.

Great Glen Trails puts special effort into rounding out the outdoor experience. Part of this includes their Quick Start programs which introduce newcomers to the sports of hiking, canoeing, kayaking, fly-fishing, and of course, mountain biking. Another cool offering is the self-guided nature tour. The first stop identifies the animals that call this land home and shows how to identify various tracks. The remaining 19 stations are spaced over a three-mile route. Wetland ecology, the history of Mount Washington Valley, and the identification of red spruce, balsam fir, and other trees are some of the subjects presented at these stations.

In addition to renting conventional mountain bikes, a recumbent and a hand-cycle are also available at the Great Glen Trails bike shop. For kids old enough to ride but too young to push the pace, Adams Trail-A-Bikes attach to an adult size mountain bike to create an off-road tandem. Kiddy trailers for babies and toddlers round out the stable of rentals for the family caravan. If none of these options fit, there is a daycare on site.

Within sight of Great Glen Trails is the Mount Washington Auto Road. It climbs nearly eight miles to the summit where 150,000 people visit annually for views from the highest peak in the Northeast. From Mount Washington's top you can see across four states, into Canada, and out to the Atlantic Ocean. A second way to the peak of Mount Washington is on the Mount Washington Cog Railway. Today, passenger cars are towed up one of the steepest tracks in the world by coal-fired steam locomotives similar to "Old Pepperass," the original engine. Signs for the Cog Railway are posted on U.S. Route 302 in Bretton Woods.

Ride Information

🕐 Trail Contacts:
Great Glen Trails, Pinkham Notch, Gorham, NH (603) 466-2333 or www.mt-washington.com

🕐 Schedule:
Memorial Day weekend through late October, 8:30 A.M. to 5 P.M.

💲 Fees/Permits:
$7 for a bike pass. Bikes, kiddy trailers, and Adams Trail-A-Bikes are available for rent on-site at the Great Glenn Trails bike shop.

❓ Local Information:
Mount Washington Valley Chamber of Commerce, North Conway, NH 1-800-367-3364 or www.4seasonresort.com— For information on the **Mount Washington Auto Road** visit www.mt-washington.com

💡 Local Events/Attractions:
Storyland, Glen, NH (603) 383-4293 — where storybook characters come to life for children • **Heritage New Hampshire,** Glen, NH (603) 383-9776 — an historical theme park • **Mount Washington Cog Railway,** Bretton Woods, NH (603) 278-5404 • **AMC Pinkham Notch Visitor Center and Lodge,** Pinkham Notch, Gorham, NH (603) 466-2727 • **Mount Washington Auto Road,** Pinkham Notch, Gorham, NH (603) 466-3988 or www.mt-washington.com

👥 Group Rides:
All the local shops run group mountain bike rides. Red Jersey Cyclery also runs a summer race series, with weekday event dates.

👥 Organizations:
White Mountain Wheel People, Jackson, NH (603) 383-4660

🚲 Local Bike Shops:
Red Jersey Cyclery, Glen, NH (603) 383-4660 or www.redjerseycyclery.com • **Boardertown,** Glen, NH (603) 383-8981 or — rentals available • **Joe Jones Ski and Sports,** North Conway Village, NH (603) 356-9411 or www.joejonessports.com • **Moriah Sports,** Gorham, NH (603) 466-5050 • **Great Glen Trails** sales, rental, and repair shop, Pinkham Notch, Gorham, NH (603) 466-2333

🅝 Maps:
USGS maps: Mount Washington **Great Glen Trails trail map** — available on site, or in advance by calling Great Glen Trails

The third option for assault on the summit is the heartiest: hike up! Trails depart from spots around the mountain, but be cautious of their difficulty and the history of deadly shifts in weather conditions on Mount Washington. The Appalachian Mountain Club (AMC) Pinkham Notch Visitor Center and Lodge in Gorham is the best place to get trail information, including weather forecasts. The AMC *White Mountain Guide*, available at the Visitor Center, is the most popular resource for basic information on hiking trails in New Hampshire and Western Maine. Epic mountain bike rides can be planned from the maps in the guide—all White Mountain National Forest land is open to fat tires except the Appalachian Trail and designated wilderness areas. The common sense rule is to stay on designated trails and avoid heavily hiked trails.

MilesDirections

0.0 START by heading out on Glen Meadows Sluice, and turn right past the bridge onto Clementine Wash. Ride along the field, past the weather station.

0.6 At the sign marking intersection #23, turn right onto Hairball Passage. A "T" intersection with Libby Trace comes up quickly. At this intersection turn right again.

1.0 Turn right at intersection #51, then bear left at the first fork. A short rise ends at Great Angel Station.

1.1 Continue past the station, through intersection #52, and pick up Great Grumpy Grade. Great Grumpy Grade becomes Glen Meadows Sluice, which returns to the lodge.

2.3 The short loop has ended. Work up an appetite on the other trails, then return for a sandwich at the lodge deli and enjoy the view of fields and mountains from a table on the deck.

Mount Washington Auto Road Bicycle Hill Climb

In 1997, Tyler Hamilton of the United States Postal Service cycling team crushed the record time in the Mount Washington Auto Road Bicycle Hill Climb by five minutes and won an Audi for it. In 1999, after coming in 13th in the Tour de France, he knocked another 1 minute 35 seconds off his own mark and won another Audi. Hamilton, a native of Massachusetts, floated up the 7.6 mile Auto Road in 50 minutes and 21 seconds. The women's race record also fell in 1999 when 18 year-old Canadian Genevieve Jeanson shaved 10 minutes off the women's mark, finishing ninth overall at 1:01:57.

If an hour seems a little long for such a short distance, consider that the Mount Washington climb ascends 4,600 feet with average grades of 12 percent—and the steepest inclines of over 22 percent come in the last mile to the summit. If this ride sounds like fun, plan ahead because the Auto Road is open to cyclists only once a year, and you have to enter the race.

The race typically runs in August to avoid harsh summit conditions. All proceeds go to benefit the environmental education and outreach mission of The Tin Mountain Conservation Center, who runs the race. Contact them at Tin Mountain Conservation Center, P.O. Box 1170, Conway, NH 03818 or (603) 447-6991 or www.tinmtn.org.

CAUTION!

Be prepared for unexpected weather and other natural dangers when hiking Mount Washington. Though beautiful many days, well over 100 people have perished on its slopes.

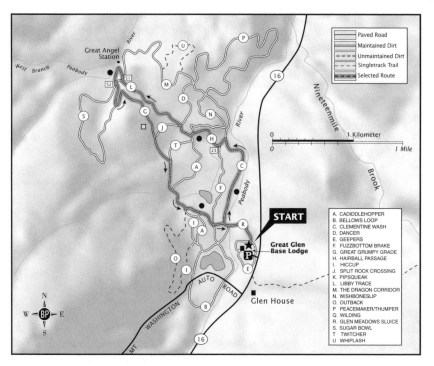

		Paved Road
		Maintained Dirt
		Unmaintained Dirt
		Singletrack Trail
		Selected Route

A. CADIDDLEHOPPER
B. BELLOWS LOOP
C. CLEMENTINE WASH
D. DANCER
E. GEEPERS
F. FUZZBOTTOM BRAKE
G. GREAT GRUMPY GRADE
H. HAIRBALL PASSAGE
I. HICCUP
J. SPLIT ROCK CROSSING
K. PIPSQUEAK
L. LIBBY TRACE
M. THE DRAGON CORRIDOR
N. WISHBONESLIP
O. OUTBACK
P. PEACEMAKER/THUMPER
Q. WILDING
R. GLEN MEADOWS SLUICE
S. SUGAR BOWL
T. TWITCHER
U. WHIPLASH

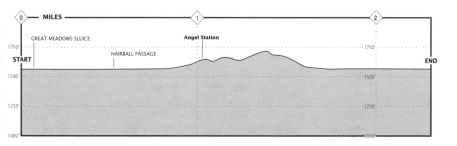

Cherry Mountain Loop

Ride Summary

A long day awaits voyagers along the Cherry Mountain Loop. Nearly 30 miles of distance combines with a heavy sum of gravity to keep you on the bike for many hours. You'll go up, up, up, and down much too briefly. The aerobic challenge comes of course from the climbing, and though singletrack trail skills won't come into play along the pavement and maintained gravel route, long, steep descents demand the ability to ride within your limit. And speaking of limits, watch the speed limit when falling down Cherry Mountain Road and the road through Jefferson Notch, for there's bound to be oncoming car traffic.

Ride Specs

Start: From Lower Ammonoosuc Falls eastern trailhead parking area, off U.S. Route 302
Length: 29.1-mile loop
Approximate Riding Time: 4½ hours
Difficulty Rating: Extended climbs make this a difficult loop physically, but it's not technically challenging.
Trail Surface: Maintained gravel roads and pavement
Lay of the Land: Mountainous, with the Israel and Ammonoosuc rivers flowing along valley floors north and south, respectively, of the Dartmouth Range
Elevation Gain: 2,578 feet
Land Status: Public roads
Nearest Town: Twin Mountain, NH
Other Trail Users: Hikers and motorists
Wheels: Mountain bikes are best, though low-geared hybrids may be suitable if descents are taken slowly

Getting There

From North Conway, NH: Follow NH 16 / U.S. 302 north. Continue on U.S. 302 after NH 16 departs right in Glen. Drive through Crawford Notch State Park. Pass Bretton Woods Ski Area and Fabyan's Restaurant. One mile beyond the restaurant, you pass Old Cherry Mountain Road on the right. Continue another mile on U.S. 302, crossing over the Ammonoosuc River before turning right into the paved parking area. **DeLorme: New Hampshire Atlas & Gazetteer.** Page 44, B-1

L ong climbs and descents define the Cherry Mountain Loop. The views and scenery along the way may seem distracting on the trip up and all too blurred to enjoy at speed on the way down. The section of the ride over Jefferson Notch takes you into the White Mountain National Forest, though you'll still be in unspoiled countryside the entire day.

In 1885, Oscar Stanley learned just how dramatic and violent the slopes of the White Mountains can be. Stanley lived and farmed on the north side of Cherry Mountain, just northeast of the first leg of the route. One July morning a cloudburst loosened soil and rocks from Owlshead, high above his land. The slide it caused swept a million tons of debris two miles down the mountain to the val-

ley—right over Stanley's home. Stanley's cattle and crops were destroyed, and his farmhand died days later from injuries received when the barn collapsed on top of him. Forest now hides the swath cut by the disaster, but Stanley Slide Brook reminds visitors of the steep and rugged wilderness that characterizes Northern New Hampshire.

The ride begins by following the northern bank of the Ammonoosuc River, where you'll set your warm-up pace to the sounds of rushing water over rounded boulders and 15-foot waterfalls. Shortly past Lower Falls begins the long climb up Old Cherry Mountain Road. This gravel route sees little car traffic and rises to views of the northern Presidential Range. To the west runs Deception Brook. And part of Old Cherry Mountain Road follows the Deception Brook Esker—a miles-long sand and gravel deposit left from the area's last glacial period.

Before beginning the second steep ascent to the top, you enjoy a flat section. Cherry Mountain Trail departs to the west at the height of land on Old Cherry Mountain Road. Cherry Mountain Trail is not a part of the chapter loop, but might be worthy of exploration. It's an out-and-back route of roughly seven miles with steep sections throughout. It connects with other trails in the White Mountains' hiking network, but ends at Mount Martha. Martha's Mile continues on to the Owlshead Trail, but the descent from there is a steep, long, difficult one down the path of Stanley's Slide.

Continue along Old Cherry Mountain Road, then suffer a brief stint on pavement until the smooth gravel of Valley Road. The flat Valley Road winds for three miles across the valley floor where open fields and towering mountains fill the view. The bridge over the South Branch River marks the last cool spot to rest before the vertical battle over Jefferson Notch.

Jefferson Notch Road climbs forever, seeming to never crest or descend. Caps Ridge Trail departs left of Jefferson Notch Road at the height of land, offering a one-mile side-trip to a granite outcrop that faces the boulder-strewn Ridge of the Caps. The shortest hike to any Presidential Range summit above 5,000 feet is the 2.5-mile trip over Caps Ridge Trail to Mount Jefferson, which the Appalachian Mountain Club estimates takes two hours and 40 minutes. It is a difficult route with much scrambling (ascending using hands and feet) over exposed rock and ledge.

After passing the sign marking Jefferson Notch the loop enters a long descent along Jefferson Brook. Expect to ride the brakes much of the way and absorb a good amount of washboard chatter through your arms and shoulders, as stutter bumps form at many of the turns. You'll emerge onto paved Base Road, which later comes out at Fabyan's Restaurant and a variety store. This is the last place to get a drink or some food before the remaining few miles along U.S. Route 302 back to the start area.

The White Mountain National Forest Service promotes mountain biking along the Cherry Mountain Loop. Logging and storms, however, have damaged the trails cutting between Old Cherry Mountain Road and Jefferson Notch Road. If interested in exploring the various trails off of Old Cherry Mountain Road and Jefferson Notch, bring a good map and expect a difficult ride.

Scenic riding in the White Mountains.

Ride Information

🕐 Trail Contacts:

White Mountain National Forest Service, Ammonoosuc Ranger District, Bethlehem, NH (603) 869-2626

🕐 Schedule:

Roads are not plowed in winter, though theoretically they're open for riding.

❓ Local Information:

Bethlehem Chamber of Commerce, Bethlehem, NH (603) 869-2151 • **Twin Mountain Chamber of Commerce,** Twin Mountain, NH (603) 846-5407

💡 Local Events/Attractions:

The loop passes a few miles from the **Mount Washington Cog Railway,** (603) 278-5404 or 1-800-922-8825

🛏 Accommodations:

Twin Mountain Chamber of Commerce lodging referrals, Twin

Mountain, NH 1-800-245-8946 • **Zealand Campground** is 200 yards beyond the start of the ride. First come, first serve. (603) 869-2626

👥 Organizations:

White Mountain Wheel People, Glen, NH (603) 383-4660

🚲 Local Bike Shops:

Red Jersey Cyclery, Glen, NH (603) 383-4660 or *www.redjerseycyclery.com* **Littleton Bicycle Shop,** Littleton, NH (603) 444-3437 • **Boardertown,** Glen, NH (603) 383-8981 *or www.mwv.org/bt*

Ⓝ Maps:

USGS maps: Mount Washington, NH

Cresting at 3,009 feet, Jefferson Notch Road is the highest public road in New Hampshire.

The nicest stretch of the ride is along Valley Road. Presidential Range is in the background.

MilesDirections

0.0 START by riding the abandoned railroad grade east from the parking area, past the gate and signboard. Pass the Lower Falls at 0.5 miles.

1.1 Turn left onto graveled Old Cherry Mountain Road. Cross the railroad tracks and begin climbing.

4.7 Reach the top of the hill.

8.5 Turn right onto New Hampshire 115 North.

10.3 Cross the railroad tracks and take the first right onto Valley Road.

13.0 Cross the bridge over the South Branch River.

13.3 Turn right onto Jefferson Notch Road. There is a large sign here for Jefferson Notch.

18.8 Crest the climb of Jefferson Notch. Descend down Jefferson Notch Road to Base Road.

22.1 Turn right onto Base Road.

26.7 Turn right onto U.S. Route 302, and pass Fabyan's Restaurant and a variety store.

28.0 Turn right onto Old Cherry Mountain Road. Take the immediate left onto the side road that leads to the Lower Ammonoosuc Falls Hiking Trail.

29.1 Finish. Wash off in the cool water of the Ammonoosuc River.

Alternate Start: The parking area for the Caps Ridge Trail, at the height of Jefferson Notch Road.

Lower Falls of the Ammonoosuc River.

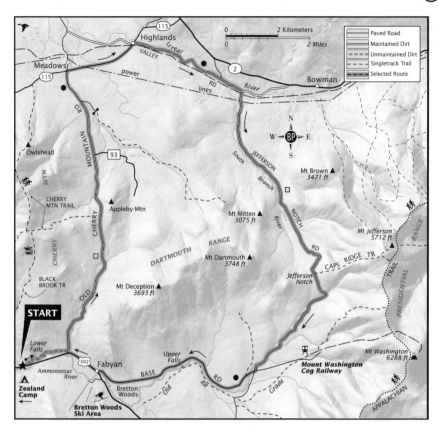

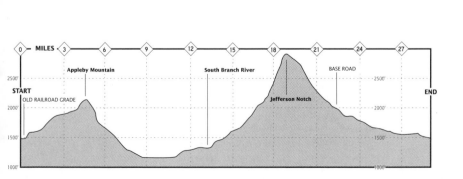

Phillip's Brook
Backcountry Rec. Area

Ride Summary

Terrain. Terrain. Terrain. It's what Phillip's Brook Backcountry Recreation Area is all about. You'll find great mountain biking along both chapter loops, or you can blaze your own ride with maps and advice from the Phillip's Brook staff. Of the two trip options described in this chapter, the Three Gate Loop offers a moderate workout in the hilly terrain. For the Long Mountain Loop, expect a very challenging climb and rougher trail conditions. Either way, you'll be in remote country, alone with the mountains and the moose prints.

Ride Specs

Start: The Three Gate Loop begins at the Phillip's Brook lodge. The Long Mountain Loop takes off from the junction of the Jodrie Brook Trail and Robert's Brook Trail by Phillip's Brook.

Length: Three Gate Loop, 7.3-mile loop; Long Mountain Loop, 9.2-mile loop

Approximate Riding Time: Three Gate Loop, 1½ hours. Long Mountain Loop, 1½ hours.

Difficulty Rating: Minimal technical challenges, with the exception of the two miles at the top of the Long Mountain climb which is very hard. The Three Gate Loop is easy to moderate, with one meaningful climb. Long Mountain Loop is difficult due to elevation and loose surfaces.

Trail Surface: Gravel logging roads and wide singletrack trails over rocks and loose or muddy soil. Rolling doubletrack with some steep grades and many natural obstacles.

Lay of the Land: Mountainous region of new growth forests, with some areas of clearcut

Elevation Gain: Three Gate Loop–633 feet; Long Mountain Loop–1,843 feet

Land Status: Private land with owners consent to allow recreational usage

Nearest Town: Stark, NH

Other Trail Users: Hikers, campers, anglers, dogsledders, cross-country skiers, snowshoers, and hunters (in season)

Wheels: Mountain bikes only

Getting There

From Groveton, NH: Take U.S. 3 South and turn left onto NH 110 east. Continue on NH 110 for 13 miles. Turn left onto Paris Road. Cross the single lane bridge and go through the stop sign at the Dewey Hill Road intersection. Follow Paris Road to the right where it forks two miles from NH 110. Continue another 1.4 miles to the Phillip's Brook Backcountry Recreation Area and Paris Field office. It is on the right after a sharp left bend in the road.

From Berlin, NH: Follow NH 110 northwest for 12 miles. Turn right onto Paris Road. (From Paris Road the directions are the same as above.) *DeLorme: New Hampshire Atlas & Gazetteer:* Page 50, K-5

S ilence. Pure natural silence. And after dark, blackness. The blackest of night under the clearest of skies. No reflection from nearby streetlights, and no hum of autos on the interstate in the distance. What interstate could even be in the distance when the last stretch of broken pavement ended 14 miles away? You're out there for sure at Phillip's Brook Backcountry Recreation Area.

Rural scenery turns to remote landscape not far north of New Hampshire's Lakes Region and outlet shopping centers. A bit farther onward lies Phillip's

Brook Backcountry Recreation Area. Located between Stark and Dixville Notch, it's not exactly hard to find or to get to. What is hard to find is an undertaking similar in concept and promise to the one Bill Altenburg operates. Altenburg's enterprise, Timberland Trails Incorporated, leases this 24,000-acre valley of timberland from International Paper Company (IPC) for the pursuits of outdoor enthusiasts. Though traditionally paper companies have allowed private citizens access to their land, formal arrangements that would bring in large numbers of users are not usually made.

Since 1898, IPC has managed sustainable foresting in the Phillip's Brook area. While they still harvest timber from the valley, trails and non-active logging roads are open for non-motorized recreation. That means just about everything can cross paths out in the woods, from mountain bike group rides to guided llama treks arranged through the Phillip's Brook Backcountry Recreation office.

With over 75 miles of trails available, a trip to the Backcountry rightly demands an extended visit. Mountain bikers willing to be fully self-reliant can plan days of epic riding, biking from tent site to tent site or between the multiple yurts spaced about the valley. Yurts are large framed circular structures covered with canvas or other material. At Phillips Brook they come with bunks, mattresses, a propane cookstove, a woodstove, and a few other niceties.

For those who prefer extended day trips, sans panniers or bike trailer, the lodge on Phillip's Pond makes a great base to ride from. The lodge comes complete with bunks, showers, a kitchen stove, a refrigerator, and generator powered lighting. Bring your own bike tools, and save some time for the wood-fired hot tub.

The two loop options discussed here exemplify the diversity of terrain available at Phillip's Brook Backcountry Recreation Area. Each follows logging roads for a good portion of its mileage, but the *Three Gate Loop* includes only a "moderate" climb, while the *Long Mountain Loop* challenges riders with a relentless three-mile ascent. The elevation gain along each route leads to multiple areas with broad open views of the valley and mountains, including clear-day sightings of Mount Washington and other peaks in the Presidential Range.

Three Gate Loop can be ridden from the door of the Phillip's Brook lodge. Pedaled counterclockwise, you will enjoy a shallow descent until crossing Phillip's Brook where coasting transitions into climbing. In autumn, freshly fallen leaves cover the trail as it rises through a corridor of color, only to emerge to finer open views of the White Mountains.

From the high ground you will lose elevation on the way back to the lodge road. The first trail to pass on your right is the Nelson Brook Trail, which runs four miles to the Nelson Brook yurt. Next on the right comes North Pond Loop, which connects to South Pond loop. Together, these circle Phillip's Pond for an extended version of *Three Gate Loop*.

Ride Information

🚲 Trail Contacts:

Phillip's Brook Backcountry Recreation Area, Timberland Trails, Inc., Conway, NH 1-800-TRAILS-8

🕐 Schedule:

Open year-round

💡 Local Events/Attractions:

Nash Stream Forest, New Hampshire Department of Forests and Lands, Concord, NH (603) 271-2214– New Hampshire's largest state forest, Nash Stream Forest abuts Phillip's Brook Backcountry Recreation Area's western border and offers many additional miles of gravel roads and trails over its 39,600 acres

🛏 Accommodations:

Phillip's Brook, Dummer, NH 1-800-TRAILS-8 – The log cabin lodge on Phillip's Pond holds eight to 12 people and is $55 per person per night. Yurts are $26 per person per night. The fire tower is $16 per person per night.

👫 Group Rides:

Guided llama or dogsled trips can be arranged certain weekends by calling **Phillip's Brook**, 1-800-TRAILS-8.

🚌 Public Transportation:

North Country Transportation (NCT) runs demand responsive door to door service from Berlin to anywhere within Coos County, including Phillip's Brook. NCT will allow bicycles and provide a bike trailer for groups with advance reservations. Call 1-888-997-2020 for more information.

🚌 Intercity Bus Service:

Concord Trailways, 1-800-639-3317 or *www.concordtrailways.com* – They offer daily service to Berlin from Boston and Concord.

🚲 Local Bike Shops:

Moriah Sports, Gorham, NH
(603) 466-5050
Tobin's Bike, Lancaster, NH
(603) 788-3144
Croteau and Sons Bicycle, Berlin, NH
(603) 752-4963

Ⓝ Maps:

USGS maps: *Three Gate Loop* – Dixville Notch, NH; Dummer Pond, NH. *Long Mountain Loop* – Dummer Pond, NH •
Trail information and topographic maps – available at Phillip's Brook Backcountry Recreation Area office at the Paris Field Trailhead

As healthy as the climb along the *Three Gate Loop* might seem, the one along the second ride option is something else altogether. The *Long Mountain Loop* ascent takes up the majority of the first half of the nine-mile circuit. It begins as a pure logging road climb followed near the top by more climbing through wide singletrack. Described in its simplest formula, the *Long Mountain Loop* goes up, around the Long Mountain yurt, and descends for a really long time.

Terrain at the end of the Long Mountain climb and the beginning of the descent represents the greatest technical challenge as it is very steep and rocky. This section loses elevation at such a rapid pace that the profile of the remaining downhill roll stays rather shallow but fast.

If not already apparent, Phillip's Brook Backcountry Recreation Area is not a small suburban forest with paved nature paths and parking lots at the trailheads. Alone, the gravel auto road to the lodge would make a rough enough mountain bike route for some. Other riders may want a dawn to dusk adventure up mountains and over ridgelines. Whether it's an epic trip into remote country, or just a very quiet vacation spent drifting in a canoe on Phillip's Pond, the Backcountry offers a remoteness few ever have the opportunity to experience.

MilesDirections – Three Gate Loop

0.0 START from Phillip's Brook lodge via the access road.

2.3 Cross the bridge over Phillip's Brook and pass around the gate. Turn left at the intersection.

2.4 Follow the doubletrack that departs to the left.

6.0 Turn left at the "T" intersection after the bridge. Immediately cross another wooden bridge. Nelson Brook Trail passes to the right. Later, pass the North Pond Loop.

7.0 Go right at the "T" intersection with the lodge access road. Pass through the gate.

7.3 Back at the lodge, find something cold to drink in the fridge.

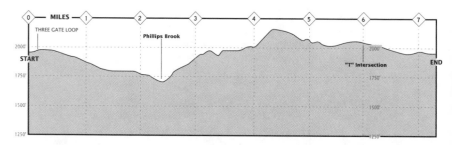

MilesDirections – Long Mountain Loop

0.0 START up Jodrie Brook Trail, marked with blue flags, over a rolling course that pitches up near the 2.0-mile point.

2.2 Pass a logging road on your left. Continue straight, uphill, with the blue flags.

3.4 Pass the junction with the Long Mountain Col Trail.

3.7 Roll left through a log landing. The trail becomes narrow and enters the woods at the far corner of the landing.

4.6 Pass in front of or behind Long Mountain yurt. The trail becomes Robert's Brook Trail on the opposite side of the shelter. Follow the yellow flags into a sharp descent.

6.1 A grassy trail continues straight at a 90-degree left in the main trail. Take the main trail left into an immediate climb.

7.9 Long Mountain Col ski trail comes in from the left.

9.2 With a final rush of speed, the loop ends.

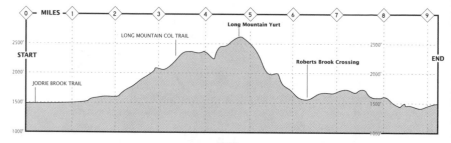

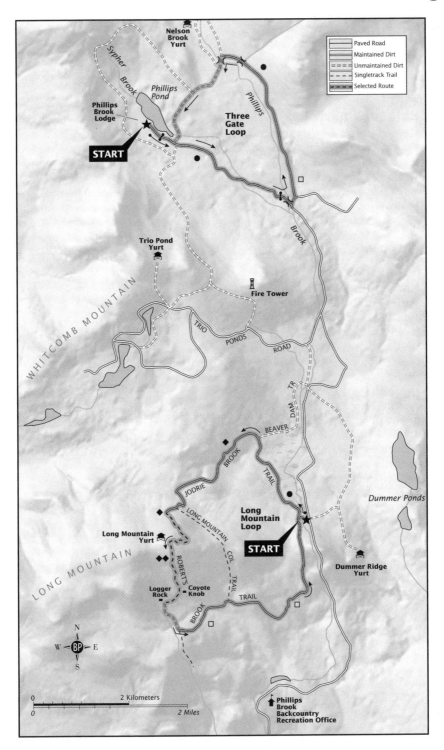

Paved Road
Maintained Dirt
Unmaintained Dirt
Singletrack Trail
Selected Route

Nelson Brook Yurt

Sypher Brook

Phillips Pond

Phillips Brook Lodge

START

Three Gate Loop

Phillips Brook

Trio Pond Yurt

Fire Tower

TRIO PONDS ROAD

WHITCOMB MOUNTAIN

DAM TR

BEAVER

JODRIE BROOK

TRAIL

Long Mountain Yurt

Long Mountain Loop

START

Dummer Ponds

LONG MOUNTAIN

ROBERT'S BROOK TRAIL

Logger Rock

Coyote Knob

COL TRAIL

TRAIL

Dummer Ridge Yurt

N
W E
S

0   2 Kilometers
0   2 Miles

Phillips Brook Backcountry Recreation Office

The Balsams Wilderness

Ride Summary

In the most rugged and wild country of Northern New Hampshire you'll find great mountain biking, and even greater luxury accommodations. The Balsams Grand Resort Hotel maintains a vast network of cross-country ski trails within their 15,000 acres of private wilderness. These trails are used in the summer for biking, hiking, and nature tours. Off the resort grounds, abandoned roads and two-wheel drive gravel roads double the available miles of terrain. No set route has been given, due to the variety of technical challenges and diversity of terrain. Beginners can leave The Balsams Mountain Bike and Nature Center with a few pointers and a staff-suggested plan for an easy route. Experienced riders can simply take off with a resort map—and hope to find their way home by dinnertime.

Ride Specs

Start: From the Balsams Mountain Bike and Nature Center at the Balsams Grand Resort Hotel

Length: The on-site network includes 30 miles of hiking/biking trails and over 30 more miles of hiking-only trails.

Approximate Riding Time: At your discretion

Difficulty Rating: The Balsams rates its trails for difficulty and includes this information on its summer trail map. Routes vary from easy to difficult with steep grades forming much of the challenge on the difficult trails.

Trail Surface: Grass covered cross-country ski trails and woodland cross-country ski trails with steep hills in sections, although flatter routes do exist

Lay of the Land: Remote, mountainous, heavily forested terrain frames the maintained trails of The Balsams.

Land Status: Private hotel resort land

Nearest Town: Colebrook, NH

Other Trail Users: Walkers, hikers, and joggers

Wheels: Mountain bikes only

Getting There

From Berlin, NH: Follow NH 16 North to Errol, NH. Turn left onto NH 26 West. Follow for 10 miles through Dixville Notch to the Balsams Grand Resort Hotel. The entrance road is well marked by signs. Turn right onto the entrance road and follow signs to the Mountain Bike and Nature Center.

From Lancaster, NH: Follow U.S. 3 North to Colebrook, NH. Turn right onto NH 26 East. Continue on NH 26 for seven miles. The Balsams Grand Resort Hotel will be on your left. Turn left onto the entrance road and follow signs to the Mountain Bike and Nature Center. *DeLorme: New Hampshire Atlas & Gazetteer:* Page 50, C-6

You open the curtains of your hotel room to the 32 acres of Lake Gloriette below. Mountains of upturned bedrock rise to 3,000 feet in the background with their jagged faces and sheer cliffs shrouded by a light mist. Your day has begun, and it will be your day at The Balsams Grand Resort Hotel. With just over 200 rooms, The Balsams has a staff of 400 ready to prepare your breakfast, pack you a picnic for a morning ride, and provide you the very best of luxury resort life.

What began in 1866 as a 25-room summer guesthouse now stands as one of the premiere resort destinations in the world. Ski, golf, and vacation reference guides utter nothing but superlatives about the Balsams' food and accommodations, and its unspoiled setting in Dixville Notch. Their American vacation package packs more into the day and night than you would ever think possible this far into the Great North Woods of New Hampshire. For hotel guests, three meals each day and all activities are complimentary. Those complimentary activities go a long way when you consider they include play at the Panorama Golf Course, and in winter, downhill skiing at the Balsams Wilderness Ski Area.

The resort is recognized as a national historic landmark by the National Trust for Historic Preservation, and is one of the 100 Historic Hotels of America (HHA). The Balsams earned its HHA honor because of its age, its importance to local history, and the faithful preservation of its original architecture. It is the only resort in New Hampshire to have earned both a four-diamond and a four-star rating from the nation's major travel clubs.

Beyond the service and attention lavished on its guests, the Balsams strives to educate visitors about the natural wonders surrounding Dixville Notch. The estate covers 15,000 acres, an area larger than Manhattan. Staff naturalists lead seminars and nature walks, guiding you to the best spots in the area to view flora and fauna. The Balsams is a partner in the New Hampshire Watchable Wildlife Program, and provides meals and accommodations for program technicians doing research in Dixville Notch. This relationship benefits all, as the aim of the Watchable Wildlife Program adds to the breadth of experiences the resort seeks for its guests.

The Balsams and Dixville Notch State Park both maintain hiking trails. One popular destination is Table Rock, an exposed outcrop that offers views of Lake Gloriette, the resort, and Sanguinary Ridge beyond. Routes over Table Rock are part of the Dixville Notch Heritage Trail, a component of the New Hampshire Heritage Trail System.

The Resort on Lake Bloriette

When you do manage to fit in your mountain bike ride, you'll travel over The Balsams' cross-country ski network. This means obstruction-free paths, with singletracks being little more than a solitary line worn down the center of a wide, grassy trail. This is the type of terrain many people like, but before hitting the trail, notice again the mountains all around. You are not in Kansas anymore Dorothy; you're in the North Country of New Hampshire. Pick a loop in harmony with your aerobic desires. In the area to the far west of the hotel, grades can be a true challenge, though the climbs are not long by cycling standards. From Lake Gloriette to Mud Pond, the total elevation gain is less than 500 feet, making this area to the north of the hotel a good start for many. For the best advice on the lay of the land and ride options personalized to your needs, speak with the Mountain Bike and Nature Center staff.

Dixville Notch is the first town in the U.S. to vote in primary elections

Ride Information

🕐 Trail Contact:
The Balsams Grand Resort Hotel, Mountain Bike and Nature Center, Dixville Notch, NH (603) 255-3400

🕐 Schedule:
The resort is open for the summer from mid May through mid October. During the ski season, it's open mid December through early April.

💲 Fees/Permits:
$5 per person for a day trail pass (free to hotel guests).

❓ Local Information:
The Balsams Grand Resort Hotel, Dixville Notch, NH or *www.thebalsams.com* • **Dixville Notch Information Center** (open May to October), Dixville Notch, NH (603) 255-4255 • **North Country Chamber of Commerce** (open June to October), Colebrook, NH (603) 237-8939

🔱 Local Events/Attractions:
Dixville Notch State Park, Dixville, NH (603) 823-5563 • **Mount Rain Aviation,**

Errol Airport, Errol, NH (603) 482-3323 *Accommodations:* • **The Balsams Grand Resort Hotel,** Dixville Notch, NH 1-800-255-0800 (in New Hampshire) or 1-800-255-0600 (in Canada and the remainder of the U.S.)

🚴 Local Bike Shops:
The Balsams Mountain Bike and Nature Center, Dixville Notch, NH (603) 255-3400 — rentals and repairs • **Tobin's Bike,** Lancaster, NH (603) 788-3144 • **Croteau and Sons Bicycle,** Berlin, NH (603) 752-4963 • **Moriah Sports,** Gorham, NH (603) 466-5050

🅝 Maps:
USGS maps: Dixville, NH; Lovering Mountain, NH; Blue Mountain, NH; Diamond Pond, NH • **The Balsams Map and Guide** — available on-site or with summer vacation package requests

MilesDirections

The Balsams does not plan set routes for its vast and varied trail network. Rather, speak with the Mountain Bike and Nature Center staff to help you chart a loop suitable to your interests and skill level. Whether you're a resort guest or day-user, the staff will cater to your needs. Both experienced and novice riders will benefit from their expertise.

Flume Brook

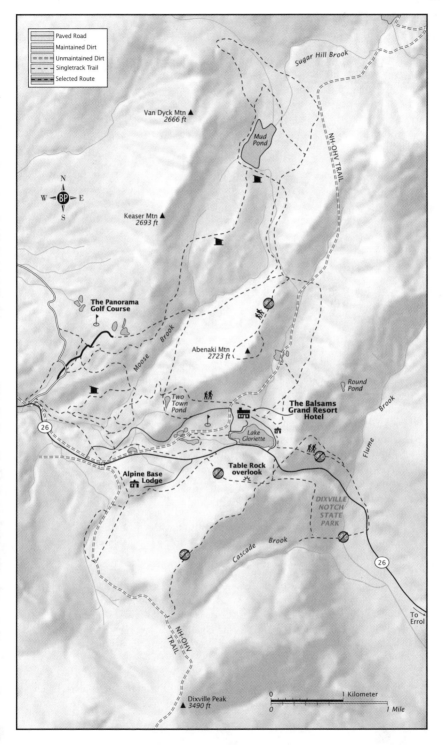

National Watchable Wildlife Program

If moose were hippie rockers, then Pittsburgh, New Hampshire, would be their Woodstock. Tourists and resident sightseers would be the flower children digging the mangy scene and Moose Alley would be the New York State Thruway on the third weekend of August 1969. This is all a stretch of the imagination though, because you won't find Woodstock-like crowds in Pittsburgh, New Hampshire, nor will you find a hoofed mammal able to play the Star Spangled Banner left-handed.

While Pittsburgh's Moose Alley has its degree of fame, many more, lesser-known opportunities for wildlife viewing exist throughout New Hampshire and Maine. Both states participate in the National Watchable Wildlife Program, a cooperative effort between federal, state, and private organizations, which provides people with the opportunity to view wildlife in their natural habitat. The program began in 1990 as a way to responsibly promote wildlife viewing, with the hope that everyday folk might gain a greater appreciation for, and conservation ethic toward, animals they typically knew only from photographs.

In New Hampshire, Watchable Wildlife efforts are directed by the Fish and Game Department, while Maine Inland Fisheries and Wildlife manages its state's efforts. The strong New Hampshire program boasts 90 sites designated for wildlife viewing. These vantage points may be simple salt licks or wallows into which road salt drains, or they may be more intricate, as is the viewing blind off of New Hampshire 26 through Dixville Notch. The blind sits on one of New Hampshire's busiest moose trails and offers onlookers the security of a shelter from which to observe.

The fervor to observe wildlife is one of the fastest growing recreational quests in the country. Annually, 30 million Americans plan their travel with the expectation of seeing animals in their natural habitat. With the huge amount of forested and coastal land in New Hampshire and Maine, the potential exists to add millions of dollars to state economies. Dangers abound as well, since attracting people into the woods brings them out of their element and places them into situations where they are easily viewed as threats. By designating sites for viewers to watch from, animals can pass unmolested over their established routes. This makes them less likely to become agitated or frightened, to attack, or to flee—all of which risk harm to the animals.

The impact of human presence on the established patterns of wildlife is a topic that naturalists continue to debate. One question they hope to answer is: "How close can we get before it's too close?" Even at distances that seem to us reasonable, animals may sense movement or unfamiliar scents and assume a threat. They may alter feeding habits and other routines in order to remove themselves from a perpetual defensive posture. To monitor this, behavior patterns and species populations are being studied near Watchable Wildlife sites. Scientific data is the best evidence to support the viability of drawing people into nature so that the appreciation instilled in them might spill over into their daily lives.

One way to locate Watchable Wildlife sites is to stumble upon them. They are marked with brown and white signs displaying a pair of binoculars. For a more precise approach to discovery in New Hampshire, order the New Hampshire Wildlife Viewing Guide from the New Hampshire Fish and Game Department. The guide lists 73 viewing spots around the state, with directions to each location and descriptions of the animals you might expect to see. Information on Maine wildlife can be found through Maine's Department of Inland Fisheries and Wildlife, though you'll need to contact their Information and Education branch for specific details about the Maine Watchable Wildlife Program. For details on the National Watchable Wildlife Program, with links to the federal and private organizations that support it, visit *www.gorp.com/wwldlife/wwhome.htm*.

For more Watchable Wildlife Program info:
- New Hampshire Fish and Game Department, 2 Hazen Drive, Concord, NH 03301; (603) 271-3211
- NH Watchable Wildlife website: *www.wildlife.state.nh.us/education.html*
- Department website: *www.wildlife.state.nh.us/home.html*
- Maine Department of Inland Fisheries and Wildlife, 284 State Street, 41 State House Station, Augusta, ME 04333-004; (207) 287-3303
- Educational Programs and Information website: *www.state.me.us/ifw/edu.htm*
- Department website: *www.state.me.us/ifw/homepage.htm*

Honorable Mentions

White Mountains Region

Compiled here is an index of great rides in the White Mountains region that didn't make the A-list this time around but deserve recognition. Check them out and let us know what you think. You may decide that one or more of these rides deserves higher status in future editions or, perhaps, you may have a ride of your own that merits some attention.

(E) Conway Town Trails

Centered between the outlet stores of Conway and North Conway waits a limited but convenient network of trails developed by local citizens. The loop begins at the town canoe launch, on the Saco River behind the Conway police station. You'll ride southwest along the Saco River, turn north before crossing U.S. Route 302, and finally head back through Redstone to the canoe launch again. Under six miles in all, it's still a very convenient, crowd-free place amidst an area thousands of people vacation in each year. *DeLorme: New Hampshire Atlas & Gazetteer:* Page 45, J-11

(F) Lower Nanamocomuck from Albany Covered Bridge

The Lower Nanamocomuck Trail begins northwest of Albany Covered Bridge, off Deer Brook Road in Albany, New Hampshire. The trailhead is reached from the Kancamangus Highway (NH 112), six miles west of Route 16. The trip utilizes fire roads and a marked, singletrack cross-country ski trail along the Swift River. Obstacles on the singletrack require intermediate skills to negotiate. The route can be ridden out and back or as a loop with a return to the parking area via the Kancamangus Highway. Either way, 14 miles of terrain will be covered. Midway through the ride, there is an option to take the footbridge at Rocky Gorge to cut the loop to eight total miles. This ride is within the White Mountain National Forest. The Saco Ranger Station at the intersection of New Hampshire 16 and the Kancamangus Highway has hiking and mountain bike maps of trails in their jurisdiction. The AMC White Mountain Guide is perhaps the best trip planning and mapping resource for self-guided excursions. The number for the Saco District Ranger Station is (603) 447-5448. *DeLorme: New Hampshire Atlas & Gazetteer:* Page 44, J-7

(G) Sawyer River/Pond Trails Loop

Technical riding over rocks and roots highlights this long, advanced loop. Narrow trails, forest service roads, and dirt roads combine for a four to six-hour trip. This ride is accessible from Sawyer River Road, off state U.S. Route 302 west of Bartlett, New Hampshire, or off Bear Notch Road, which runs between the Kancamangus Highway (NH 112) and U.S. Route 302. Use the Upper Nanamocomuck Trail to connect the Sawyer Pond and Sawyer River Trails. All routes are within the White Mountain National Forest and fall under the purview of the Saco Ranger District. The ranger station is a good source for the ever-changing trail conditions throughout the region. Contact them at (603) 447-5448. *DeLorme: New Hampshire Atlas & Gazetteer:* Page 44, I-3

(H) East Branch River Loop

This ride starts on Forest Service Road 87 / East Branch Road, off the north side of the Kancamangus Highway (NH 112), four miles east of downtown Lincoln, New Hampshire. It is a flat 6.5-mile trip that runs along the East Branch of the Pemigewassett River. For a loop return on the Wilderness Trail, portage across the river is necessary, but there are boulders that allow this to be done. On the west side of the river, one-third of a mile from the portage, is Franconia Falls, a popular destination for the hikers with whom you'll share the return leg of the loop. This is an hour ride. Services, including three cycling shops, are located in Lincoln. You are within the Pemigewassett Ranger District of the White Mountain National Forest on this ride. Their number is (603) 536-1310. *DeLorme: New Hampshire Atlas & Gazetteer:* Page 43, H-14

(I) Franconia Notch Recreation Path

New Hampshire's trademark, the granite face of the Old Man of the Mountain, can be viewed from this 10.5-mile recreation trail which runs the length of Franconia Notch. The beach at Echo Lake, views of the Franconia and Kinsman mountain ranges, and the waterfalls at Flume Gorge and the Basin are other popular attractions. Grades are suited to beginners and families, but all cyclists should enjoy the quiet of this paved pathway. Though autos are not allowed, bikers share the path with walkers and rollerbladers. Parking at the southern trail end is available at the Flume visitor center in Lincoln, New Hampshire. More parking is available at the northern terminus at Echo Lake and at various intersections along the way. Ride time is at the discretion of individuals. The number for Franconia Notch State Park is (603) 823-9513. *DeLorme: New Hampshire Atlas & Gazetteer:* Page 43, I-12

(J) Success Pond Loop

Over 30 miles will be ridden on this advanced loop that utilizes the Success ATV/Trail Bike Area route and the remote, unpaved Success Pond Road. Distance, loose surfaces, and short steep climbs can challenge you along the singletrack and logging roads of the ATV trail, which is marked along its course. Traveling New Hampshire 16 North out of Berlin, New Hampshire, there will be signs for OHRV parking at the intersection with Mason Street. Turn right across the bridge and turn left at the next stop sign onto Hutchins Street. Travel 0.7 miles farther to the next OHRV sign and let the other signs guide you to the trailhead. The New Hampshire Bureau of Trails number is (603) 271-3254, and they show this route on their ATV and Trail Bike Guide. *DeLorme: New Hampshire Atlas & Gazetteer:* Page 49, B-12

Maine's

South
Coast

Maine's South Coast

Most of Maine's population lives within its South Coast region, though even that fact does little to get in the way of available land for mountain biking. Stand in the heart of Portland and things look typically urban, but just 20 minutes away and you're in the countryside. Out there are long, quiet rides like those at Lake Arrowhead and Ossipee Mountain. These rides are typical of the abandoned or little used roads that abound in the South Coast west of the Maine Turnpike.

The region's population and major attractions hug the seaboard from Freeport, Maine, south to the New Hampshire line. The attractions begin with L.L. Bean and the outlet shopping of Freeport, before moving down to Portland with its Olde Port historic district. Farther south the beaches of Old Orchard and Saco form the draw. Next down the line is Kennebunkport with its seaside village atmosphere, which is mirrored farther on in Ogunquit and York Harbor.

Most of the following rides are concentrated along the seaboard to keep things accessible for the greatest number of mountain bikers. Some are circuit type rides, while other like those at Mount Agamenticus have a huge amount of terrain, and the relative renown to match. Enjoy.

Portland

Gulf of
Maine

Kennebunkport

Atlantic
Ocean

Ogunquit

York
Harbor

Mount Agamenticus

Ride Summary

Mount Agamenticus goes by the names Aggie, Mount A, and sometimes, the Big A. Whatever you decide to call it, the terrain here is the most expansive to be found in Southern Maine or Seacoast New Hampshire. A myriad of abandoned roads and game paths have become the routine destination for hundreds of mountain bikers. A hilly layout, coupled with multiple wetlands, ponds, and streams make Mount A a challenging place to ride even on a good day.

Ride Specs

Start: From the bottom of Mount Agamenticus summit access road
Length: 9-mile loop
Approximate Riding Time: 1½–2½ hours
Difficulty Rating: Difficult. Muddy in the spring and bony through the summer.
Trail Surface: Worn single and doubletrack, repetitive climbing, one long climb, and many eroded sections
Lay of the Land: Rolling terrain, mostly wooded with multiple wetlands
Elevation Gain: 990 feet
Land Status: Mix of town and state owned property
Nearest Town: York, ME
Other Trail Users: Hikers, equestrians, ATVs, cross-country skiers, snowshoers, and hunters (in season)
Wheels: Mountain bikes only

Getting There

From Kittery, ME: Take I-95 North to York, ME. Get off I-95 at the Yorks / Ogunquit / U.S. 1 exit (Exit 4). Turn left at the end of the off-ramp. The parking lot is 6.7 miles from the ramp. Immediately cross the bridge over I-95 and take the last right turn before the commuter parking lot, onto Chases Pond Road. Bear left where Chases Pond Road merges with Mountain Road. Continue on the main road, which later becomes Agamenticus Road. Park in the area just before the tar transitions to dirt. The uphill paved road leads to the summit of Mount Agamenticus, but you'll be riding there not driving. **_DeLorme: Maine Atlas & Gazetteer:_** Map 1, A-4

O n a busy summer afternoon, the one thing harder than climbing Mount Agamenticus in the middle ring is finding a parking spot at the base of the access road. The license plates come from all over because the local secret was given up long ago. New Hampshire riders make the 15-minute trip north from the state border, and Massachusetts folks with gas to burn often show up too. A Quebec tag may be seen during the height of summer tourism.

Fat tires rolled through the woods around Mount Agamenticus years before the sport grew into mainstream popularity. For solitary roadies exploring the game trails with their new wheeled toys, or for possies of tuned-in enthusiasts hammering out three-hour doubletrack joyrides after work, Mount Agamenticus was the place. Through the late '80s and early '90s, the "Sunday Morning Ride" forever paired good times with Mount Agamenticus. These word-of-mouth gatherings drew

dozens and often broke apart once into the woods, but they'll forever stand as the beginning of mountain biking in Southern Maine.

The town of York promotes the Agamenticus Wilderness Reserve as the largest undeveloped forest on the Atlantic coastal plain. When riding, you will be on land owned separately by the town, the York Water District, the Kittery Water District, and the State of Maine. The Mount Agamenticus trail network is extensive and complicated. As a result, getting lost on any ride over it is a common problem. The area also gets very muddy in the spring and after rainy periods, which makes it popular with some users but not with land managers. They watch the condition of these woods, and in recent years have put up gates to keep jeeps and other 4x4s off the trails. They now also require permits for ATVs.

The loop enters the woods at one of the gates erected to keep out the 4x4s. The first downhill is difficult—steep and rocky with exposed tree roots to throw riders from any rhythm they may try to establish. The terrain remains rocky and typically wet until past Folly Pond when a stretch of smoother terrain lulls one into a sense of ease. Once through the smooth stuff, you can expect loose surface climbs and descents, along with some rocky flat sections for the rest of the ride.

True to the laws of mountain biking, the most difficult bit of trail comes just before you're out of the woods. That stretch is a boneyard uphill that's hard to ride even as a downhill. Once the rocks are dispensed with, a gradual climb on gravel Mountain Road returns you to the parking lot, where it just wouldn't be right to stop just yet.

The final leg is a nice workout for some, a ferocious battle with gravity for others. It starts up the Mount Agamenticus access road and then darts left into the woods onto an off-camber doubletrack climb. The mix of canted technical terrain and continuous elevation gain makes it difficult. The final leg to the top of the mountain runs up a former ski slope, with slippery surfaces and steep grades. Stay to the exposed rock so as not to erode the soil, but be warned that the rock turns greasy on damp days and dewy mornings.

Once at the top, check out the distant view of Mount Washington from the deck of the summit lodge, or stop to see the horses at Agamenticus Stables. The trip down to the parking lot uses the paved access road. There are many steep sharp corners, and cars will be approaching from the opposite direction.

With the typical delays of summer traffic in York county resort towns, Mount Agamenticus might be the best place to get away from it all. If unfamiliar with the trails, then ride during the weekend between mid-morning and early afternoon. During these times there should be plenty of friendly faces on the popular routes, but not so many that you'll feel cramped.

Broken chain repair.

Ride Information

Trail Contact:
York Parks and Recreation, York Village, ME (207) 363-1040

Schedule:
Year-round

Local Information:
York Chamber of Commerce, York, ME (207) 363-4422 or 1-800-639-2442 • Ogunquit Chamber of Commerce, Ogunquit, ME (207) 646-2939

Local Events/Attractions:
Agamenticus Horse Stables, Agamenticus Village, ME (207) 361-2840 • The Kittery Outlets, U.S. Route 1, Kittery, ME

Organizations:
Team Grimace, Ogunquit, ME (207) 646-0376 or www.teamgrimace.com

Local Bike Shops:
Berger's Bike Shop, York, ME (207) 363-4070 • Wheels & Waves, Wells, ME (207) 646-5774 • Bretons Bike Shop, Wells, ME (207) 646-4255

Maps:
USGS maps: York Harbor, ME

Names...

The Sixty-Forty Trail also goes by a more popular, obscene name coined for its difficulty. Ride The _ _ _ _ Trail to figure out the answer yourself.

MilesDirections

0.0 START on the paved road, heading in the direction you drove in from.

0.2 Turn right and pass the York and Kittery Water Districts gate onto the doubletrack Sixty-Forty trail. (Bikes are allowed, but ATVs need permits.)

0.8 Follow the trail to the right at the earthen dam forming Folly Pond. At the top of the first rise turn right onto a doubletrack. The pond will be to your back. Bear left at the first trail split, and then cross through two successive stone walls spaced 10 yards apart.

1.0 Turn left at the first trail split, near Welchs Pond and start a gentle climb.

1.6 Pass a swamp and come to a "triangle" trail junction with an island of trees in the middle. Turn left.

2.0 Ride along with a wetland to the right.

2.9 After the doubletrack splits and rejoins around an island of trees, turn right at the next trail junction. There is a faint tree marking here 10 feet off the ground that points back in the direction you came.

3.3 After crossing a seasonal stream, turn right onto a singletrack and then right again a few seconds later onto a doubletrack. Follow the doubletrack to its end where it transitions through the trees into a worn, uphill singletrack. This trail then alternates between single and doubletrack and is typically wet.

4.3 Turn left at the trail junction. A tree on the right has a faint marking pointing back in the direction you came.

4.6 A downhill run passes the remains of a wrecked bus. Turn right, onto a technical uphill, at the "T" intersection.

5.3 Bear left at the trail split, away from the typically wet doubletrack popular with ATV riders. Marking the intersection are a smooth rock with chainring gouges across the top and a large birch tree just after it to the left of the trail. Cross through a stone wall.

5.4 Turn right at the intersection with the Fifty-Fifty Trail, marked by an old tire on the ground nearby.

6.0 Welchs Pond Trail comes in from the right, but continue on Fifty-Fifty. Cross Hoopers Brook at the bottom of a rocky downhill, and then try to ride the eroded climb on the other side.

6.3 Turn right, uphill, onto gravel Mountain Road. Watch for cars.

6.9 Turn left by the parking lot onto the paved access road. Take the first left onto the doubletrack Nature Trail.

7.7 Cross a former expert ski trail and then an overgrown trail with a ski lift. At the third abandoned ski trail turn uphill, picking lines over the exposed rock. Continue climbing to the lodge at the summit of Mount Agamenticus.

8.1 Descend the paved access road from summit. Watch for cars around the many steep, sharp corners.

9.0 Mount Agamenticus conquered.

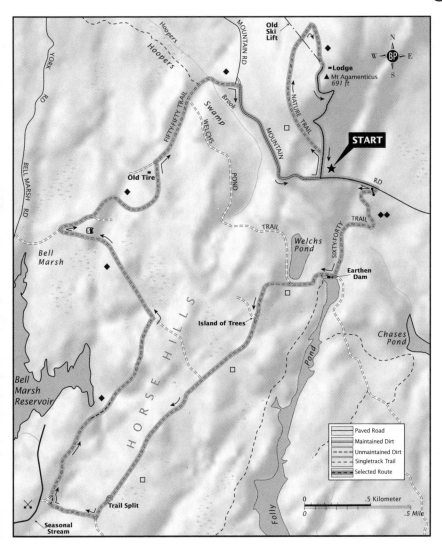

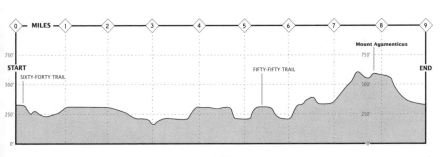

Tatnic Hill Loop

Ride Summary

The summertime popularity of the Ogunquit / Wells Beach area has taken its toll on rideable open space. One need only head west though to find a simple little mountain bike loop. Tatnic Hill offers the principle challenge on the ride, while a mix of paved and maintained dirt roads act as supporting cast. The mixed terrain probably won't appeal to mountain biking purists, but those who believe any trail is worthy of exploration will be able to make a time of it.

Ride Specs

Start: From the side of Cheney Woods Road
Length: 8.7-mile loop
Approximate Riding Time: 1½ hours
Difficulty Rating: Technically easy, with short rutted or eroded moderate sections. One 20-foot portage over rocks to cross the stream. This section can be avoided. Physically easy, due to generally firm surfaces and no meaningful hills
Trail Surface: Flat, minor hills. Unmaintained roads, dirt and paved roads
Lay of the Land: Rural forested countryside, home to moose and deer
Elevation Gain: 202 feet
Land Status: Town roads
Nearest Town: Wells, ME
Other Trail Users: Hikers, equestrians, motorists, and hunters (in season)
Wheels: Mountain bikes only

Getting There

From Wells, ME: Head south on U.S. 1. At the intersection of U.S. 1 and ME 9B, turn right onto ME 9B West. After four miles, turn left onto Cheney Woods Road. Park to the right another mile later when the pavement ends. *DeLorme: Maine Atlas & Gazetteer.* Map 2, E-4

L ike the Wild West, the East had its share of cattle rustlers. The ones in Wells, Maine, hid out in the Robbers' Caves on Tatnic Hill, which you pass on this ride. It seems that stealing livestock in those rugged days was more of a family business than the fault of a lone deviant, and most likely the thievery was done largely for survival. But whatever the reason, the stealing threatened the livelihood of neighbors who struggled just as hard to live on the frontier—and Wells was a frontier in the 18th Century. The problem was eventually taken care of, with true frontier justice, when the neighbors banded to reclaim their livestock and drove the thieves from their settlement.

Throughout the area of Wells, west of the Maine Turnpike, the remains of colonial roads can be still be found. They remain open for logging, for access to camps and property that would otherwise be land-locked, and for fire fighting vehicles. Today, the colonial roads over Tatnic Hill probably see more moose than human traffic. The quiet makes it a cure-all for vacationing riders tired of the beach crowds

or for local residents who haven't explored enough of their area. This loop over Tatnic Hill puts up a moderate challenge in some sections, but on the whole the off-roading is easy.

The wide gravel section of Cheney Woods Road gives a good warm-up and room for partners to ride abreast while they talk. After the right turn onto the grassy track, consider the possibility of hidden obstacles or ruts, but press on to the smooth gravel ahead. Enter the tree-sheltered corridor of a narrow country road, pass a home, and then ride opposite the horse fence of Racealong Stables.

Pavement interrupts the journey for a while, but the setting is rural and traffic will be minimal. An old cemetery set above the grade comes up on the left, just beyond the wide right bend in Tatnic Road. After the left at the stop sign and the continuation onto Hill Road, the tarmac disappears and the going roughens up. The crest of Tatnic Hill comes in the first quarter mile on the abandoned track. For a visit to the Robbers' Caves, walk east (right) into the woods here. Hunt for the out-crop with what looks to be a chimney vent running up through it.

The greatest challenge on the loop comes over the next two miles. The terrain rolls easily, but minor erosion has exposed rocks on some grades and vehicle ruts will be encountered. Ruts are a particular pain because once in one, it decides which way you'll go. The best way to avoid this is to ride the flat ground through the middle of the two tracks.

Expect bugs, puddles, and mud during the spring or after heavy rainfall. The mud is a good place to scout for signs of moose. Even in populated southern coastal Maine, the half-ton cousin of the deer can be seen. Look for a cloven hoof print with two toes.

After passing a stone cottage that appears to be straight out of "Hanzel and Gretel," an intersection will come up. The planned route turns to the right, but to be completed requires carrying the bike on rocks over water at a washed out bridge.

If the confidence of anyone in the party is in question, a left at this intersection will avoid the portage and knock some distance off the trip. Either way, the finish is on pavement, which though unfortunate is hard to avoid with no expanse of open public land in the area.

So, the ride has ended and some cool event to cap the day is needed. The ocean beaches of Wells, Moody, or Ogunquit can take care of that. Since the beaches are the draw to this area, it makes sense to experience them by mountain bike. No fancy conversion is needed to shift into sand cruiser mode, just check the local paper for the tide watch and ride the firm wet sand when crowds are low and the water is out. A bike is also the best way to get through the heavy traffic that comes with summer, especially at bottlenecks like Ogunquit center. When busy, the drive from the Wells line to the center takes a half-hour, but it's only 10 minutes by bike.

A scroll from north to south of other attractions in the area includes the Wells National Estuarine Research Reserve, located on a 1,600-acre preserve of beach, marsh, and woodland. There are seven miles of trails to walk. Tours of the habitat run daily through the summer and on weekends in spring and autumn. Laudholm Farm, a 19th Century saltwater farm, is a high point of the site.

Farther south on U.S. Route 1 is the Wells Auto Museum. Motels, restaurants and other businesses catering to tourism also line this stretch of road. Ogunquit, the next village down the line, offers a center of small shops, boutiques and art galleries. From near Ogunquit center, the Marginal Way cliff-walk runs along Maine's rocky coast out to Perkins Cove—another popular area that can take a chunk of time to reach by car. Lobster boats moor in the cove, and fishing and sailing charters are

Ride Information

Trail Contacts:
No contact, as the ride is on town roads or abandoned town roads.

Local Information:
Wells Chamber of Commerce, Wells, ME (207) 646-2451 • Ogunquit Visitor Information, Ogunquit, ME (207) 646-5533 • Laudholm Farm and Wells National Estuarine Research Reserve, Wells, ME (207) 646-1555 • Ogunquit Chamber of Commerce, Ogunquit, ME (207) 646-2939

Local Events/Attractions:
Marginal Way cliff-walk, Ogunquit, ME • Wells Auto Museum, Wells, ME (207) 646-9064 • Tully's Beer & Wine, Wells, ME (207) 641-8622 • Ogunquit Playhouse, Ogunquit, ME (207) 646-2402

Local Bike Clubs:
Team Grimace, Ogunquit, ME (207) 646-0376 or www.teamgrimace.com

Local Bike Shops:
Wheels & Waves, Wells, ME (207) 646-5774 • Bretons Bike Shop, Wells, ME (207) 646-4255 • Berger's Bike Shop, York, ME (207) 363-4070 • Cape Able Bike Shop, Kennebunkport, ME (207) 967-4382 – they run road rides and mountain bike rides and offer family paced rides • Bikes, Blades, and Boards, Kennebunk, ME (207) 967-3601 or 1-800-220-0907

Maps:
USGS maps: North Berwick, ME

available. If there are still hours in the day, sit for a play at the Ogunquit Playhouse, where some of the finest summer theatre in Maine has been performed since the 1930s. Or hit Tully's Beer & Wine in the Aubuchon plaza on U.S. Route 1, just south of the Wells Auto Museum. Tully's stocks cigars, wine, and beer from around the world. Drop some coin on a loaf of bread from the bakery next door to complete a carbo-packed meal.

MilesDirections

0.0 START uphill on Cheney Woods Road.

0.9 At the transition to pavement, a grassy doubletrack heads off to the right. Follow the doubletrack as it shortly turns to dirt. Pass Racealong Stables on the left.

1.9 Turn left onto Tatnic Road. It bends sharply to the right a half-mile up, and then continues to a stop sign.

3.0 Turn left at the stop sign. At the 90-degree right turn that follows, continue straight across the road. This dirt track is Hill Road, though it may look like a driveway. Immediately, driveways split to the right and left and Hill Road continues up the abandoned track between them. The first rise crested is Tatnic Hill and the Robbers' Caves are through the woods to the right.

4.6 Pass a stone cottage on the way to an intersection. The "good" road turns sharply to the left. You're going to follow the route as it turns right and then rolls left through an area of timber cutting. At the washed out bridge a mile up, use the rocks on the right to portage across the water. *[**Option.** If the rocks aren't an attractive route or are underwater, return to the intersection at mile 4.6 and continue on the "good" road. Turn left on ME 9B West, and turn left again under a mile later onto Cheney Woods Road.]*

5.8 After the washed out bridge, exit the woods onto Hickory Lane. Turn left on Hickory Lane, and 0.2 miles farther turn left again on Loop Road.

6.2 Turn left on ME 9B West.

7.8 Turn left on Cheney Woods Road and return to the start.

8.7 Arrive at your vehicle.

Alternate Starts: Tatnic Hill is a less than seven-mile road ride from many motels and residences near Wells Beach and Ogunquit village. Taking Tatnic Road out is one option to access the loop.

Start of the Fall Foliage Challenge.

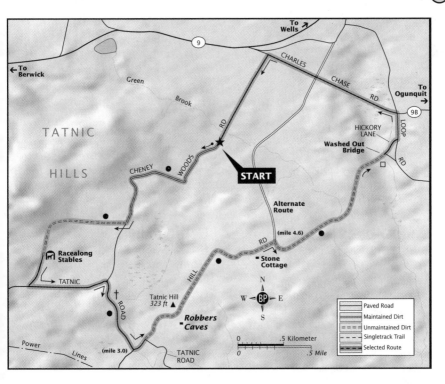

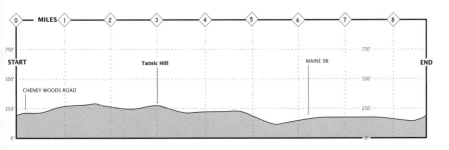

Kennebunk Bridle Path

Ride Summary

Anyone in the Kennebunkport area who is up for a simple ride might want to explore the Kennebunk port Bridle Path. The trail is about the only off-road terrain available in the immediate area and offers a healthy way to spend an hour. A singletrack section begins beyond Maine 9 for some riding that will test your skills. If that sounds unappealing, stick to the Bridle Path, and then bike into Kennebunkport center. You can even continue north along the ocean toward Walkers Point.

Ride Specs

Start: From the parking lot of Sea Road School in Kennebunk, ME

Length: 5.6-mile out-and-back

Approximate Riding Time: 45 minutes

Difficulty Rating: Easy. The ride follows community trails. The singletrack on the ocean side of Maine 9 adds a degree of challenge to the ride.

Trail Surface: Smooth, flat gravel, with some loose surfaces along the singletrack

Lay of the Land: Flat unpaved community recreation trail that weaves through woods and marsh.

Elevation Gain: 46 feet

Land Status: Community sponsored recreational trail

Nearest Town:
Kennebunk and Kennebunkport, ME

Other Trail Users: Hikers and joggers

Wheels: Hybrids, trailers, kids' single-speeds, and mountain bikes are fine along the first miles of the Bridle Path. Mountain bikes only on the singletrack.

Getting There

From Kennebunk, ME: Head southeast on ME 35. After crossing the bridge over the railroad tracks, you will see Tom's of Maine on the right. Take the next right turn onto Sea Road. Continue for 0.3 miles and turn right into the parking lot of Sea Road School. When school is in session, park in the dirt turn-off to the side of ME 9 at the bridge over the Mousam River. The trail intersects ME 9 on the northeast side of the bridge.

From Kennebunkport, ME: Follow ME 35 northwest for approximately three miles from the junction of ME 9 and ME 35 (Port Road). Turn left onto Sea Road. Continue for 0.3 miles before turning right into the parking lot of Sea Road School. When school is in session, park in the dirt turn-off to the side of ME 9 at the bridge over the Mousam River. The trail intersects ME 9 on the northeast side of the bridge. *DeLorme: Maine Atlas & Gazetteer.* Map 3, D-1

The tidal waterways Branch Brook, Kennebunk River, and Mousam River drain the Maine coastal plain west of the Kennebunks into the Atlantic Ocean. Two of the three define town boundaries. To the south, Branch Brook separates Kennebunk from Wells, while to the north, the Kennebunk River cuts the line between Kennebunk and Kennebunkport.

Settlement began here 10 years after French explorer Samuel de Champlain first anchored off this section of Maine's coast in 1604. Hostilities with the native inhabitants of the land began almost immediately. The Europeans established the

settlement of Cape Porpus, but by 1689 the natives had repossessed the land. Lieutenant General Sir William Pepperrell stepped in to finally rest the property into European hands in the early 1700s. Cape Porpus was reincarnated, so to speak, and the town became known as Arundel and grew from a new village centered on Burbank Hill.

Farming, sawmills, and gristmills formed the basis of the settlement's early economy, but shipbuilding and sea trade were to bring the region the prosperity that is evidenced today by the old stately homes that line the main streets of Kennebunk and Kennebunkport. The first half of the 19th Century saw over 1,000 schooners, clippers, and other vessels emerge from the shipyards of the Kennebunks. At peak production, 100 ships were built in a single year.

The advent of steel hulls and the waging of the American Civil War sparked the decline in production for the shipyards along the Mousam and Kennebunk rivers. Kennebunkport began its transition into a summer resort community, where visi-

tors came for the beaches and other natural beauties. Today, the draw of coastal scenery, grand old homes, sailboats resting in their slips, and the boutiques of Dock Square make Kennebunkport one of the most popular destinations in Maine. These attractions are augmented by a cultural atmosphere popular with artists, photographers, and writers. Authors have published novels using the town as the setting, and in the case of Booth Tarkington, even written from a schooner tied dockside in the harbor.

Just as the sea brought people and goods to and from the Kennebunks, so too did the railroad. On the chapter ride you'll follow an abandoned rail line now used as an underground utility corridor and community recreation path. The trip is a basic one, starting from the Sea Road School, with no big bumps or other pitfalls to worry about as the legs stretch out.

The Rachel Carson National Wildlife Refuge borders both sides of the trail. In addition to views of the flora and birds in the refuge, the trail runs a parallel course to the Mousam River. The singletrack paths that depart into the woods are off limits to bikes, so riders tempted by narrow trails will have to wait until the route changes beyond Maine 9 to a nicely beaten, more challenging singletrack path that follows the same flat course of the rail line.

The trail next travels on raised bed across a saltwater marsh, with grasses and wildflowers to line your way, as well as the occasional thorny branch to watch for. Forest envelops you again on the far side of the marsh until soon you reach the trail end at Sea Road. To continue the ride on to Dock Square, take a right on Sea Road. Continue along the ocean before the route loops back inland to the traffic light at the intersection with Maine 9. Turn right at the light to roll into the village.

Ride Information

📞 Trail Contacts:
Kennebunk Parks and Recreation Department, Kennebunk, ME (207) 985-6890

🕐 Schedule:
Open year-round

❓ Local Information:
Kennebunk-Kennebunkport Chamber of Commerce, Kennebunk, ME, (207) 967-0857

📍 Local Events/Attractions:
Webhannet Golf Club, Kennebunk, ME (207) 967-2061 • Saint Anthony's Monastery, Kennebunkport, ME (207) 967-2011

🚲 Local Bike Shops:
Cape Able Bike Shop, Kennebunkport, ME (207) 967-4382 – they run road rides and mountain bike rides and offer family paced rides • Bikes, Blades, and Boards, Kennebunk, ME (207) 967-3601 or 1-800-220-0907 • Bretons Bike Shop, Wells, ME (207) 646-4255 • Wheels and Waves, Wells, ME (207) 646-5774

🗺 Maps:
USGS maps: Kennebunk, ME; Kennebunkport, ME

A trip beyond the Dock Square via Ocean Avenue will lead to Saint Anthony's Monastery, a meticulously kept Tudor estate on a point of land northeast of town. Iron gates lead to lush grounds and gardens. Shrines and Saint Anthony's Chapel offer a silent refuge from the more heavily touristed places outside the gates.

Rachel Carson's Silent Spring

The book Silent Spring *led a revolution of social, scientific, and legislative change in the most revolutionary decade of the 20ᵗʰ Century. Rachel Carson's 1962 book brought the words "ecology" and "environment" out of the vernacular of researchers and professional specialists and into livingroom debates across the country. She also confronted the public with a frightening prophesy: If left unchecked, humankind's will and modern power to manipulate the interwoven natural systems of the planet would one day destroy the very lands, rivers, and air that allow life.*

Carson's book dealt a great deal with insecticides (particularly DDT) and touched on industrial and radiological contamination. She noted documented cases of the loss of bird, fish, animal, and human life attributable to the chemical poisoning of the earth. Whether it was because the public was ready to listen or the message was too powerful to ignore, Silent Spring *changed the attitudes of millions.*

Today, the Rachel Carson National Wildlife Refuge protects over 5,000 acres of marsh, shoreline, and forest along the Maine coast. Named in her honor and managed by the United States Fish and Wildlife Service, the refuge is spread over 10 parcels from Kittery to Cape Elizabeth. It preserves precious habitats from development and other threatening human intrusions. Visit the refuge headquarters off of Maine 9 on the way into Kennebunkport from Wells to learn more about Rachel Carson and marsh ecology. And pick up a copy of Silent Spring. *Though written 38 years ago, this classic is well worth reading today.*

MilesDirections

0.0 START toward the Sea School parking lot's exit. Make a right turn before coming to Sea Road, onto the trail that cuts across the school driveway. The trail leads behind residences and crosses neighborhood streets.

2.1 Cross Maine 9. The trail continues as a singletrack on the opposite side of the road.

2.8 The trail ends at Sea Road across from the Webhannet Golf Club. Turn around and return by the same trail to conclude the ride on dirt. *[**Option.** Or, turn left onto Sea Road for a paved road and smooth finish back to the Sea School.]*

5.6 Ride ends at the school parking lot.

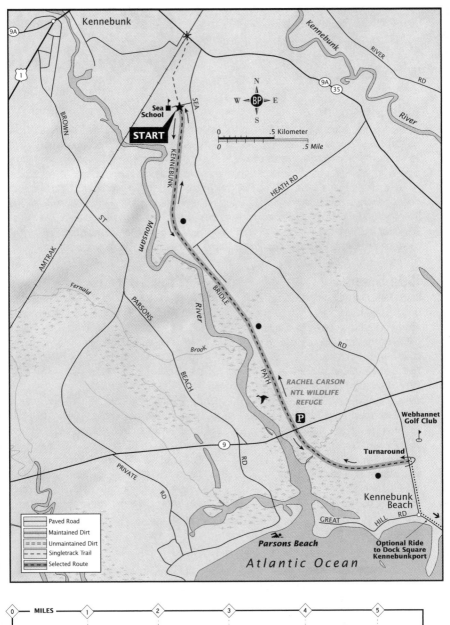

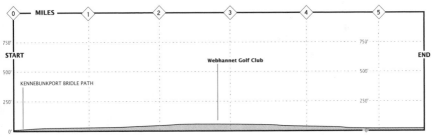

Clifford Park In-town Loop

Ride Summary

Trails are scarce in this region of Maine, due in part to the buildings and roadway infrastructure that support the summertime tourism economy of Old Orchard Beach, Saco, and Biddeford. Clifford Park offers an oasis from the waves of visitors and country clutter stores. Despite its semi-urban surroundings, the park boasts some challenging off-road terrain. Wilderness adventure is not to be had on the chapter ride, but many trail thrills will be found. The trip begins on an abandoned road before following a doubletrack spur. This spur loops to eventually rejoin the central park loop. The three-mile ride affords short rocky downhills, climbs up tight singletrack, and quiet privacy by the sounds of The Falls. The loop is too short to exhaust anyone on just one lap, so plan on riding your own variations. There's a map-board of trails located at the Clifford Park parking lot to help you.

Ride Specs

Start: From Clifford Park in Biddeford, ME
Length: 3-mile loop
Approximate Riding Time: 30 minutes
Difficulty Rating: Moderate due to surface variety and trail obstacles
Trail Surface: Mixed sections of smooth or rocky doubletrack and singletrack with wet areas and minor elevation changes
Lay of the Land: Large forested park nestled within an area of heavy commercial and residential development
Elevation Gain: 46 feet
Land Status: Town park
Nearest Town: Biddeford, ME
Other Trail Users: Hikers, joggers, and cross-country skiers
Wheels: Mountain bikes only

Getting There

From Saco, ME: Follow ME 9 South across the Saco River into Biddeford. ME 9 South turns left at a set of lights and becomes Pool Road / ME 9 South. Take this left and Clifford Park will be 0.5 miles farther on the right. Park in the lot before the tennis courts.

By Bus: Shuttle Bus offers service from Portland and Old Orchard Beach to Main Street in Biddeford. From the bus stop proceed south on Alfred Street and turn left on Pool Road. Clifford Park will be 0.5 miles farther on the right. Schedule Information, (207) 282-5408 or *www.shuttlebus-zoom.com*.
DeLorme: Maine Atlas & Gazetteer: Map 3, C-2

Throughout Maine, rivers split settlements into sister towns or twin cities. Biddeford and Saco have shared such a relationship since each was incorporated in 1631. They prospered by the power of their great textile mills, situated on opposite banks of the Saco River. The architectural legacy of these mills still dominates the main road from Saco through downtown Biddeford, where modern businesses now fill many restored spaces.

The area boasts a strong tourism economy, with large numbers of travelers heading to Old Orchard Beach, Ferry Beach State Park, and the Scarborough beaches. Found more to the north of Biddeford, motels, restaurants, water parks, and other amusement centers cater to the summer crowd. There are spots that get

unruly with summer revelers, especially at night, and other places where a family would feel right at home.

Sometimes being a mountain biker means searching out trails where you didn't think any could exist. A look at any map of the seaboard in the Biddeford and Saco area reveals the lack of open public spaces, aside from beaches. Clifford Park distinguishes itself in this respect by offering a number of good trails packed into a confined area. Dozens of spurs and connectors lead off the main loop to new challenges. Longer trails used by ATVs head out beyond the Clifford Park boundary. Except for big hills, all the obstacles one might wish for can be found, including rocky drop-offs, downed trees, and tight, twisting singletrack. In the spring there'll be mud too, and plenty of it in certain areas.

Immediately into the ride, you climb a small rise to a false flat before reaching a second, rather eroded climb that gives the day's first challenge. You continue on smooth doubletrack before reaching a tighter section of trail beyond a small gravel pit. The singletrack loops back toward the heart of Clifford Park, where more technical riding awaits. Alternating between singletrack and doubletrack, the route becomes scattered with rocks, puddles, and shallow elevation changes. Trail surfaces also vary between exposed rock, mud, gravel, and sand. Throughout the woods, you will often see blocks of granite standing alone or piled haphazardly from Biddeford's now defunct quarrying industry.

After passing within earshot of The Falls, where West Brook cascades 20 feet over jagged rock, you rejoin the main park loop doubletrack. Other trails branch off to the left, returning in a short distance to the chapter loop. You'll bypass these though, coming soon upon a muddy section where consecutive turns head you on a short, difficult singletrack climb to the knoll above the Clifford Park tennis courts and playground. From here, it's a quick trip home to the parking lot to reset your bearings and strike out on a loop of your own making.

An active citizens group, Saco Bay Trails, has made great efforts throughout the Saco Bay area to secure trail access for hikers, mountain bikers, and equestrians. While many of their current trails are best for short nature walks, two trails in progress should pique a mountain biker's attention. One is the CMP Trail, which runs seven miles from the Saco River to Scarborough along a Central Maine Power transmission line. The second trail is the Eastern Trail, an abandoned railroad grade just east of U.S. Route 1 in Saco. A project backed by many advocates, the Eastern Trail is expected to run through Maine coastal towns from South Portland to Kittery, covering 50 miles. In the grand vision, it would be the local leg of the East Coast Greenway, the planned mountain biking highway stretching from Calais, Maine to Key West, Florida. Imagine that.

Ride Information

◐ Trail Contacts:
Biddeford Department of Parks and Recreation, Biddeford, ME (207) 283-0841

◐ Schedule:
Open year-round

◐ Local Information:
Biddeford/Saco Chamber of Commerce, Saco, ME (207) 282-1567 • **Town of Biddeford,** Biddeford, ME or www.lamere.net/biddeford

◐ Organizations:
Saco Bay Trails, Saco, ME (207) 282-0514 or www.sacobaytrails.org

◐ Local Bike Shops:
Bicycle Habitat, Saco, ME (207) 283-2453 • **Quinn's Bike and Fitness,** Biddeford, ME (207) 284-4632 • **Cape Able Bike Shop,** Kennebunkport, ME (207) 967-4382

◐ Maps:
USGS maps: Biddeford, ME

MilesDirections

0.0 START by biking through the opening in the fence and turning right uphill onto the gravel road. Pass a doubletrack that departs to the left.
0.2 Pass a second doubletrack departing to the left. Take a right at the next doubletrack, marked by a large rock outcrop to the right.
0.5 Homes come into view. Turn left here. Head through a grassy area and cross gravel-fill along the edge of a swamp. Continue through a small gravel pit and straight up a rise into the woods. When homes come into view again, the trail loops left, back toward the park's center.
1.0 Pass a low ledge and come to a "T" intersection. Turn right onto the doubletrack. The trail narrows and splits. Follow the left fork, away from the small rock slab. Pass a water hole on the left. Turn right at the "T" intersection with the doubletrack.
1.4 Beyond the abandoned granite quarry site the trail splits. Bear left. Midway down a shallow rocky singletrack descent, there is a blue tarp in the woods to the left.

1.6 Turn left at the "T" intersection. At the next intersection continue straight across the intersecting trail, over a hump, and down to The Falls. At The Falls, the trail loops back left, toward the center of Clifford Park.
1.9 Continue across the four-way intersection with a long sandy trail. Turn right at the next intersection, onto the doubletrack. Pass an industrial fence on the right.
2.3 Bear left through a muddy area. Houses and buildings are in view. Immediately beyond the mud, turn right onto a grassy singletrack. Turn right again 300 feet later through an opening in the trees onto a tight, uphill singletrack. The Clifford Park playground can be seen from the top of the hill. Turn left up the bermed turn.
2.6 Turn right at the four-way intersection with the doubletrack. Turn right at the "T" intersection with the gravel road and descend to the parking lot.
3.0 One loop down.

The Falls.

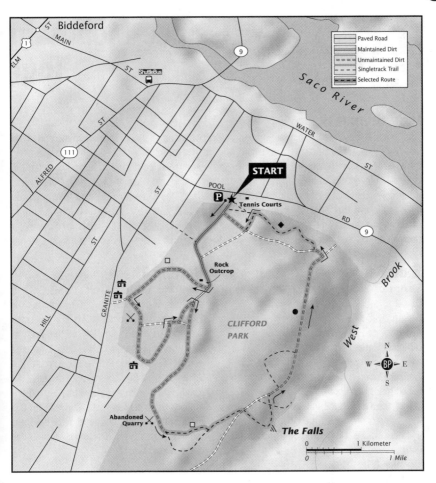

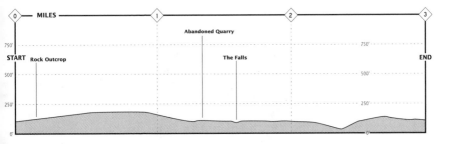

Ossipee Mountain Tour

Ride Summary

This "out in the country" loop near Portland challenges your endurance, and toward the end of the ride tests your ability as a mountain biker. A maintained gravel access road climbs up and along the side of Ossipee Mountain. You negotiate a rutted abandoned track that leads into a flat trip along smooth fast doubletrack. Along this doubletrack you pass the site of a washed out dam where water flows below concrete walls that toppled years ago. You climb a paved road that loops you back to the trail that brought you past Ossipee Mountain. After retracing familiar terrain back to McLucas Road, you can climb up to the fire tower and enjoy the spectacular views from the top of Ossipee Mountain. Otherwise continue down the access road back to the start of the ride.

Ride Specs

Start: From McLucas Road, near Waterboro Center
Length: 13.5-mile circuit
Approximate Riding Time: 2 hours
Difficulty Rating: Moderate. Hilly, with generally good trail surfaces in dry conditions
Trail Surface: Gravel, paved, and unmaintained roads and doubletrack
Lay of the Land: Rural forested countryside, with one prominent mountain, flat valley land, and the sizable Little Ossipee Pond to the north
Elevation Gain: 1,172 feet
Land Status: Town roads (mostly abandoned ones)
Nearest Town: Waterboro, ME
Other Trail Users: Hikers, motorists, ATVs, snowmobiles, and hunters (in season)
Wheels: Mountain bikes only

Getting There

From Saco, ME: Head north on ME 5. From the junction of ME 5, U.S. 202, and ME 4 in East Waterboro, continue for 1.8 miles to Waterboro Center. Turn left at the flashing light. Continue through the stop sign and across Old Alfred Road. Drive past the Waterboro Fire Station and onto Ossipee Hill Road. Take the immediate right after the fire station onto McLucas Road. Continue for 0.3 miles and park to the side of the road, past the cluster of homes. *DeLorme: Maine Atlas & Gazetteer:* Map 2, A-4

A trip by car from Waterboro Center to Kennebunk Landing on the seacoast takes little more than an hour. Triple that time if you're going by bike. If you were to go by oxen, and happen to be dragging a two-masted schooner, give yourself three days. And remember, the oxen and schooner option only works in the winter when the snow is deep enough for the ship's cradle to slide.

Undeterred by the sneers of doubting neighbors, Captain Josiah Swett and his son William set out in 1818 to build a two-masted schooner, not only from the trees of Ossipee Mountain, but more impressively, from atop Ossipee Mountain—near the present-day fire tower. Swett's plan was to drag the finished ship overland—

consider that Ossipee Mountain was largely an unbroken forest at the time with primitive, windy roads—to Kennebunk Landing, where his son would take over the helm and sail her to the West Indies. Needless to say, the locals thought he was out of his mind. But that's just what he did.

The schooner was called the *Waterboro*, and it ended up taking 50 oxen from the farms of Waterboro and the surrounding towns to slide the 43-ton ship the entire 25 miles to the ocean. But once there, with William Swett as captain, the Waterboro sailed off to the West Indies. To the right, 1.6 miles into this ride, you'll pass the Captain Swett Cemetery, marked by a plaque and fencing.

Over 100 years after the Swetts sailed their ship off Ossipee Mountain an inferno ravaged the forested land of Waterboro. The fire of October 1947 came after 108 days of no rain and ultimately burned 20,000 acres. It scorched the mountain and homes throughout town on its 10-day rage. To appreciate nature's power to cleanse and heal, consider that only a few decades ago charred woodland cradled nearly every mile of this ride.

Where fire conquered Ossipee Mountain, the typical mountain biker may not be so lucky. Your assault begins with a gradual climb that steepens before the dust gets coughed out of the lungs. Though grades vary, the struggle against gravity continues to alternate between loose and hard-packed surfaces until the McLucas Road transition to abandoned doubletrack. The abandoned section takes a slightly downhill course through a rutted, sometimes muddy area along the hillside.

A stint on gravel road interrupts the divine doubletrack riding, and you then return to the woods at the sharp bend in Ross Corner Road. The clear flat track

runs northwest over good trail surfaces. About two miles into the ride, a well-worn trail departs to the left where the chapter loop heads straight into a short rocky downhill. The diversion onto the well-worn trail leads out of the forest canopy and into a sandy area by a washed out dam. An alternative route to reaching the dam is to head straight where the chapter loop turns right—just past mile 4.7. Manage a few sharp twists in the path. At the top of the rise and before the sandpit, depart to the left onto the singletrack. Cross a section of jagged rocks and walk through the opening in the brush ahead and to the left.

Away from the dam site and back onto the chapter loop, the final section of doubletrack west of Ross Corner Road clears the woods soon enough. Homes begin to appear well before the transition from gravel road to pavement. It's a rolling ride on Clark Bridge Road out to the turn onto Ross Corner Road. A respectable climb follows, with sinister flats that deceive one into a false sense of accomplishment.

Familiar scenery returns on McLucas Road, until the 1.1-mile climb to the fire tower. The first fire tower was constructed in 1918 to keep a lookout on approaching forest fires from the nearby towns. After the fire of 1947, the tower was condemned and in 1954 a new tower was built. Open views of the countryside are well worth the leg-burning climb to the top. Just beyond the tower, on the western side of Ossipee Mountain, a wide granite ledge offers a similarly spectacular overlook. While resting above the splendor of Maine's forested hills refresh yourself with the thought of the extended downhill ride all the way home.

Ride Information

● Trail Contacts:
There are no trail contacts as these are abandoned town access roads or paved roads.

◔ Schedule:
Open year-round

◕ Local Events/Attractions:
Little Ossipee Pond offers fishing, boating, and lakeside cottage rentals. A public boat launch sits off of ME 5, 0.4 miles beyond the flashing light that signals the turn for the ride start. • The Taylor House Museum, Waterboro, ME – open Saturdays from 1:00 P.M. to 3:00 P.M. • Town of Waterboro – For local events, visit the their webpage at www.mixnet.net/~waterboro

● Accommodations:
Blackburn's Campground borders the ride start on one side, and Little Ossipee Pond on the other. Waterboro Center, ME (207) 247-9966

● Mountain Bike Tours:
Backcountry Excursions, Touring Hostel and Lodge, Limerick, ME (207) 625-8189 or www.backcountryexcursions.com

● Local Bike Shops:
Goodrich's Bike Shop, Sanford, ME (207) 324-1381 • Gorham Cycles, Gorham, ME (207) 839-2770

● Maps:
USGS maps: Waterboro, ME

The broken dam, never repaired after wash-out.

MilesDirections

0.0 START the ride up gravel McLucas Road.

1.4 Continue on the flat road to where another gravel road turns uphill to the left. A logging highway bends to the right, but continue straight on the abandoned doubletrack. Pass the Captain Swett Cemetery.

2.5 Turn left onto the paved Ross Corner Road. Continue 0.1 miles to the sharp left bend in the road. Two gravel trails come into the paved road here. Turn onto the gravel trail to the right, which is actually an abandoned portion of Middle Road.

4.7 Continue straight where the more traveled trail banks left into a sandy area by a washed out dam. Immediately enter a short, rocky downhill. Turn right at the first doubletrack. If you reach a river flowing through an oasis of sand, you just missed the turn. The doubletrack soon crosses a buried culvert before opening onto gravel road. Farther on, the gravel transitions to pavement.

7.5 Ride along Clark Bridge Road with a clear view across open fields to the left. Pass a derelict barn, a farmhouse, and more derelict out buildings. Turn right immediately beyond these onto Ross Corner Road.

8.8 Climb to the top of the hill, where the pavement transitions to gravel. Turn left at the hilltop back onto gravel McLucas Road. Continue straight on McLucas Road, which will soon transition to unmaintained doubletrack.

9.9 Soon after passing Captain Sweet Cemetery again, make a right turn off McLucas Road up the steep gravel car road toward the fire watchtower.

10.4 At the gate to the right, turn uphill again. Manage a steep difficult climb to the fire watchtower. Continue to the left past the tower and onto a singletrack that leads to an exposed granite overlook of the northwestern countryside. Return to McLucas Road by the same route that brought you up.

12.1 Turn right onto McLucas Road. After a flat section, enjoy a long downhill run.

13.5 The end.

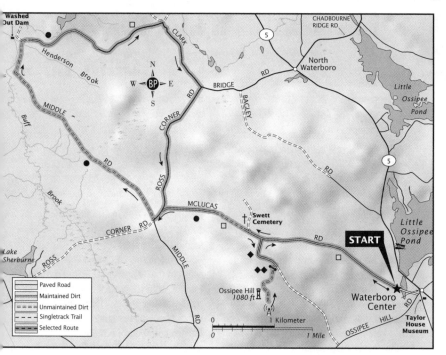

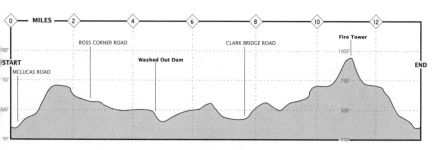

Lake Arrowhead Dam Loop

Ride Summary

The Lake Arrowhead Dam Loop starts and finishes by the shallow water of Lake Arrowhead. You'll warm up on an unmaintained gravel cut-through road before a bit of pavement sends you around to the dirt again. Once off the tarmac, a secluded ride along the Never-ending Trail begins. Things soon point up for about a mile, which makes the moderate grade more strenuous than might be expected. After the long climb, one steep difficult downhill is part of the loop. It deserves caution and attention.

Ride Specs

Start: From the Lake Arrowhead Dam, off of New Dam Road
Length: 9.6-mile loop
Approximate Riding Time: 1½ hours
Difficulty Rating: Low technical difficulty overall, with one difficult rocky and eroded downhill. Physically easy, with few demanding climbs and one difficult descent.
Trail Surface: Doubletrack, gravel roads, abandoned roads, and paved roads.
Lay of the Land: Rural forest with minor grades and one hill to climb. Some clearcut acreage in process of reclamation.
Elevation Gain: 470 feet
Land Status: Private property abuts the abandoned town roads and active roads of the chapter loop.
Nearest Town: Waterboro, ME
Other Trail Users: Motorists (even on the roads in the woods), ATVs, and snowmobilers
Wheels: Mountain bikes only, though hybrid riders can explore all but the downhill portion of the ride at mile 4.1

Getting There

From Waterboro, ME: Follow U.S. 202 / ME 4 North to the junction of ME 5. At the junction turn left onto ME 5 North. Continue on ME 5 north for four miles. Turn right onto Silas Brown Road. At the stop sign turn right onto Chadbourne Ridge Road. Soon after passing between Lake Arrowhead (to your left) and Little Ossipee Pond (to your right), turn left at the base of the hill onto New Dam Road. Follow this for 2.8 miles to the bridge. Park to the left in the grass and gravel area by the boat launch. *DeLorme: Maine Atlas & Gazetteer.* Map 2, A-4

For the riders who began traveling North Waterboro's local trails in the mid 1980s, the much-forgotten dirt roads east of Lake Arrowhead don't have proper street names. Instead they go by monikers like the Never-ending Trail, Outer Toothpick, and Skidder Sin. Mention these in the right circles and you'll no doubt illicit tales of great crashes—and probably get to see the small but worthy scars that linger—or hear wistful remembrances of riders pedaling through silent forest corridors, while three bike lengths ahead a hawk in flight scouts the terrain.

But not all of life's leisure time is spent in the saddle. Most of the other local diversions tend to revolve around the water. Lake Arrowhead, born from a dammed river, is the hot spot for anglers and boat captains—especially those who have become familiar with its shallow depths. Out at Love Island the depths increase, and so too does the fun. The island seems to unite this mixed community of summer residents and locals. It's also the kind of place where grandchildren might have to wait in line behind their grandparents for a run at the rope swing.

The only line you'll find on this ride, however, will be the one of trucks with boat trailers jockeying for their shot at the boat launch. It's here that your mountain bike trek starts. Across the pavement, a gateway of branches hides the secret of an overlooked and unmaintained gravel road. The road diverges from the Little Ossipee River on a flat run out to paved Doles Ridge Road. You'll encounter areas that puddle during wet times, but it's uncomplicated going on the whole. Trails to the right of Doles Ridge Road head down to the river and often lead to secluded fishing holes. Another popular fishing spot sits at the intersection with Maine 117 in Hollis, sight of a good alternate start for the loop.

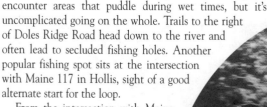

From the intersection with Maine 117, it's back onto dirt again, traveling on an unmarked gravel road that soon transitions to doubletrack. Trails and unmaintained roads branch off for the remainder of the ride, but most dead-end at log landings or loop back to the main route.

After the successive intersections about a half-mile onto the doubletrack, a settlers cemetery hides to the left. Many of the gravestones have toppled over or sunk into the earth. A few remain upright at the head of depressions in the ground. The cemetery signals the start of a long gradual climb up the Never-ending Trail. Loose surfaces and minor erosion along the ascent make things interesting, but the search for the top ends in a little more than a mile. Next begins a difficult section on the steep and eroded doubletrack of Skidder Sin. Parts of the

267

incline are stepped, where there will be nothing but a six to 12-inch free fall from the top of large roots and rocks until touchdown on terra firma again. For kicks, there are some overhanging branches to maneuver around. Skidder Sin is short though, and an aberration given the overall ease of the trail surfaces.

The rhythm of climbing and descending continues with another climb. This one starts in the woods on a snowmobile trail before it emerges on pavement by a home to the right. It's the last lengthy climb before a flat section on gravel road and a minor vertical insult leading into a long shallow descent. Earlier in the loop this descent had been the "...long gradual climb up the Never-ending Trail."

On the final leg of the route through the woods, expect sandy sections and a wide track cleared by recent logging. There will be a puddle covering a stone fill where the trail floods between two wetlands, particularly after several days of rain. Farther on, at a culvert, the trail makes an uncharacteristic dip. New Dam Road and the parking area aren't far beyond this.

Ride Information

Trail Contacts:
There are no trail contacts as these are either active or abandoned town roads.

Schedule:
Open year-round

Local Events/Attractions:
Lake Arrowhead, North Waterboro, ME – *recreational boating and fishing* • **Little Ossipee Pond,** Waterboro Center, ME – *recreational boating and fishing*

Mountain Bike Tours:
Backcountry Excursions, Touring

Hostel and Lodge, Limerick, ME (207) 625-8189 or *www.backcountryexcursions.com*

Local Bike Shops:
Goodrich's Bike Shop, Sanford, ME (207) 324-1381 • **Gorham Cycles,** Gorham, ME (207) 839-2770

Maps:
USGS maps: Waterboro, ME; Limington, ME

MilesDirections

0.0 START on the opposite side of the pavement from the parking area, by the sign for New Dam Road, and ride the unmaintained gravel road.

0.7 Turn right onto paved Doles Ridge Road. Continue to the stop sign at Maine 117.

1.7 Turn right at Maine 117 and cross the bridge over the Little Ossipee River. Turn right onto the gravel Chadbourne Ridge Road (the Never-ending Trail) immediately after the bridge.

2.0 The more traveled part of the road bends right at a house. Instead, follow the well-worn doubletrack that goes left of the house.

2.7 A trail comes in from the right at an island of trees. At the intersection immediately after this, roll to the right. Begin a long gradual climb.

4.1 At the flat section atop the climb turn left, uphill, just before passing through a clearcut area. Begin a rough steep descent on Skidder Sin.

4.9 Turn right (away from Hollis) at the snowmobile trail junction, onto Lord Road (Brickhouse Road). You'll first climb through the woods and then on pavement before coming to the four-way intersection with Chadbourne Ridge Road (the Never-ending Trail).

6.1 Turn right at the stop sign onto the dirt portion of Chadbourne Ridge Road. Pass homes and then a communications tower.

7.8 Roll left where a snowmobile trail departs to the right. Another trail comes in from the right. At the intersection immediately following, bear left of the island of trees and enter a trail with many sandy sections.

9.4 Turn right onto paved New Dam Road.

9.6 Reach your vehicle. If Lake Arrowhead calls you in for a swim, be wary of the currents near the dam.

Alternate Starts: Try starting at the intersection of Doles Ridge Road and ME 117 at the Little Ossipee River in Hollis, ME.

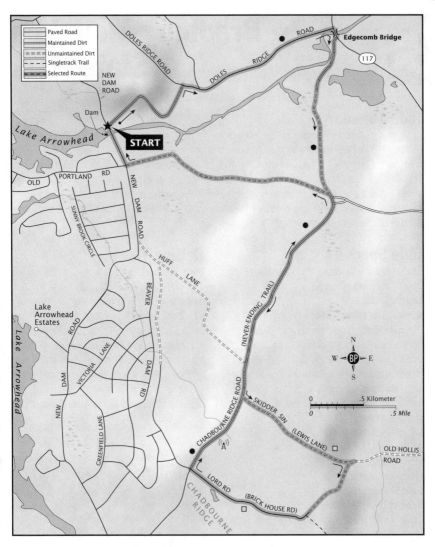

36

Bradbury Mountain State Park

Ride Summary

Great mountain biking exists just four miles from the popular outlet shopping center of Freeport, Maine. The ride begins on an easy doubletrack trail well marked with white blazes, and then enters a harder doubletrack on the Northern Loop Trail before embarking on the truly difficult Boundary Trail. The Boundary Trail is a primitive singletrack along an old stone wall. The reward comes at the summit of Bradbury Mountain where one can survey the countryside and Casco Bay. Even without a mountain bike, the park and Bradbury Mountain make a great natural discovery just out of the shadow of commerce and tourism.

Ride Specs

Start: From the Bradbury Mountain State Park parking area, off Maine 9

Length: 5-mile loop

Approximate Riding Time: 1 hour

Difficulty Rating: Technically easy start on doubletrack leads to difficult singletrack of rocks and roots. Physically difficult due to the technical nature of the Boundary Trail.

Trail Surface: Doubletrack and singletrack, with rocks, loose surfaces, and sharp grade changes to watch out for

Lay of the Land: Rolling forest with boulders and bog areas. Bradbury Mountain is the primary feature.

Elevation Gain: 324 feet

Land Status: State park

Nearest Town: Freeport, ME

Other Trail Users: Hikers, equestrians, and cross-country skiers

Wheels: Mountain bikes only

Getting There

From Freeport, ME: Take I-95 North to ME 125 (Exit 20). Take ME 125 north for 0.1 miles to a stop sign and a sign for Bradbury Mountain State Park. Turn left here onto Pownal Road. Follow Pownal Road for just over four miles (it turns into Elmwood Road) to the intersection of ME 9. At the intersection turn right onto ME 9 North. Bradbury State Park is on the left, 0.6 miles ahead and marked by a large sign. *DeLorme: Maine Atlas & Gazetteer.* Map 5, C-5

People rely on his parkas to keep them alive in sub-zero temperatures, on his tents to shelter them in the deepest of winter, and on his hiking boots to get them from Mount Katahdin to Springer Mountain, or just across the University of Maine, Orono campus, after a January snowstorm. Mr. Leon Leonwood Bean probably couldn't have imagined that his first 100 pairs of Bean boots would start a business with a revenue today in excess of one billion dollars. But, he probably didn't figure on 90 of those original 100 sales being returned due to faulty stitching. That was in 1911.

L.L. Bean refunded his customers' money without argument. He took his lesson and corrected the faults of his boot, the same boot L.L. Bean, Inc., sells today for hunting, autumn walks in the woods, and puddle splashing on the way to school. By being steadfastly honest, demanding the best quality and function from his products, and backing everything he sold with a 100 percent satisfaction guarantee, L.L. Bean's reputation spread across the state, then across the country. Today his original one-man enterprise is recognized worldwide.

Mr. Bean passed away in 1967, handing the company presidency over to his grandson, Leon Gorman. The business has grown remarkably, and yet very little has changed. They still back their 16,000 products with an unsurpassed guarantee, company employees still trek into the woods to test the goods they sell (just as Mr. Bean always did), and the company is still headquartered out of Freeport, Maine.

Today, the L.L. Bean store on Main Street in Freeport serves as the anchor for a thriving retail center. Restaurants, shops, and factory outlets fill downtown buildings and spread south along U.S. Route 1. Over 3.5 million people per year visit Freeport, making it one of the most popular destinations in the state. As with most of Maine though, the land outlying its well-visited areas quickly fades to rural, which is what you need for a good bout of mountain biking.

Bradbury Mountain State Park is four miles west of the L.L. Bean store and the center of Freeport. A fair sized park at 590 acres, it boasts ball fields, a playground, and a hiking trail to the rocky summit of Bradbury Mountain. The mix of doubletrack and single-track trails within the park boundary allows you to challenge yourself and your bike, and yet you're always within two miles of help. From the peak you can see Casco Bay to the east. During spring and fall migrations osprey, red-tailed hawks, and eagles may be seen flying the thermals overhead.

Acquired in 1991, the 100 acres of Knight Woods in the southern portion of the park serve as the warm-up venue for the ride. The first half mile will take you on a flat doubletrack course, before the body loosens up on a short twisting downhill. You'll pass a spur to the Snowmobile Trail, and then ride along a rock wall before turning back toward the Bradbury Mountain State Park headquarters.

Many erosion control dams cut across the doubletrack Northern Loop Trail. These four-inch high black strips flex

when ridden over and are not likely to cause a pinch-flat. Off the Northern Loop Trail and onto the Boundary Trail, the dams go away and hard technical riding begins. Rocks and sharp elevation changes keep the challenge high on this primitive singletrack. To your right runs one of the many stone walls throughout the region. Closer to Bradbury Mountain, you'll cross three wooden bridges before another trail joins the Boundary Trail for the final distance to the summit.

From the top of Bradbury Mountain you'll descend the Northern Loop Trail back to the parking area. Another, slightly longer option would be to follow the marked Tote Road Trail down to the Ski Trail and back home. Maintain a low speed for either route, as both are typically crowded with hikers and other bikers.

L.L. Bean has been open every minute of every day since 1951.

Ride Information

📞 Trail Contacts:
Park Manager, Bradbury Mountain State Park, Pownal, ME (207) 688-4712

🕐 Schedule:
Open year-round

💲 Fees/Permits:
$1 per person

❓ Local Information:
Freeport Merchants Association, Freeport, ME 1-800-865-1994 or *www.freeportusa.com*

Accommodations:
Bradbury Mountain State Park, Pownal, ME (207) 688-4712 – *There are 41 primitive sites for year-round camping.*

🚲 Local Bike Shops:
L.L. Bean, Inc. 95 Main Street, Freeport, ME (207) 865-4761 • **National Ski and Bike,** Freeport, ME (207) 865-0523 • **Yarmouth Bicycle Shop,** Yarmouth, ME (207) 846-1555 • **New England Mountain Bike,** Falmouth, ME (207) 781-4882 • **Bath Cycle & Ski,** Woolwich, ME (207) 442-7002 • **Haggetts Cycle Shop** Portland, ME (207) 773-5117 • **Back Bay Bicycle Portland,** ME (207) 773-6906 • **Cycle Mania,** Portland, ME (207) 774-2933 • **Allspeed Bicycle & Ski,** Portland, ME (207) 878-8741

🗺 Maps:
USGS maps: North Pownal, ME

MilesDirections

0.0 START by facing the ball field. Ride to the right corner of the parking lot onto Knight Woods Loop. Cross Maine 9 and bear right, away from the Link Trail. Continue counter clockwise around the doubletrack Knight Woods Loop. White blazes will mark your way.

0.6 The trail joins with a snowmobile trail where it then rolls left across a wooden bridge. Stay with the white blazes as the snowmobile trail departs from the main trail.

1.2 After riding a straight course along a stone boundary fence on the right, connect back to the out leg of the Knight Woods Loop at a "T" intersection. Turn right at the intersection. Continue back across Maine 9 to the parking area.

1.4 Turn right at the signboard by the ball fields. Follow the blue blazed Northern Loop Trail around the left edge of the ball fields. You will begin climbing gently past the Ski Trail.

1.9 Turn right at the Boundary Trail. You'll cross a wooden bridge and ride a long course along the stone boundary wall marking the park perimeter. The Boundary Trail has orange blazes.

3.4 The Summit Trail joins from the right. Continue left (uphill) with the blazes.

3.6 At the Bradbury Mountain summit, head left onto the doubletrack Northern Loop Trail. Blue blazes guide you downhill to the parking lot.

5.0 Reach the parking area and your vehicle.

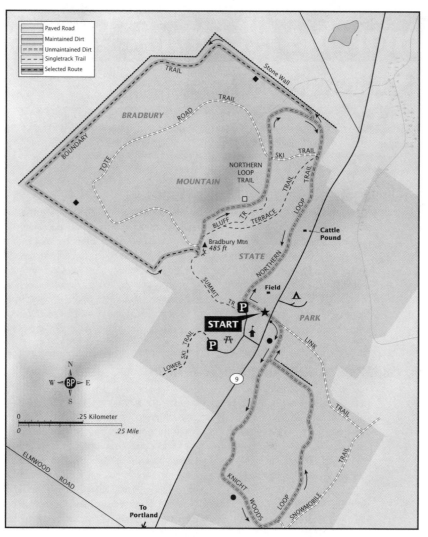

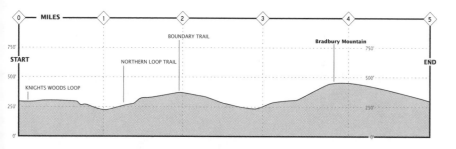

Honorable Mentions

Southern Coast Region

Compiled here is an index of great rides in the Southern Coast region that didn't make the A-list this time around but deserve recognition. Check them out and let us know what you think. You may decide that one or more of these rides deserves higher status in future editions or, perhaps, you may have a ride of your own that merits some attention.

(K) University of Southern Maine Woods

Located at the University of Southern Maine campus in Gorham, the university woods offer a 10-mile network of single and doubletrack trails. Gorham Bike and Ski, on Main Street in the center of town, runs weekly off-road rides and a Wednesday night racing series in the summer. They also sponsor the Alden Hill Challenge, an annual Maine Mountain Bike Series event, on the campus trails. Call Gorham Bike and Ski for the lowdown on the university woods, or for group ride schedules. Contact them at (207) 773-1700 or visit www.gorhambike.com. To get to the campus, take Exit 6 off of Interstate 95 though Portland, then follow Maine 25 west for seven miles. Once into Gorham, look for the USM signs. *DeLorme: Maine Atlas & Gazetteer:* Map 5, E-2

(L) Highwater Trail Along the Wild River

A difficult loop using the Highwater Trail and the Wild River Trail gives an 18-mile test of endurance and perseverance. The ride starts across from the Hastings Campground road, off of Maine 113 near its intersection with Wild River Road in Hastings, Maine. The Highwater Trail travels the northwest bank of the Wild River for nine miles before crossing it at the Spider Bridge and returning to the parking area via the Wild River Trail and Wild River Road. Short, steep climbs and stream crossings add to the other natural obstacles such as rocks and blowdown. Earlier river crossings can shorten the trip by many miles, though bridges may be washed out—and the river runs too fast in spring to consider fording it. There may be hiking traffic on the trails and autos on Wild River Road. Wild River Campground is at the center of the loop. This ride is within the Evans Notch Ranger District of the White Mountain National Forest. The ranger station has a mountain bike map of the trail and can be reached at (207) 834-2134. *DeLorme: Maine Atlas & Gazetteer:* Map 10, C-1

(M) Turner Property

The state operates 15 miles of trail along the Androscoggin River from Turner to Auburn, Maine. The route falls under the jurisdiction of the ATV Program, so you'll share the woods with motorized users. Take Turner Center Bridge Road from Maine 117 to find the trailhead parking lot, which is near the river. Once into the woods, you'll be on abandoned road and doubletrack. Views of farm pasture and second growth hardwoods frame your ride over the rolling terrain. For a map of the trail, call the ATV Program at (207) 287-4958. *DeLorme: Maine Atlas & Gazetteer:* Map 11, D-4

(N) Jay to Farmington ATV Trail

This abandoned rail line runs 14 miles from Jay to Farmington, site of the University of Maine, Farmington campus. The Jay trailhead sits off Maine 4, with TNS Cyclery located right nearby. Most maps, including the DeLorme: Maine Atlas & Gazetteer, still show the rail line, so you might opt to pick up the trail at a convenient intersection along its route. Expect minimal grade change, which is a nice break in this hilly area. Also, sections of sand interrupt typically easy pedaling on the gravel surface. Call the Maine ATV Program office at (207) 287-4958 for a map. *DeLorme: Maine Atlas & Gazetteer:* Map 19, E-5

(O) Mount Blue State Park

A collection of shared-use trails adorns the Mount Blue State Park network in Weld, Maine. While hiking trails are off-limits, 25 miles of gravel roads, singletrack, and doubletrack welcome mountain bikers. Doubletrack trails are typically moderate to difficult, while gravel roads offer a physical challenge over easier surfaces. Camping is available on site and trails are posted with ATV markings. The state ATV trail map outlines the network, and more detailed maps are available at park trailheads. From U.S. Route 2, follow Maine 142 north to Weld. Call Mount Blue State Park at (207) 585-2738 for more information. *DeLorme: Maine Atlas & Gazetteer:* Map 19, C-3

(P) Baxter State Park

The Baxter State Park perimeter road will take you 43 miles from end to end of this 201,000-acre state park. Though the gravel road is open to cars, mountain bikers can find their challenge in the long climbs and descents on the route. Regrettably, bikes are prohibited from the many miles of trails. With the heaviest auto traffic to the south near the Mount Katahdin trailheads, a stay at one of the park's more northern campgrounds makes a good base from which to ride. The Baxter Park Authority, at (207) 723-5140, manages the park, which is 18 miles northwest of Millinocket, Maine. *DeLorme: Maine Atlas & Gazetteer:* Map 51, D-1

From Augusta

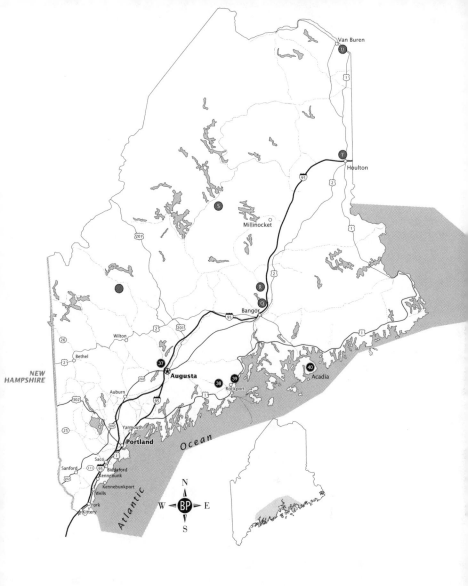

To Acadia

From Augusta to Acadia

The Augusta to Acadia rides are pulled from the Kennebec/Moose River Valleys, Mid Coast, and Downeast/Acadia regions of the state. They are spread across a large amount of land, much of which is distinct. Riding in the valley area of Maine's capital Augusta sees little in the way of extended elevation gains. While the ride near Augusta uses a state sponsored OHRV trail to keep things on the up-and-up, rural and abandoned roads are easily found anywhere in the area.

Throughout the Mid Coast region of Maine popular seaport villages form the attraction for visitors. One can take windjammer cruises from many of the harbors or go deep-sea fishing or island hopping. When it's time to bike, one should know that though elevations are low so close to the ocean, the area's focal point, Camden, is known as the place where "the mountains meet the sea."

The northernmost ride covered in Maine travels within a small portion of the most family-friendly biking network in America—if not the world. That network consists of the carriage trails in Acadia National Park. Here, beside the Atlantic Ocean, sits 40,000 rolling and unspoiled acres with over 55 miles of smooth gravel paths on which to chart a day's adventure.

Summerhaven ATV Trail

Ride Summary

At the northwest edge of Augusta lies six miles of fast paced mountain bike terrain. At times you'll feel you're on a roller coaster as banked turns swoop downhill on a freewheeling run. The Summerhaven ATV Trail—an OHRV (Off-highway Recreational Vehicle) trail established by the state—invites experienced riders to rocket over rolling and twisting doubletrack. Intermediate riders can hammer out their own pace to test fitness and skill. Intrepid beginners will enjoy the challenge of this well marked and very rideable loop.

Ride Specs

Region: Kennebec and Moose River Valley
Start: From the Summerhaven ATV Trail and Tyler Pond boat launch access road, off of Summerhaven Road
Length: 6.0-mile loop
Approximate Riding Time: 1½ hours
Difficulty Rating: Technically moderate overall, due to sketchy gravel trail surfaces and grade changes. Physically moderate due to some short but steep hills and sandy sections that are hard to pedal
Trail Surface: Fast doubletrack over gravel and loam surfaces worn down by ATVs, short sections of unpaved road, as well as open gravel pits and sand pits to negotiate
Lay of the Land: Generally flat, forested land with numerous areas of open sand/gravel excavations
Elevation Gain: 283 feet
Land Status: State sponsored recreational trail

Nearest Town: Augusta, ME
Other Trail Users: ATVs, motorcyclists, and snowmobilers
Wheels: Mountain bikes only (unless you want to ride a dirt bike or an ATV)

Getting There

From Augusta, ME: Take I-95 North to ME 27 North (Exit 31). Turn onto ME 27, away from Augusta center. Three miles farther look for the Wicked Good Restaurant on the right. Turn left across from the restaurant onto Summerhaven Road. Bear right where Sanford Road departs to the left. Just under one mile from ME 27, turn left onto the gravel access road marked with the boat launch sign. Park in the cleared lot on the left at the top of the access road. *DeLorme: Maine Atlas & Gazetteer:* Map 12, B-5

M aine's largest and busiest seaport at that time, Portland, wanted the honor. Bangor, the lumber shipping center on the Penobscot River, had its points to make. But when the political dust settled, it was the old Plymouth Colony trading outpost of Augusta, midway between Portland and Bangor, who emerged as the capital of the fledgling state of Maine. The year was 1727.

The Maine Department of Conservation is counted among the many state departments that call Augusta home. Under the Department of Conservation's wing rests the Bureau of Parks and Lands with its All Terrain Vehicle (ATV) Program. Through use of public lands and access agreements with private landowners, the ATV Program administers a vast network of ATV and snowmobile trails throughout the state of Maine, routes totaling thousands of miles. While some of these loops run through the northern wilderness, the Summerhaven ATV Trail remains the most convenient in the network to population centers. The remaining Maine ATV Trails are touched upon in the Honorable Mentions section to follow. You're encouraged to explore the remote woods of Vacationland.

The chapter loop begins along the ridge northeast of Tyler Pond. While trails depart to the right, each intersection is clearly marked by signs bearing ATV symbols that point out the proper route. These ATV signs appear off and on throughout the loop, directing you in the right direction.

Early on, you'll pass a small clearing with views of Tyler Pond to the left. An abandoned auto may still mark the spot as well. Beyond the clearing you'll turn up a small rise and ride a flat section. Then you descend a twisting bermed chute, a nice joyride that you may regret hitting too slow the first time through.

Beyond the turn-off for Fairbanks Pond you'll need to pay closer attention to trail markers. Though arrows point out all turns, there are fewer ATV signs marking the trail. This is especially true at the first gravel pit. As you make your way through a former excavation, turn right at the "T" with an abandoned road, and then immediately roll left away from the second pit. Your course will continue on worn doubletrack, where the frequent passing of ATVs has loosened many surfaces and banked the numerous turns.

Gravel road crossings appear in the middle of the loop. Look for the posted signs that warn you in advance of the crossings. Along this section of the ride a small gravel pit with a short sand slope challenges the legs and traction. This pit serves as a primer for a monster excavation that comes up later. On the start to the final third of the ride you'll come upon a giant sandpit. This is a challenging trail surface for a mountain bike. To avoid plowing to a quick stop, ride along the right rim of the pit—the several unconnected sections of short trail provide for a firmer ride.

More small gravel pits will come and go on the remainder of the loop, but the trail leans toward twisting doubletrack and wider abandoned roads. As a note to anyone riding the Summerhaven ATV Loop in the fall, particularly in the weeks before deer season, local hunters often use these pits to sight their rifles. If the sound of gunfire becomes a worry, the gravel Sanford Road (Old Belgrade Road) runs parallel to the trail and to the left. The road accompanies the trail beginning at the big sandpit and will return you to Summerhaven Road. Once to Summerhaven Road, a left turn on the pavement gets you back to the parking area.

Ride Information

🕐 Trail Contacts:
Maine Bureau of Parks and Recreation, Augusta, ME (207) 287-4958

🕐 Schedule:
Open year-round

❓ Local Information:
Kennebec Valley Chamber of Commerce, Augusta, ME (207) 623-4559

🔱 Local Events/Attractions:
Maine State Museum, Augusta, ME (207) 287-2301 • **Children's Discovery Museum,** Augusta, ME (207) 622-2209 • **Maine Statehouse,** Augusta, ME (207) 287-1400 • **Old Fort Western,** on the Kennebec River, Augusta, ME (207) 626-2385

🚲 Local Bike Shops:
Auclair Cycle and Ski, Augusta, ME (207) 623-4351 • **Poulin Cycle,** Augusta, ME 1-800-773-1852 • **Hilltop Bike and Ski,** Manchester, ME (207) 623-6219 • **CM Cycle,** Waterville, ME (207) 873-5490

🅝 Maps:
USGS maps: Augusta, ME; Belgrade, ME

MilesDirections

0.0 START toward Summerhaven Road. Turn left at the marked trail just prior to the pavement.

0.4 Turn left at the marked intersection.

0.9 Turn left uphill, with the direction arrows at the marked intersection.

1.3 Carve through a series of downhill bermed turns. Bear left where the trail to Fairbanks Pond comes in.

1.5 Bear left again, following the arrow for snowmobile trails South 29 and Club Loop. A wetland will be on your left before a sandy section of road climbs up to a loose gravel surface. Bear right at the fork, following the arrow nailed to the tree rather than continuing under the forest canopy. Continue across the sandpit and straight into a manageable climb. Avoid the climb that heads up steeply to the right of the sandpit.

1.9 Turn right at the "T' intersection with the rocky gravel road, Mount Vernon Road. Bear left immediately, through a grassy section. Bear left again onto the worn-down ATV trail.

2.3 Cross a gravel road where ATV signs are posted. Continue up a small hill with concrete blocks laid down for erosion control.

2.5 Turn right at the "T" intersection.

2.9 Cross Old Belgrade Road, a gravel road, and continue with the ATV trail markers.

3.3 Emerge from the woods into a small gravel pit. Continue straight across the access road and up a sandy slope on the other side. There is an ATV trail sign at the top of the slope.

3.4 Cross the gravel Mount Vernon Road. Stay with the well-worn ATV trail as others branch off. Pass a caution sign for the gravel pit. Descend left into the huge excavation and plot your own course along its sandy length, or try to piece together the several short unconnected trails along the right rim.

4.0 Bear right at the end of the sandpit, toward the small fence with the orange signs. On approach to the fence, look for the marked ATV trail that re-enters the woods to the left.

4.8 Turn right with the trail. Immediately veer left at the ATV trail sign. Ride along the right rim of a small gravel pit.

5.1 Turn left at the "T" intersection. Ignore the upcoming right that breaks off from the ATV trail. Come to Sanford Road and continue across.

6.0 You are finished.

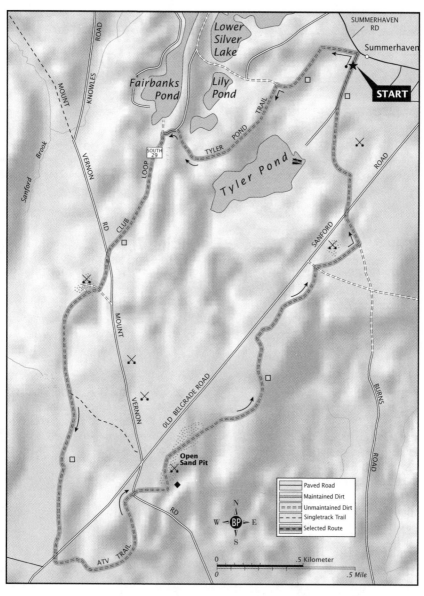

Legend:
- Paved Road
- Maintained Dirt
- Unmaintained Dirt
- Singletrack Trail
- Selected Route

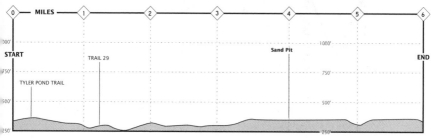

Camden Snow Bowl Sampler Loop

Ride Summary

This short, hard loop waits just a few miles from the center of popular Camden, Maine. While day-trippers and vacationers browse about the downtown shops and look out over Camden Harbor, you'll start your ride up Ragged Mountain, the peak for the Camden Snow Bowl. After negotiating a climb up the ski slopes, a technical singletrack leads you into the woods where a mix of tight trails, doubletrack, and abandoned roads are to be found. The last mile of the loop is a steep drop to the bottom that refreshes you for another trip around the three-mile course.

Ride Specs

Start: From the base of Ragged Mountain at the Camden Snow Bowl
Length: 3-mile loop
Approximate Riding Time: 30 minutes
Difficulty Rating: Technically difficult due to steep sections and rocky trails. Physically difficult due to climbs and descents over technical terrain.
Trail Surface: Grassy ski slopes, rocky singletrack, doubletrack, and unmaintained gravel roads with loose or slippery areas
Lay of the Land: Hilly forested land surrounding ski slopes of Ragged Mountain
Elevation Gain: 604 feet
Land Status: Town property
Nearest Town: Camden, ME
Other Trail Users: Hikers, cross-country skiers, snowmobilers, and hunters (in season)
Wheels: Mountain bikes only

Getting There

From Rockport, ME: Drive U.S. 1 North into Camden. Just beyond the Rockport / Camden town line, turn left after the Subway sandwich shop onto John Street. You'll come to a stop sign at Mechanic Street, a road that originates from the center of Camden. Turn left at the stop sign. Follow the main road (and the small signs with the skier illustration) to the Camden Snow Bowl. Turn left into the ski area, 3.4 miles from U.S. 1. Park in the large gravel lot at the base of the mountain. *DelLorme: Maine Atlas & Gazetteer.* Map 14, D-3

M aine's mountain bike racecourses tend to be very hard and technical. You'll often find short but steep climbs, chainring-smashing rocks, and a peppering of exposed roots. On the morning of event day, the trails are sometimes little more than deer paths, which local course designers have dressed with ribbon in order to wear in the groove for a great hometown singletrack. Water, rather than soil, dominates spring trail conditions, as brook crossings become cold rivers to wade through. The courses are beautiful in a grueling way, and riding one makes a lot more sense than staying home on a Sunday to mow the grass. The Camden Snow Bowl Sampler Loop is a typical Maine racecourse.

The annual start of the Maine Mountain Bike Series, the Spring Runoff, travels up and around little Ragged Mountain (1,300 feet), which lies just west of the popular vacation spot of Camden. True to Maine racecourse tradition, it's a very difficult ride, and mile-for-mile one of the toughest you're likely to encounter along the coast. By summer, the rocks that everyone slid over in the Spring Runoff appear as fields of trail mines, and the hills riders could only run up offer just enough dry traction for a leg-burning workout.

Ignoring the difficulty of hitting the course after snowmelt, a summer or fall ride goes like this: You begin as unsuspecting prey to the mountain as you roll across the grass at the base, before dodging up the ski slope and off into a short singletrack spur. You cross from the singletrack to the T-bar lift and then ride directly up at granny-gear pace. After switching to another steep ski slope climb, you enter the woods on an undulating singletrack that introduces the day's first extended section of rocks and roots.

Returning to doubletrack, two trails fork to the right on a course to the top of Ragged Mountain. These are side-trips, though, and not on the chapter loop, which narrows past the two splits and degrades as it scribes a taxing climb past a cabin. You emerge onto an unmaintained rocky road that descends. The subsequent intersection with the logging road begins a chicane that sends you back toward the Camden Snow Bowl. You cross a snowmobile bridge and two turns later enjoy a very fine stretch of singletrack as you weave into a rough descent. Use caution on the descent as wetness may linger on lower slopes, causing wheels to slide sideways over slick rocks.

KEEP ALL BODY PARTS INSIDE TOBOGGAN UNTIL YOU COME TO A COMPLETE STOP !!!!

Once out to the grass-covered ski slope you can turn up to the top of Ragged Mountain for views of Bald Mountain and Penobscot Bay to the north, unless you're a purist who only climbs mountains from the base. In that case, continue downhill to the finish of the chapter loop and walk up.

If the Snow Bowl Loop sounds too hard, and its sister ride described in the Camden Hills State Park chapter doesn't appeal to you, the paved roads of the Camden and Rockport area make a great way to explore Mid-coast Maine. In Camden you might want to ride up the paved Mount Battie Auto Road, which leads to summit views of Camden Harbor and Penobscot Bay. An alternative trip leaves at Chestnut Street from Camden center, heading south to the peninsula east of Rockport Harbor. Beauchamp Road in Rockport returns you north along the harbor.

The large islands of the area also make exceptionally popular summer day-trips for cyclists. Vinalhaven's roads are mostly paved and are serviced by ferry from the state dock off U.S. Route 1 in Rockland, Maine. East of Vinalhaven, and accessible by ferry from Stonington on the tip of Deer Isle, waits Isle Au Haut. Dirt roads and stretches of pavement lace Isle Au Haut, portions of which lie within Acadia National Park.

Ride Information

ⓣ Trail Contacts:
Camden Parks and Recreation, Camden Snow Bowl Manager, Camden, ME (207) 236-3438

ⓢ Schedule:
Trails are open for riding from snowmelt onward, but don't expect dry terrain until mid June in a typical year.

ⓘ Local Information:
Rockport/Camden/Lincolnville Chamber of Commerce, Camden, ME (207) 236-4404 or 1-800-223-5459 or *www.camden-me.org* • **Camden Snow Bowl,** Camden, ME or *www.midcoast.com/~snowbowl*

ⓔ Local Events/Attractions:
Ferry service to Vinalhaven, ME, from Rockland, ME, Maine State Ferry Service, (207) 624-7777 • **Ferry service to Isle au Haut,** ME, from Stonington, ME, Stonington Dock Co. and Ferry Service, (207) 367-6516

ⓐ Accommodations:
Towne Motel, Camden, ME (207) 236-3377 – *offers nice rooms and reasonable rates within walking distance to downtown Camden*

ⓑ Intercity Bus Service:
Concord Trailways, 1-800-639-3317 or *www.concordtrailways.com*

ⓛ Local Bike Shops:
Oggibike, Camden, ME (207) 236-3631 • **Brown Dog Bikes,** Camden, ME (207) 236-6664 or *www.browndogbike.com* • **Maine Sport Outfitters,** Rockport, ME (207) 236-7120 • **Birgfeld's Bicycle Shop,** Searsport, ME (207) 548-2916

ⓝ Maps:
USGS maps: Camden, ME; West Rockport, ME

MilesDirections

0.0 START at the base of the mountain, and then turn to the right between the lodge and the ski trails. Continue past the last lift, a T-bar, onto the farthest ski slope. Turn uphill, keeping to the right edge of the slope. At the stand of birch trees, turn right onto a short singletrack that goes into the woods. Emerge from the woods and back onto the ski slope. Cut across to the T-bar. Ride uphill along the T-bar until the next cross-mountain trail.

0.2 Turn left away from the T-bar. Continue across the mountain to the slope with the ski racing starter houses. Turn uphill on the slope, following the worn groove as it moves left across the mountain. You'll pass a doubletrack that leads into the woods.

0.4 The ski slope turns upward steeply just ahead. Turn left into the woods onto the singletrack. Follow the uphill trail at the immediate split.

0.6 Pass a 12-foot spur trail to a doubletrack on the left. Come to the "T" intersection with another doubletrack. Turn right and then follow the trail left at the next two forks.

0.9 Pass a small cabin located a short distance to the left of the trail.

1.6 Intersect an unmaintained gravel road at an island of trees. Turn left along a flat section before beginning a fast rocky descent. A trail will join from the right.

2.1 Turn right at the gravel road, and then immediately turn left onto a narrower trail. Houses will be in view before this turn. Cross a decrepit snowmobile bridge.

2.3 Turn right onto the doubletrack just beyond the snowmobile bridge. Immediately turn right again onto the singletrack that may be marked with lime green ribbon. The singletrack soon follows along the edge of a steep slope with "Private Property" signs to the right. Join a second trail and turn right. Cross pallets laid down across a brook. Climb up the steep slope to join another singletrack, and ride the rocky descent until it emerges onto the ski slope for the final bonus run to the bottom.

3.1 You have completed a Maine Race loop.

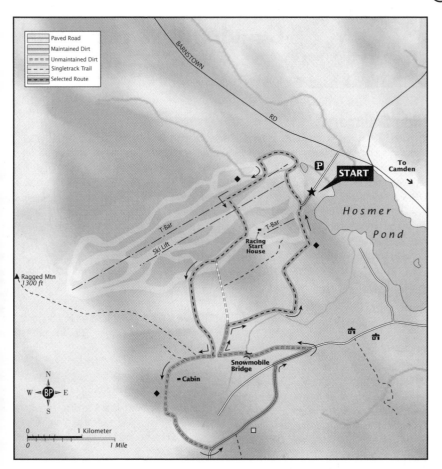

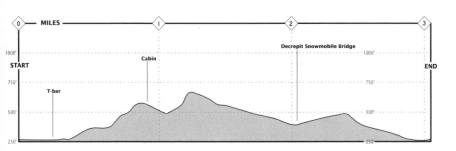

Camden Hills State Park
Shared-Use Trails

Ride Summary

Camden, "Where the mountains meet the sea," has attracted wide-eyed vacationers since the 19th Century, but not until recently has it drawn visitors due to its spectacular mountain biking opportunities. Now you can ride the super-technical singletrack, Summer Bypass, which pulls out all the stops in its rocky, challenging course. Before reaching the Summer Bypass, you'll tackle the doubletrack Snowmobile Trail, which offers a slightly lesser threat than the anticipated Summer Bypass does. On return from the midpoint of the ride, you'll have a long shallow climb followed by a second run at the Summer Bypass. As an option for riders seeking a less difficult trip overall, the alternate start location, mentioned in the cues, gives access to a nice six-mile ride on gated gravel roads through Camden Hills State Park.

Ride Specs

Start: From Camden Hills State Park, off U.S. Route 1, two miles north of downtown Camden
Length: 10.6-mile out-and-back
Approximate Riding Time: 2½ hours
Difficulty Rating: Technically difficult due to rocks, roots, and other trail obstacles along the doubletrack and singletrack sections. Physically difficult due to length, an extended section of technical singletrack, and a long gravel road climb.
Trail Surface: Rocky, twisting singletrack and doubletrack sandwiched around an open leg of gravel road
Lay of the Land: Hilly, forested countryside sloping down to the Atlantic Ocean
Elevation Gain: 1,519 feet
Land Status: State park
Nearest Town: Camden, ME
Other Trail Users: Hikers, equestrians, snowmobilers, and hunters (in season)

Wheels: Mountain bikes only, though hybrids will manage the gravel road section beginning at the "Alternate Start" (in the Miles/Directions section)

Getting There

From Camden, ME: Follow U.S. 1 North for approximately two miles. Camden Hills State Park is on the left and marked by a large brown sign. *DeLorme: Maine Atlas & Gazetteer:* Map 14, D-4

amden village's attraction comes from its deep roots as a shipbuilding and sailing port. The downtown buildings and homes remind one of an era when Maine led the world in ocean commerce. Many of the boats now ported in Camden Harbor haul in lobsters and fish for the local restaurants or head out with tourists on sport-fishing and windjammer tours. Clearly, the water remains an integral part of life in Camden Harbor.

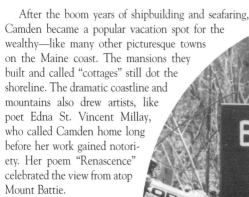

After the boom years of shipbuilding and seafaring, Camden became a popular vacation spot for the wealthy—like many other picturesque towns on the Maine coast. The mansions they built and called "cottages" still dot the shoreline. The dramatic coastline and mountains also drew artists, like poet Edna St. Vincent Millay, who called Camden home long before her work gained notoriety. Her poem "Renascence" celebrated the view from atop Mount Battie.

Integrated into Camden's modern-day character are many cultural offerings, from live summer performances at the Camden Opera House, to jazz festivals, to gallery exhibits. While lunching at harbor-side restaurants, an off-shore yacht race may be going on, or a canoeist may be testing the calmer waters of Lake Megunticook. It's a town of variety, where New York style mingles with country comfort.

Until recently, rangers turned mountain bikers away from the 30 miles of trails in Camden Hills State Park's 5,474 acres. The prohibited routes included many underused sections, even along gravel and abandoned roads. The Fiddlehead Cycling Club worked with park officials to gain rider access to certain trails, including the chapter route. They came out to work at trail maintenance days and designed and built the Summer Bypass Trail that cuts around a notoriously wet section of the Snowmobile Trail. The Fiddlehead Cycling Club also drew support from the International Mountain Bike Association (IMBA), ultimately winning the battle against a small faction of people determined to keep bikes out.

The route you'll ride, thanks to your local friends, leaves from the camping area and climbs a short access road past the water tower. It then covers the difficult Snowmobile Trail on an up and down rocky course. Soon into the trip comes the Summer Bypass Trail. The Summer Bypass epitomizes classic, technical Maine singletrack. It weaves between trees spaced a bar-width apart, crosses brooks and seasonal runoff paths, and switches back on itself only to turn again in the right direction. Laid out to keep steep elevation changes to a minimum, the challenge of the trail creates the fun.

All hardship goes away on return to the Snowmobile Trail. You'll have to cross a shallow brook, but after the ski hut foundation it's gravel roads for three miles out until the turnaround at Youngtown Road. You'll climb on the return, and then tackle the Summer Bypass again for a final memory of trail cut from scratch by mountain bikers.

Ride Information

Trail Contacts:
Park Manager, Camden Hills State Park, Camden, ME (207) 236-3109

Schedule:
At the discretion of the Park Manager, trails may be closed to prevent damage.

Fees/Permits:
$2 per person

Local Information:
Rockport/Camden/Lincolnville Chamber of Commerce, Camden, ME (207) 236-4404 or 1-800-223-5459 or *www.camdenme.org*

Local Events/Attractions:
A full calendar of local events can be found at *www.camdenme.org*

Accommodations:
Campsites are available at Camden Hills State Park, Camden, ME (207) 236-3109

Restaurants:
The Sea Dog Brew Pub, Camden, ME, (207) 236-6863 • **The Waterfront,** Camden, ME (207) 236-3747

Intercity Bus Service:
Concord Trailways 1-800-639-3317 or *www.concordtrailways.com*

Organizations:
The Fiddlehead Cycling Club, Camden, ME (207) 236-4592

Local Bike Shops:
Brown Dog Bikes, Camden, ME (207) 236-6664 or *www.browndogbike.com – sales and rentals delivered to vacation lodgings* • **Oggibike,** Camden, ME (207) 236-3631 • **Maine Sport Outfitters,** Camden, ME (207) 236-7120 • **Birgfeld's Bicycle Shop** Searsport, ME (207) 548-2916

Maps:
USGS maps: Camden, ME; Lincolnville, ME

Camden Harbor covered up for winter.

MilesDirections

0.0 START from the Camden Hills State Park tollbooth. Turn right at the fork onto the paved road toward the camping area. Continue straight, soon coming to signs for Mount Megunticook trails and shared-use trails. Follow these signs.

0.2 Bear left toward the Mount Megunticook trails. Veer right where the actual Mount Megunticook Trail leaves to the left (no bikes allowed up the mountain). Continue past the water tower onto the white-blazed Snowmobile Trail.

1.2 Signs announce the boundary of the hunt-restricted zone. To the left of the boundary, another sign points to the singletrack Summer Bypass Trail. Turn left onto Summer Bypass and follow its blue blazes on a winding course.

2.2 Pass double blazes and rejoin the Snowmobile Trail. Turn left, cross Spring Brook, and then pass the foundation and chimney of a former ski hut. The trail becomes a gravel road.

2.8 Pass Zeke's Trail on the left. Begin a short downhill and at the bottom slow or stop for a bridge that is missing some boards.

3.5 Unpaved Bald Rock Road comes in from the right.

5.3 Come upon the trailhead parking lot at Youngtown Road. Turn around and return on the gravel road you just descended.

8.3 Pass the ski hut foundation. Cross Spring Brook, and take the first right onto the single-track Summer Bypass. Follow the blue blazes.

9.4 Turn right at the "T" intersection with the Snowmobile Trail.

10.6 End of ride.

Alternate Starts: There is a parking lot at the northern trailhead, off Youngtown Road by its intersection with ME 173 in Lincolnville. A large sign marks the trail. This is the start for easy gravel road riding, with a long-ish but not steep climb.

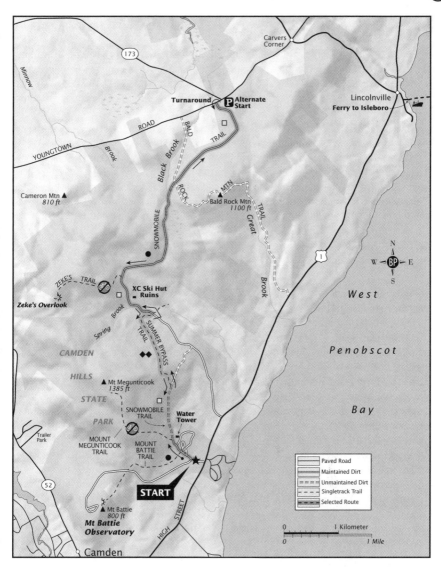

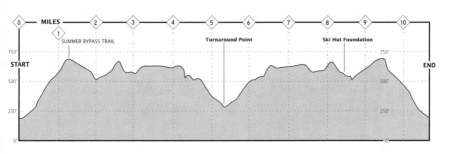

Acadia National Park Carriage Trail: The Eagle Lake Loop

Ride Summary

Within Acadia are mountains, rivers, lakes, and over 55 miles of gated gravel roads for the cyclist to explore. This ride gives you only a glimpse of the varied terrain, but it's perfect for anyone looking for an exhilarating morning or afternoon pedal. Groups will have no problem staying together and kid trailers and hybrid bikes roll smoothly along the Lake Loop that encircles Eagle Lake. Lake Loop's scenery, easy terrain, and proximity to Eagle Lake make it a popular ride in the summer.

Ride Specs

Start: From the Eagle Lake Carriage Trails parking area
Length: 6.3-mile loop
Approximate Riding Time: 1 hour
Difficulty Rating: Easy, with one lengthy hill
Trail Surface: Smooth, gated gravel roads, wide enough for groups of riders to pedal abreast
Lay of the Land: Island with forest, open areas of exposed bedrock, and expertly maintained paths cut into steep hillsides
Elevation Gain: 656 feet
Land Status: National park
Nearest Town: Bar Harbor, ME
Other Trail Users: Hikers, joggers, cross-country skiers, and equestrians
Wheels: Child trailers, hybrid bikes, or single-speed children's bikes will ride well on many carriage paths. Mountain bikes can easily handle all carriage paths.

Getting There

From Bar Harbor, ME: Head west on ME 233. Take the first left after the posted turn for Park Loop Road and Cadillac Mountain (the left is signed "Eagle Lake Carriage Trails"). Alternate parking is located 100 yards farther up on the right. Many alternative parking areas are available. Consult a road map or the official Acadia National Park Map for the most convenient one.

Park Shuttle Bus: (Memorial Day to Labor Day) Island Explorer offers a shuttle to and from the Bar Harbor Village Green and the Eagle Lake Parking Area. From Bar Harbor take the Eagle Lake Bus (Number 5). Each bus carries five bicycles. For more information and rates call Downeast Transportation at (207) 667-5796. *DeLorme: Maine Atlas & Gazetteer:* Map 16, B-3

By force of wind and water, eroded earth crept eastward off the North American continental plate toward the sea where it met with volcanic ash, seaweed, and other deposits to form the early foundation of Acadia National Park. Magma then surged from within the earth to transform the bedrock into the coarse-grained granite that marks much of the area's geology today.

Millions of years of erosion rounded the land surrounding Acadia to form a single mountain ridge, stretching from east to west. Glaciation later swept through the area, carving out lakes and valleys and forming the cliff-walled inlet of Somes Sound—in the end creating out of the single ridge 17 separate mountains. The last glacier retreated some 100,000 years ago and left the north face of Acadia's mountains sloped and smooth, while fracturing the granite of the south faces into jagged steps. Climatic changes finally forced the enormous sheets of ice—which ranged in thickness from 3,000 to 9,000 feet—to recede. The melt-off raised the ocean level to the point where Acadia was cut off from the mainland, leaving only its peaks exposed as islands.

A cadia National Park is the most visited national park per acre in the United States.

The Acadia region has felt the tread of humanity's footsteps for only a few thousand years due to these geological changes. Ancient tools and pottery of the Red Paint People mark the legacy of the first known inhabitants. Much later, at the time of the European arrival to North America, the Abenaki Indians wintered on Pemetic, which translates to "sloping land." The progress of exploration in the New World, followed by the growth of the United States, slowly brought non-native settlements to the island. Farming, shipbuilding, and fishing were the means by which these people made their livings.

By mid 19th Century, the powerful and placid beauty of the Maine coast spurred development of the tourism industry. Restaurants and inns for the "summercators" fueled the area's presence as a resort community. Some of the wealthiest families in history such as the Astors, Rockefellers, Pulitzers, Vanderbilts, and Morgans built summer homes on nearby shores.

Development hasn't always spurred conservation, but these wealthy summercators preserved Acadia National Park for later generations. The families came for the land's rugged beauty, but saw the ease with which it might be destroyed by development. In 1901, Charles W. Eliot, then president of Harvard University, formed the land trust that gathered properties into the first national park acquired entirely through private land donations.

The mention of Acadia's carriage paths brings a smile to any cyclist acquainted with the roads. Built to preserve horse drawn travel, and to ward off the intrusion of the automobile, John D. Rockefeller, Jr. initiated the construction of the single lane gravel roadways. Today, the 55 miles of carriage paths remain closed to motorized vehicles. This means that cyclists, walkers, equestrians, and cross-country skiers can journey along the coast and up to the mountains without tons of steel bearing down on them.

For the chapter loop, you'll have an easy time pedaling on a wide, fantastically maintained carriage road around Eagle Lake. It's a popular route no matter the time of year. You'll begin from the boat launch parking lot on the south side of Maine 233, riding clockwise around the water. The loop travels a flat course for the first few miles before turning east and climbing away from the water. The ascent here on the middle third of the loop is not harsh, though it is a change from the effortless beginning. Past the climb you'll drop to the second numbered intersection of the day, then roll down and up again on a shorter more gradual course before a flat stretch home.

Upon completing the ride you may decide to further explore Acadia or participate in one of the park programs. Rangers lead hikes to several mountains, as well as nature walks for children. They give presentations on park history, from its geological formation to the lives of those who have called it home. On summer evenings free slide-lectures and concerts are put on at campground amphitheaters. All are welcome to these shows.

Bar Harbor

Bar Harbor and the towns surrounding Acadia National Park have thrived as vacation destinations for over 100 years. Fascination with Downeast coastal village culture brings people back time and again to take in the local character. Boutiques, galleries, shops, ice cream parlors, and fishing charters give character to these small Maine towns. The harbors fill with charter boats, whale watching cruises, and vacation boats. During the early morning hours you can catch the lobstermen setting out to bait their traps. Mount Desert Island offers dramatic landscapes, fine dining, and shopping along with a selection of accommodations. The town offerings, along with the serene and wild surf of the Atlantic Ocean and the rugged geology of Acadia, make Mount Desert Island the largest and most diverse vacation destination on the Maine coast.

Consider a daytime excursion to the Abbe Museum where Native American artifacts and cultural history are on display. Nearby, the Nature Center offers exhibits on the natural history of Acadia. The wildlife logbook at the Nature Center is a place for children and adults to record the animals they have seen while at Acadia.

To enjoy the natural gifts of Acadia, bike up the Cadillac Mountain auto road to open summit views of the island and the Gulf of Maine. Or visit Somes Sound, the only fjord on the East Coast of America, where the power of glaciers carved the great gorge from solid rock. Whatever your choice or desire, bring your bike to this cycling friendly place to appreciate it all up close.

Ride Information

📞 Trail Contacts:

Park Superintendent, Acadia National Park, Bar Harbor, ME (207) 288-3338

🕐 Schedule:

Trails are open year-round.

💲 Fees/Permits:

The Acadia National Park entrance fee is $5 per vehicle, or $3 per person if you bike in. Fees cover a one-week visit.

❓ Local Information:

Acadia National Park, Bar Harbor, ME (207) 288-3338 or *www.acadia.net/anp* • **Acadia Information Center**, Ellsworth, ME (207) 667-8550 or 1-800-358-8550 • **Bar Harbor Chamber of Commerce**, Bar Harbor, ME (207) 288-3393 or 1-800-288-5103 or *www.barharborinfo.com* • **Southwest Harbor/Tremont Chamber of Commerce**, Southwest Harbor, ME 1-800-423-9264 or *www.acadia.net/ swhtrcoc* • **Mt. Desert Chamber of Commerce**, Northeast Harbor, ME (207) 276-5040 (summer) • **Schoodic Peninsula Chamber of Commerce**, Gouldsbouro, ME (207) 963-7658 • **Deer Isle/Stonington Chamber of Commerce**, Stonington, ME (207) 348-6124 (summer) or *www.acadia.net/ deerisle* • **Vermont Transit** 1-800-552-8737 – *operates a Boston to Bar Harbor bus during the summer* • **Concord Trailways** 1-800-639-3317 or *www.concordtrailways.com – summer service from Bangor and Portland*

📍 Local Events/Attractions:

Wildwood Stables, Mount Desert Island, ME (207) 276-3622 – *offers horse drawn carriage rides, and has stall space for the horses of vacationers to Acadia National Park*

🛏️ Accommodations:

Blackwoods and Sewall Campgrounds, Acadia National Park, ME 1-800-365-2267 – *Tent sites at campgrounds cost from $8 to $13 per night. Trailers up to 35 feet can be accommodated at specific sites.*

👥 Organizations:

The Friends of Acadia is a citizen group that helps maintain the vitality of the national park. Visit them at *www.foacadia.org.*

🚲 Local Bike Shops:

Bar Harbor Bicycle Shop, Bar Harbor, ME 1-800 824 2453 or *www.barharborbike.com* • **Acadia Bike and Canoe**, Bar Harbor, ME (207) 288-9605 • **Kind Cycle**, Bar Harbor, ME (207) 288-0444 • **Northeast Harbor Bike Shop**, Mount Desert, ME (207) 276-5488 • **Southwest Cycle**, Southwest Harbor, ME 1-800-570-8579 • **Maine Mountain Bike**, Ellsworth, ME 1-800-400-4950 • **Wheels of Bar Harbor**, Bar Harbor, ME 1-800-491-9433

🗺️ Maps:

USGS maps: Bar Harbor, ME; Salisbury Cove, ME; Southwest Harbor, ME; Seal Harbor, ME

MilesDirections

0.0 START by heading left from the boat launch. Ride clockwise along the shore of Eagle Lake.

2.0 Come to Intersection 7. Turn right, with the sign for the Around Lake Loop. Soon begin a gradual climb.

3.9 Roll down to Intersection 8 for another right turn, again following the sign for the Around Lake Loop.

6.0 When the Maine 233 overpass comes into view, turn right for the boat launch parking (or continue straight if you parked in the lot on the north side of Maine 233.)

6.3 Welcome back.

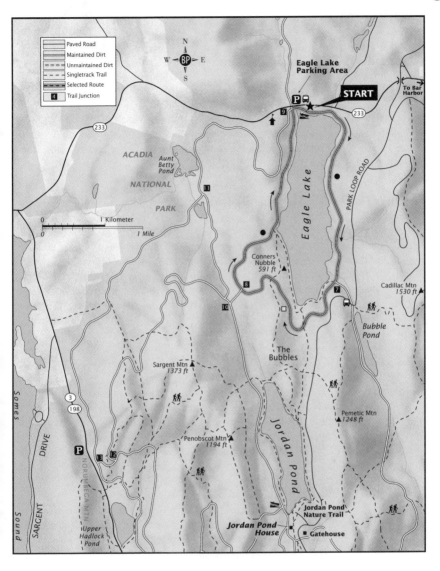

Legend

- Paved Road
- Maintained Dirt
- Unmaintained Dirt
- Singletrack Trail
- Selected Route
- 4 Trail Junction

Eagle Lake
Parking Area

START

To Bar
Harbor

233

ACADIA

Aunt
Betty
Pond

NATIONAL

PARK

11

0   1 Kilometer
0   1 Mile

9

Eagle Lake

Conners
Nubble
591 ft

8

10

7

Cadillac Mtn
1530 ft

Bubble
Pond

The
Bubbles

Sargent Mtn
1373 ft

Pemetic Mtn
1248 ft

Penobscot Mtn
1194 ft

Jordan Pond

3
198

P

13 12

NORUMBEGA MTN

Jordan Pond
Nature Trail

Upper
Hadlock
Pond

Jordan Pond
House

Gatehouse

Somes

SARGENT   DRIVE

Sound

PARK LOOP ROAD

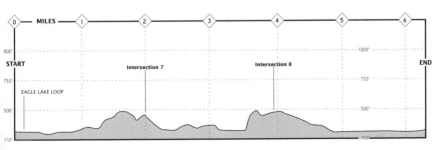

MILES   0   1   2   3   4   5   6

START

EAGLE LAKE LOOP

Intersection 7

Intersection 8

END

000'   1000'

750'   750'

500'   500'

250'   250'

Honorable Mentions

Augusta to Acadia

Compiled here is an index of great rides from Augusta to Acadia that didn't make the A-list this time around but deserve recognition. Check them out and let us know what you think. You may decide that one or more of these rides deserves higher status in future editions or, perhaps, you may have a ride of your own that merits some attention.

Ⓠ University Forest, Orono, Maine

Orono is home to the University of Maine. The trails in University Forest offer about 10 miles of well-used singletrack, doubletrack, and gravel roads. Though the terrain is rather flat, mud, roots, and loose surfaces build the challenge. Find the trails east of the paved recreation path, which lies beyond the university field house and athletic fields. The university dairy farm sits at the north end of the confined, but worthy, trail network. Information can be gathered from the Recreational Sports Office at the University of Maine, Orono, (207) 581-1081. *DeLorme: Maine Atlas & Gazetteer:* Map 23, A-3

Ⓡ Lagrange to Medford ATV Trail

The abandoned Bangor and Aroostook Railroad line has been converted by the state into a 12-mile long recreational corridor. The wide, gravel trail starts in South Lagrange, off of Maine 16. It heads north on a flat course through Medford Center to a picnic area on the Piscataquis River. The trail is close to Interstate 95 and the University of Maine, Orono campus. Call the Maine ATV Program for maps and details, (207) 287-4958. *DeLorme: Maine Atlas & Gazetteer:* Map 33, C-2

Ⓢ Carrabassett River Trail

Located across the road from Sugarloaf/USA, the sprawling mountain resort, the Carrabassett River Trail gives a secluded trip along the north side of the Carrabassett River. The trail runs a section of abandoned rail grade on a shallow pitch downhill from west to east. A loop can be done, or you can return on paved roads for a little more distance and some hill work. Enjoy the quiet of the river and majesty of 3,000-foot mountains around. Traveling north on Maine 16 / Maine 27 past Sugarloaf/USA, you'll cross the Carrabassett River and soon see the abandoned Bigelow rail station on the right. The trail begins behind this abandoned depot stop. Get trail details from the Sugarloaf Area Chamber of Commerce, (207) 235-2100. *DeLorme: Maine Atlas & Gazetteer:* Map 29, D-4

(T) Houlton to Phair Junction ATV Trail

A 40-mile recreational corridor along rail line abandoned in 1983 begins less than one mile from Interstate 95 in Houlton, Maine. You'll cross rivers, pass picnic spots and wetlands, and pedal through isolated woods along the trip. Gravel trail surfaces make it a non-technical ride, though the distance brings fitness into play. The small towns along the way offer convenience stores and restaurants to fill your hunger needs. Take Interstate 95 to Houlton and get off at the U.S. Route 1 North exit. The abandoned rail runs east of U.S. Route 1 initially, from nearby the State of Maine Tourist Information Center. The trail crosses back and forth over U.S. Route 1 many times as it travels toward Presque Isle. Contact the Maine ATV Program office for a map, (207) 287-4958. *DeLorme: Maine Atlas & Gazetteer:* Map 53, A-3

(U) Aroostook Valley Trails

Consisting of a number of independent legs, the 75 miles of the Aroostook Valley Trails—the longest state sponsored network in Maine—allows cyclists bike to the southern border of Canada. Short travel on pavement could give you longer loop options. All legs use abandoned rail line, making them flat and obstruction free. You'll share the trails with ATVs. The longest leg travels to Van Buren, Maine, former home of carbon-fiber bike make Aegis Cycles. Aegis now calls Belfast, Maine, home. Call the state ATV Program at (207) 287-4958 for details. *DeLorme: Maine Atlas & Gazetteer:* Map 69, D-2

Appendix

Bicycle Clubs and Organizations

Regional

New England Mountain Bike Association (NEMBA) Acton, MA
1-800-57NEMBA
www.nemba.org

Seacoast Chapter of NEMBA (Coastal Maine & New Hampshire)
Rochester, NH
(603) 332-0979
http://24.1.69.170/snemba

White Mountains NEMBA
North Conway, NH
(603) 356-0233

Eastern Fat Tire Association (EFTA)
Weare, NH
(603) 529-0670
www.efta.com

Maine

Bicycle Coalition of Maine
Augusta, ME
(207) 288-3028
www.acadia.net/bikeme

Team Grimace
Ogunquit, ME
(207) 646-0376 or
www.teamgrimace.com/main.html

The Fiddlehead Cycling Club/Camden Hills Off-Road Cycling Association
Camden, ME
(207) 236-4592

Midcoast Velo
Brunswick, ME
(207) 725-4013
www.sencomp.com/mcvelo/mcvelo.htm

Maine Freewheelers
Bangor, ME
(207) 848-0722 (for group ride info)
www.maineweb.com/freewheelers

Can Am Wheelers
Norway, ME
(207) 743-9018

New Hampshire

Granite State Wheelmen
Salem, NH
(603) 898-5479
www.geocities.com/Colosseum/Loge/9605

New Hampshire Mountain Biking Association
Ashland, NH
(603) 236-4666

Team Frank (for single-speed enthusiasts)
Keene, NH
e-mail at pwilson@monad.net or visit
www.top.monad.net/~pwilson/frank.html

Heart of New England Cycling Club
Keene, NH
(603) 756-9663 (call before 9:00 PM)

White Mountain Mudskippers
Bristol, NH
(603) 744-2998

The Biking Expedition
Henniker, NH
(603) 428-7500

White Mountain Wheel People
P.O. Box 1209
Glen, NH 03838
(603) 383-4660

Friends of Massabesic Bicycling Association
Auburn, NH
(603) 483-2951
www.fomba.com

National Clubs and Organizations

American Trails
The only national, nonprofit organization working on behalf of ALL trail interests. Members want to create and protect America's network of interconnected trailways.
POB 200787
Denver, CO 80220
(303) 321-6606, *www.outdoorlink.com/amtrails*

International Mountain Bicycling Association (IMBA)
Works to keep public lands accessible to bikers and provides information of trail design and maintenance.
POB 7578
Boulder, CO 80306
(303) 545-9011, *www.greatoutdoors.com/imba*

National Off-Road Bicycling Association (NORBA) - National governing body of US mountain bike racing
One Olympic Plaza
Colorado Springs, CO 80909
(719) 578-4717, *www.usacycling.org/mtb*

Outdoor Recreation Coalition of America (ORCA) - Oversees and examines issues for outdoor recreation
Boulder, CO
(303) 444-3353
www.orca.org, info@orca.org

Rails-to-Trails Conservancy
Organized to promote conversion of abandoned rail corridors to trails for public use.
1400 16th Street, NW, Suite 300
Washington, D.C. 20036-2222
www.railtrails.org

League of American Wheelmen
190 West Ostend Street #120
Baltimore, MD 21230-3731
(410) 539-3399

United States Cycling Federation
Governing body for amateur cycling.
Colorado Springs, CO
(719) 578-4581
www.usacycling.org

USA Cycling
One Olympic Plaza
Colorado Springs, CO 80909
(719) 578-4581, *www.usacycling.org*

Dear Reader: It's the very nature of print media that the second the presses run off the last book, all the phone numbers change. If you notice a wrong number or that a club or organization has disappeared or that a new one has put out its shingle, we'd love to know about it. And if you run a club or have a favorite one and we missed it; again, let us know. We plan on doing our part to keep this list up-to-date for future editions, but we could always use the help. You can write us, call us, e-mail us, or heck, just stop by if you're in the neighborhood.

Outside America
300 West Main Street, Suite A
Charlottesville, Virginia 22903
editorial@outside-america.com

Ski Resorts
[...for mountain biking?]

Ski Resorts

Ski resorts offer a great alternative to local trail riding. During the spring, summer, and fall, many resorts will open their trails for mountain biking and, just like during ski season, sell lift tickets to take you and your bike to the top of the mountain. Lodging is also available for the weekend mountain bike junkies, and rates are often discounted from the normal ski-season prices. Some resorts will even rent bikes and lead guided mountain bike tours. Call ahead to find out just what each resort offers in the way of mountain bike riding, and pick the one that best suits your fancy.

The following is a list of many of the ski resorts in New Hampshire and Maine that say yes! to mountain biking when the weather turns too warm for skiing.

Maine

Lost Valley
Auburn, ME
207-784-1561
www.lostvalleyski.com

Shawnee Peak
Bridgton, ME
(207) 647-8444
www.shawneepeak.com

Sugarloaf/USA
Kingfield, ME
(207) 237-2000
www.sugarloaf.com

Sunday River
Bethel, ME
(207) 824-3000
www.sundayriver.com

Troll Valley Mountain Bike Park
West Farmington, ME
(207) 778-3656

New Hampshire

Attitash/Bear Peak
Bartlett, NH
(603) 374-2368
www.attitash.com

Bretton Woods
Bretton Woods, NH
(603) 278-3300
www.brettonwoods.com

Cannon Mountain
Franconia Notch, NH
(603) 823-5563
www.cannonmt.com

Cranmore
North Conway, NH
(603) 356-5544

Franconia Village Cross-Country
Franconia, NH
1-800-473-5299
www.franconiainn.com

Loon Mountain Park
Lincoln, NH
(603) 745-8111
www.loonmtn.com

Mount Sunapee
Mount Sunapee, NH
(603) 763-2356
www.mtsunapee.com

Waterville Valley Mountain Bike Park
Waterville Valley, NH
1-800-468-2553
www.waterville.com

Wildcat
Pinkham Notch, Jackson, NH
1-888-4WILDCAT
www.skiwildcat.com

Fat Tire Vacations
[Bicycle Touring Companies]

There are literally dozens of off-road bicycling tour companies offering an incredible variety of guided tours for mountain bikers. On these pay-as-you-pedal, fat-tire vacations, you will have a chance to go places around the globe that only an expert can take you, and your experiences will be so much different than if seen through the window of a tour bus.

From Hut to Hut in the Colorado Rockies or Inn to Inn through Vermont's Green Mountains, there is a tour company for you. Whether you want hardcore singletrack during the day and camping at night, or you want scenic trails followed by a bottle of wine at night and a mint on each pillow, someone out there offers what you're looking for. The tours are well organized and fully supported with expert guides, bike mechanics, and "sag wagons" which carry gear, food, and tired bodies. Prices range from $100-$500 for a weekend to more than $2000 for two-week-long trips to far-off lands such as New Zealand or Ireland. Each of these companies will gladly send you their free literature to whet your appetite with breathtaking photography and titillating stories of each of their tours.

Selected Touring Companies
Maine
Backcountry Excursions
Limerick, ME
(207) 625-8189
www.backcountryexcursions.com

New Hampshire
The Biking Expedition
(student cycling tours)
Henniker, NH
1-800-245-4649
www.bikingx.com/index.html

Elk River Touring Center
Slatyfork, WV
(304) 572-3771

Vermont Bicycling Touring
Bristol, VT
1-800-245-3868

Backroads
Berkley, CA
1-800-BIKE TRIP

Timberline Bicycle Tours
Denver, CO
(303) 759-3804

Roads Less Traveled
Longmont, CO
(303) 678-8750

Blackwater Bikes
Davis, WV
(304) 259-5286

Bicycle Adventures
Olympia, WA
1-800-443-6060

Trails Unlimited, Inc.
Nashville, IN
(812) 988-6232

Repair and
Mainte

FIXING A FLAT

TOOLS YOU WILL NEED

- Two tire irons
- Pump (either a floor pump or a frame pump)
- No screwdrivers!!! (This can puncture the tube)

REMOVING THE WHEEL

The front wheel is easy. Simply open the quick release mechanism or undo the bolts with the proper sized wrench, then remove the wheel from the bike.

The rear wheel is a little more tricky. Before you loosen the wheel from the frame, shift the chain into the smallest gear on the freewheel (the cluster of gears in the back). Once you've done this, removing and installing the wheel, like the front, is much easier.

REMOVING THE TIRE

Step one: Insert a tire iron under the bead of the tire and pry the tire over the lip of the rim. Be careful not to pinch the tube when you do this.

Step two: Hold the first tire iron in place. With the second tire iron, repeat step one, three or four inches down the rim. Alternate tire irons, pulling the bead of the tire over the rim, section by section, until one side of the tire bead is completely off the rim.

Step three: Remove the rest of the tire and tube from the rim. This can be done by hand. It's easiest to remove the valve stem last. Once the tire is off the rim, pull the tubeout of the tire.

CLEAN AND SAFETY CHECK

Step four: Using a rag, wipe the inside of the tire to clean out any dirt, sand, glass, thorns, etc. These may cause the tube to puncture. The inside of a tire should feel smooth. Any pricks or bumps could mean that you have found the culprit responsible for your flat tire.

Step five: Wipe the rim clean, then check the rim strip, making sure it covers the spoke nipples properly on the inside of the rim. If a spoke is poking through the rim strip, it could cause a puncture.

Step six: At this point, you can do one of two things: replace the punctured tube with a new one, or patch the hole. It's easiest to just replace the tube with a new tube when you're out on the trails. Roll up the old tube and take it home to repair later that night in front of the TV. Directions on patching a tube are usually included with the patch kit itself.

INSTALLING THE TIRE AND TUBE
(This can be done entirely by hand)

Step seven: Inflate the new or repaired tube with enough air to give it shape, then tuck it back into the tire.

Step eight: To put the tire and tube back on the rim, begin by putting the valve in the valve hole. The valve must be straight. Then use your hands to push the beaded edge of the tire onto the rim all the way around so that one side of your tire is on the rim.

Step nine: Let most of the air out of the tube to allow room for the rest of the tire.

Step ten: Beginning opposite the valve, use your thumbs to push the other side of the tire onto the rim. Be careful not to pinch the tube in between the tire and the rim. The last few inches may be difficult, and you may need the tire iron to pry the tire onto the rim. If so, just be careful not to puncture the tube.

BEFORE INFLATING COMPLETELY

Step eleven: Check to make sure the tire is seated properly and that the tube is not caught between the tire and the rim. Do this by adding about 5 to 10 pounds of air, and watch closely that the tube does not bulge out of the tire.

Step twelve: Once you're sure the tire and tube are properly seated, put the wheel back on the bike, then fill the tire with air. It's easier squeezing the wheel through the brake shoes if the tire is still flat.

Step thirteen: Now fill the tire with the proper amount of air, and check constantly to make sure the tube doesn't bulge from the rim. If the tube does appear to bulge out, release all the air as quickly as possible, or you could be in for a big bang.

• When installing the rear wheel, place the chain back onto the smallest cog (furthest gear on the right), and pull the derailleur out of the way. Your wheel should slide right on.

LUBRICATION PREVENTS DETERIORATION

Lubrication is crucial to maintaining your bike. Dry spots will be eliminated. Creaks, squeaks, grinding, and binding will be gone. The chain will run quietly, and the gears will shift smoothly. The brakes will grip quicker, and your bike may last longer with fewer repairs. Need I say more? Well, yes. Without knowing where to put the lubrication, what good is it?

THINGS YOU WILL NEED
• One can of bicycle lubricant, found at any bike store.
• A clean rag (to wipe excess lubricant away).

WHAT GETS LUBRICATED
• Front derailleur
• Rear derailleur
• Shift levers
• Front brake
• Rear brake

- Both brake levers
- Chain

WHERE TO LUBRICATE

To make it easy, simply spray a little lubricant on all the pivot points of your bike. If you're using a squeeze bottle, use just a drop or two. Put a few drops on each point wherever metal moves against metal, for instance, at the center of the brake calipers. Then let the lube sink in.

Once you have applied the lubricant to the derailleurs, shift the gears a few times, working the derailleurs back and forth. This allows the lubricant to work itself into the tiny cracks and spaces it must occupy to do its job. Work the brakes a few times as well.

LUBING THE CHAIN

Lubricating the chain should be done after the chain has been wiped clean of most road grime. Do this by spinning the pedals counterclockwise while gripping the chain with a clean rag. As you add the lubricant, be sure to get some in between each link. With an aerosol spray, just spray the chain while pedalling backwards (counterclockwise) until the chain is fully lubricated. Let the lubricant soak in for a few seconds before wiping the excess away. Chains will collect dirt much faster if they're loaded with too much lubrication.

Index

Euphoria...
in many different states.

The most beautiful, challenging and exhilarating rides are just a day-trip away.

Visit **www.outside-america.com** *to order the latest guides for areas near you—or not so near. Also, get information and updates on future publications and other guidebooks from Outside America™.*

For more information or to place an order, call **1–800–243–0495.**

Meet the Author

After graduating with a degree in Civil Engineering from Worcester Polytechnic Institute in 1991, Bob moved to Maine and then on to New Hampshire. In 1992 he bought his first mountain bike, an entry-level Schwinn High Plains, and adapted his enduro motorcycling skills to the pedal-powered world. Many of the initial trails he biked, including those at Mount Agamenticus and Kingman Farm, are included in this book.

In July of 1992 he entered his first mountain bike race, the Treadhead Classic, which ran in the state forest near his boyhood home. He now races in the Expert class, enjoying Eastern Fat Tire Association events above all others. Competition is a great outlet for Bob, but no more satisfying than a pedal home from work or an excursion with his wife Michelle on their mountain tandem.

In writing this book, Bob learned the true meaning of epic rides, and that ice cream is a great recovery food. Michelle, who was the first in the family to own a mountain bike, often joined him off road, as did their son, who traveled with his books and toy dinosaurs in the bike trailer. Bob's appreciation of the solitude of the trail, as well as the joyous moments when rides are shared with family and friends, makes him say about cycling: "It's all I want to do."

Author